# STRATFORD
## BLUE
# D

# STRATFORD
## BLUE

*A History of*
*Stratford-on-Avon's Local Buses*

ROBERT L. TELFER

TEMPUS

*Frontispiece*: Stratford-on-Avon would not be the place it is today without William Shakespeare, and even the establishment of Stratford-on-Avon Motor Services can be indirectly attributed to him! The birthplace of his wife, Anne Hathaway, at Shottery had been visited by tourists since at least the nineteenth century, and the lack of a regular bus service to take visitors to the village inspired George Grail and Stanley Joiner to set up in business in 1927. This early photograph shows one of their original Chevrolets posed with its crew at the American Fountain in Rother Street, with its destination board showing 'Hathaway Cottage' rather than Shottery. An identical bus is visible in the background. (*Shakespeare Birthplace Trust*)

First published 2003

PUBLISHED IN THE UNITED KINGDOM BY:
Tempus Publishing Ltd
The Mill, Brimscombe Port
Stroud, Gloucestershire GL5 2QG

PUBLISHED IN THE UNITED STATES OF AMERICA BY:
Tempus Publishing Inc.
2 Cumberland Street
Charleston, SC 29401

British Library Cataloguing in Publication Data.
A catalogue record for this book is available from the British Library.

ISBN 0 7524 2792 X

Typesetting and origination by Tempus Publishing.
Printed in Great Britain by Midway Colour Print, Wiltshire.

# Contents

*What is one of the most familiar features of the Warwickshire landscape?*

Most people confronted with such a question will hesitate for a moment, and then doubtfully suggest the 'leafy lanes', the River Avon, or even plunge off the beaten track altogether by naming the Memorial Theatre or Warwick Castle, neither of which has counterparts scattered all over Warwickshire!

Because it is true that familiarity breeds contempt, the answer, although simple, occurs to few. Wherever their native abode, whether it be Avon Dassett or Aston Cross, Warwick or Woodstock, they forget how many times a day they see the Stratford 'Blue' buses wend their way along busy streets or winding lanes, carrying passengers to and from all parts of Warwickshire. Surely, since they cover routes totalling 350 miles, the Stratford 'Blue' Motors Ltd can lay claim to being one of Warwickshire's most familiar features.

*The* Stratford-on-Avon Herald, *Friday 1 September 1950*

# Preface

This book has taken a long time to come to fruition, and it does so in the year which marks the centenary of the first motor bus service in Stratford-on-Avon.

My first journey on a Stratford Blue bus was probably around 1963 when I recall being taken to Kineton one day after school, although I remember nothing of the bus (at that time the family did not have a car, and buses were taken for granted). Some years later, after moving on to secondary school, I got to know Stratford Blue much better as part of my journey home was usually on a Kineton bus on service 32A. At this stage, I have to admit, I always preferred the more familiar Midland Red buses.

My first steps into historical research began in the late 1970s and have continued on and off ever since. The idea of writing a comprehensive history of Stratford-upon-Avon Blue Motors came some years later and it soon became clear that to give the full picture I would need to cover the period from the earliest bus services around Stratford in 1903 right up to the present day – a century of bus services. So, in addition to the chapters on the original Stratford Blue company, which operated from 1927 to 1970, there is one covering the early years and two further chapters cover the period of more than thirty years since the demise of the original company. During this time the well-known name has made a succession of comebacks, but without ever replicating the success of the original. I have also included a chapter on the associated Leamington & Warwick 'Green' buses, which perhaps only a few people will now recall.

Over the years I have met and corresponded with a vast number of extremely helpful people, all of whom have willingly shared their knowledge and experience. Amongst them are former Stratford Blue staff, local historians, transport experts, professional staff of local libraries and archive services, and officers of the specialist transport societies including the Omnibus Society, the PSV Circle, the Birmingham & Midland Motor Omnibus Trust, and the National Tramway Museum. My list of contacts runs to over a hundred names and this book would not have been possible without them; I offer my thanks to them all. Unfortunately it is not possible to mention every one of them, and to single anyone out is a difficult task, but I would like to offer my special thanks to John Bennett, Alan Giles, Peter Hale, Peter Jaques (together with the Kithead Trust, whose records proved invaluable), Malcolm Keeley, Keith Lloyd, Colin Martin, Alan Mills and Chris Taylor. I am equally grateful to the many photographers whose work is reproduced in this book. In some cases I don't know who they are as my collection has been built up over many years, but where I do know I have sought permission to use the photos, and acknowledged their efforts. Again, my thanks to all of them, whether I have been able to acknowledge them or not.

I hope that you will enjoy reading this book as much as I have enjoyed working on it. As you read through it, or browse through the pictures, I would ask you to remember all the help which has made it possible. Finally, my search for relevant photographs continues, and if anyone is able to offer any further pictures or information, an approach through the publishers would be extremely welcome.

Bob Telfer
Sheffield, March 2003

# 1

# The Origins of Public Transport
# in South Warwickshire

Public transport around Stratford had been slowly evolving for over 100 years before Stratford-on-Avon Motor Services came on the scene in 1927.

Throughout rural England, the earliest form of local public transport was the horse-drawn carrier's cart, which brought all manner of goods as well as passengers from the surrounding villages into the towns. Many ran only on market days, which in the case of Stratford meant Fridays, and almost invariably they used the town's hostelries to provide stabling for the horses. This ensured that passengers, and probably the carrier himself, had the opportunity to take refreshments before the journey home. Particularly popular in Stratford was the Old Red Lion, which in 1830 was favoured by no less than twelve carriers, while others used the Anchor, the Coffee House, the Falcon and the Mulberry Tree. On Fridays the Old Red Lion was used by carriers from Bidford (Messrs Dance and Smith), Brailes (Mr Godson), Campden (Mr Ellis), Ettington (Mr Roberts), Henley (Mr Howes), Ilmington (Mr Ayres), Kineton (Mr Golby), Pebworth (Mr Chursley) and Warwick (Mr Davis).

Stagecoaches catered for longer-distance travel, and in 1830 there were four coaches a day between Stratford and London, the *Oxonian Express* and the *Triumph* on the Holyhead run, and the *Rocket* and the *Union* running to and from Shrewsbury. The *Rocket* and the *Triumph* called at the Red Horse Hotel and the others at the White Lion. Other coaches ran to Bath, Bristol, Leicester and Nottingham. Soon after this the stagecoaches began to lose their importance as the railways started to develop, but the carriers continued to play an important role until well into the twentieth century.

A predecessor of the modern railway was the Stratford & Moreton tramway, which opened in September 1826. It was built mainly to move coal from the canal basin in Stratford, where the line terminated, into the rural hinterland, and in February 1836 a branch was opened to Shipston-on-Stour, from a junction near Darlingscott. Local traders who used the line provided their own horses and wagons and paid a toll for its use. There was also an intermittent passenger service (not always sanctioned by the owners of the line), and between 1853 and 1858 Mr Bull of the George Hotel at Shipston advertised regular trips from Moreton to Stratford and Shipston. In 1847 the Oxford, Worcester & Wolverhampton Railway (OWWR) had taken out a lease on the tramway and later took on complete management responsibility, but after the opening of the Stratford – Honeybourne branch railway the tramway suffered a drop in traffic. This led to a proposal to close it but local objections ensured its survival. In the late 1880s the Great Western Railway, who had taken over the former OWWR, upgraded the section from Moreton to Shipston via the junction at Darlingscott to railway status, enabling steam locomotives to replace the horses. North of Darlingscott the line to Stratford fell into decline and was last used in about 1904.

The first conventional railway reached Stratford in July 1859, when the OWWR opened a branch off its main line at Honeybourne. Next came the Stratford-upon-Avon Railway, which opened in October 1860 and connected the town with the Birmingham & Oxford Railway's main line at Hatton. These lines were linked within Stratford when the West Midland Railway (successor to the OWWR) opened a new half-mile stretch in July 1861. In July 1873 came the East & West Junction Railway, linking Stratford with Towcester (Northamptonshire), while the fourth and final approach to the town, from the west, came in June 1879 when the Evesham, Redditch and Stratford-upon-Avon Junction Railway opened a line from Broom Junction. Also of significance was the Alcester Railway, opened in September 1876 from a junction on the Hatton line at Bearley. The final expansion of note was the opening in 1907 (1908 for passengers) of the Great Western Railway's new Cheltenham – Stratford – Birmingham route. This involved building new lines between Cheltenham and Honeybourne via Broadway and between Bearley and Tyseley (Birmingham) via Henley-in-Arden (despite its geographical location, this direct line from Stratford to Birmingham via Henley has always been known as the *North* Warwickshire Line). Only the latter and the line to Hatton survive today.

Returning to the roads, the Brailes, Shipston-on-Stour and Stratford-upon-Avon Steam Omnibus Co. Ltd introduced what was almost certainly the first motorbus service around Stratford on 16 September 1903. The company had been registered in July and was based in Church Street, Shipston. The first vehicle was delivered from its manufacturers, the Straker Steam Co. Ltd of Bristol, at the beginning of September. It had seats for eighteen passengers and despite weighing almost six tons was described in contemporary press reports as 'a compact, comfortable conveyance'.

The service created great interest, and early experiences pointed to a promising future. At the end of the month it was reported that the omnibus had carried 500 passengers in six days, and was sometimes so full that potential passengers had been left behind. A second vehicle was said to be due for delivery and there were requests for a service to other nearby villages.

Not all comment was favourable however, and the *Herald* of 2 October 1903 contained a letter from an aggrieved motorcar driver who felt that the omnibus 'should not be allowed to remain stationary on the Clopton Bridge either to take in water or passengers'. The author, who preferred to remain anonymous, urged the municipal authorities to remove this 'inconvenience and danger'. Another correspondent, believing that the steam omnibus would stop only at certain pre-determined points, wrote to express a preference for 'the good old carriers' vans, which we can hail upon the road, and be taken up where we will'.

*Spennell's Annual Directory* for 1904 gives the pattern of operation as 'From Stratford-on-Avon, G.W. Railway to Shipston-on-Stour – 10.50 a.m. and 5.15 p.m. except on Thursdays, when the time of departure is 6.15 p.m. To Stratford-on-Avon from Shipston-on-Stour – 8.15 a.m. and 3.15 p.m. except on Fridays, when the time of departure is 1 p.m.' The fare was quoted as 1*s* each way. Brailes was not mentioned, despite its inclusion in the company's title, but may have been included in the route.

The company's first annual report, covering the period from the start of business to 30 September 1904, confirmed that a second vehicle was obtained, but already hinted at problems ahead. Estimates prior to the start of business had suggested that an annual income of £500 was needed to cover expenditure and depreciation and allow a dividend for shareholders. However the directors had not allowed for the cost of the second omnibus. The revenue forecasts had been accurate enough (in the period covered by the report passenger revenues had amounted to just over £505, with a further £43 from parcels) but expenditure had exceeded income. This was partly attributed to the mechanical unreliability of the vehicles, which had led to hiring charges as well as repair bills. The need for a crew of three on every journey was another factor. Despite the problems the Chairman, Mr Edward Sheldon, expressed cautious optimism. A total of 17,748 passengers had been carried, and he hoped that with careful management and increased revenue from both passengers and parcels the next year would show a considerable improvement.

The two 'steamers', previously registered in Worcestershire as AB53 and AB199, were still with the company in August 1905 when they became AC11 and AC10 respectively in Warwickshire County Council's heavy motor car series. AC10 had seats for twenty passengers, two more than AC11, and was even heavier at 6 tons 6½cwt. With their steel tyres (5in wide at the front, 7in at the rear) and enormous weight they caused considerable damage to the roads, despite being restricted to 5mph, and were often delayed as a result.

Unfortunately Mr Sheldon's optimism was ill founded, and the service ran for the last time in September 1905, when the Steam Omnibus Co. was due to be wound up. By March 1906 AC10 was owned by the Chelsea Flour Mills in London.

Another very early motor passenger service into Stratford was operated by Robert Newcombe of Henley-in-Arden, whose wagonette service probably started in early 1904. Mr Newcombe was a cycle dealer and repairer by trade and became one of the area's motoring pioneers in 1898 when he paid £90 for a second-hand Benz dating from about 1895 or 1896. He was not deterred by the unreliability of this very primitive machine and the following year he bought an Excelsior motorcycle and a second-hand Darracq car. The latter had pneumatic tyres, which were frequently punctured, and was said to be capable of 18mph. Next he acquired two Daimler wagonettes (essentially large open cars), each seating ten passengers, and started offering a service to Stratford at 1s 6d return. As with other mechanical marvels of the time, the wagonettes had their problems. Asked in 1934 how many journeys per day he ran, Mr Newcombe replied 'Well, we were lucky if we completed one successfully'. In between breakdowns the wagonettes sometimes reached a highly illegal 20mph, but problems with the water pumps led to boiling radiators and lengthy spells at the roadside. One of the wagonettes was registered as AC252 on 2 February 1904, but appears to have been sold to a new owner in Scotland by July.

After running the wagonettes for a time, including an ambitious trip to Bridport (Dorset), where one of them was stranded for three days because the correct grade of petrol could not be found, Mr Newcombe turned to taxicabs. Initially a brand new Humber was bought, proving an immediate success. Other taxis followed but the wagonette service to Stratford was discontinued and Mr Newcombe later established the Newcombe Garage in Henley, selling and repairing cars.

During the summer of 1905, Messrs Lyon, Clark, McNeill & Co. began their 'Leamington & District Motor Omnibus Service' between Leamington and Stratford from a garage in Russell Street, Leamington. Lyon, Clark, McNeill's first two buses, 36-seat 20/25hp Milnes-

*Right*: In the summer of 1905 the first motor bus service between Leamington and Stratford was introduced, by Lyon, Clark, McNeill & Co. This notice was placed in the *Leamington Spa Courier* of 7 July and advertises a daily service, with a 'special bus' on Wednesdays and Saturdays as well as a half-hourly Leamington – Warwick service.

*Below*: After a very short time it was decided to revise fares between Warwick and Stratford on the daily service, the through fare becoming 1s 2d from 14 July, when this advertisement was placed in the *Courier*.

---

### MOTOR OMNIBUS SERVICE.

#### PUBLIC NOTICE.

A MOTOR OMNIBUS runs twice daily from LEAMINGTON (G.W.R.) to KENIL-WORTH, WARWICK, BARFORD, WELLES-BOURNE, and STRATFORD-ON-AVON.
Omnibus leaves Leamington—9 a.m. and 2-30 p.m.
Parcels accepted by this service.
Time Tables may be obtained from the Offices in Russell Street; Mr. F. J. Land, Regent Street; or Messrs. Cooke and Sons, Warwick.

PUBLIC SERVICE of MOTOR 'BUSES between LEAMINGTON and WARWICK every half-hour, commencing at 9 a.m. (except on Wednesdays and Saturdays, when the service will be every hour) until 7 p.m., when half-hour service will be resumed.

Every Wednesday and Saturday a Special 'Bus will run to STRATFORD-ON-AVON, *via* KENILWORTH, WARWICK, BARFORD, WELLESBOURNE, and STRATFORD-ON-AVON, leaving Leamington at 10-45 and returning at 7 p.m.
Fare for the day, Five Shillings.
Tickets can be obtained at the Offices, Russell Street, Leamington, and at Mr. Hadley's, 68, Market Place, Warwick.

---

### LEAMINGTON AND DISTRICT MOTOR OMNIBUS SERVICE.

THE following ALTERATIONS IN THE FARES BETWEEN WARWICK and STRATFORD have been found necessary, and will take effect on and after TO-DAY (FRIDAY), the 14th of JULY:—
WARWICK to BARFORD, 4d.
BARFORD to WELLESBOURNE, 4d.
WARWICK to STRATFORD, 1s. 2d.
Fares from KENILWORTH to LEAMINGTON and WARWICK remain the same.
DONALD McNEILL, Manager.

---

Daimler double-deckers, were registered as AC2 and AC3 in the heavy motor car series on 26 June, and were quickly put to work on a half-hourly service along the tramway between Leamington and Warwick. The tramway had closed in early 1905 for conversion to electric traction (horse cars having been used previously) and until its reopening in July the tramway company was running horse buses, which the Leamington & District Motor Omnibus Service now competed with.

The Stratford service was running by early July, and followed a very indirect route from the GWR Station in Leamington via Kenilworth, Warwick, Barford and Wellesbourne. It ran daily, leaving Leamington at 9.00 a.m. and 2.30 p.m., and also offered a parcels service. The route via Wellesbourne was perhaps chosen to serve villages away from the railway between Warwick and Stratford, which took a more westerly route. In addition to the daily service there was a 'special bus' on Wednesdays and Saturdays which left Leamington at 10.45 a.m. for Kenilworth, where it connected with a train from London (Euston) before continuing to Kenilworth Castle, Guy's Cliffe, Warwick Castle, Shottery and Stratford. On the way back to Leamington in the evening passengers were dropped off at Milverton Station for their return train to London. The fare of 5s from Leamington included lunch in Warwick after the visit to the castle. Because of the 'special' service the service along the tramway only ran hourly on Wednesdays and Saturdays until the excursion returned at 7.00 p.m. and allowed the half-hourly frequency to be resumed.

For the daily Stratford service a third Milnes-Daimler (AC4) was acquired. AC4 was an 18-seat single-decker on an 18/20hp chassis and could carry a large amount of luggage on the roof. Like the double-deckers, it had varnished wood bodywork with what the registration authority termed a red 'undercarriage'.

MESSRS. LYON CLARK, McNEILL & Co,.
BEG TO ANNOUNCE A NEW
MOTOR BUS SERVICE
FROM
LEAMINGTON TO STRATFORD
DIRECT.
Every Monday, Tuesday, Thursday, and Friday.

|  | a.m. | p.m. |
|---|---|---|
| Leamington (G.W.R.) ............ dep. | 11-0 | ... 4-0 |
| Warwick ................................. | 11-30 | ... 4-30 |
| Wellesbourne ......................... | 12-0 | ... 5-0 |
| Stratford-on-Avon (G.W.R.) arr. | 12-30 | ... 5-30 |

|  | p.m. | p.m. |
|---|---|---|
| Stratford-on-Avon (G.W.R.) dep. | 1-30 | ... 6-30 |
| Wellesbourne ......................... | 2-0 | ... 7-0 |
| Warwick ................................. | 2-30 | ... 7-30 |
| Leamington (G.W.R.) ............ arr. | 3-0 | ... 8-0 |

Leamington to Warwick, 3d.; Warwick to Stratford, 1s. 2d.; Warwick to Barford, 4d.; Barford to Stratford, 1s.; Warwick to Wellesbourne, 8d.; Wellesbourne to Stratford, 8d.
DONALD McNEILL,
Manager.

Following electrification of the Leamington & Warwick tramway, Lyon, Clark, McNeill & Co. decided to concentrate on services to Stratford. This advertisement of 18 August 1905 announced a 'direct' service which omitted Kenilworth, but only ran on four days a week.

The electric tram service began on 12 July and soon saw off Lyon, Clark, McNeill's Milnes-Daimlers. The motorbus of 1905 was not noted for its reliability and could certainly not compete effectively with electric trams, so the half-hourly motorbus service between the two towns was discontinued in favour of the services to Stratford. During August a new service was announced 'from Leamington to Stratford direct' (i.e. not serving Kenilworth). This ran two journeys each way on Mondays, Tuesdays, Thursdays and Fridays, at 11.00 a.m. and 4.00 p.m. from Leamington (GWR Station) and at 1.30 p.m. and 6.30 p.m. from the GWR Station in Stratford. The journey, via Warwick, Barford and Wellesbourne, took ninety minutes.

At one time Lyon, Clark, McNeill & Co. had hoped to buy four additional double-deckers to provide a bus every twelve minutes between Leamington and Warwick, but the success of the tramway put paid to this. Motorbuses were in any case very unpopular in certain quarters, and this was evident from the commemorative postcard issued 'in remembrance of the Leamington, Stratford, Warwick and Kenilworth motorbuses, which expired after a short and merry life on Wednesday September 20th 1905, leaving the dust and smell behind'. This included the epitaph:

*Poorly lived, and poorly died,*
*Poorly buried, and no-one cried.*

The contrast with the similar postcard produced to mourn the passing of the horse trams 'which succumbed on May 16th 1905 to an electric shock, aged 25 years' was poignant. Below the picture of two faithful horses drawing a car at a leisurely pace along Jury Street, Warwick, the verse read:

*Let not ambition mock their useful toil*
*Their homely joys, and destiny obscure.*

The exact fate of Lyon, Clark, McNeill & Co. is not known, but their involvement in local public transport in the Leamington area ceased, and the *Warwick & Warwickshire Advertiser* of 23 September 1905 reported that the buses were to be transferred to London. Public road transport in the Leamington, Warwick and Stratford areas was now once again dependent on horse power, with mechanical propulsion confined to the rails.

Although the occasional charabancs were to be seen with parties of day-trippers, it was to be some time before regular operation of motorbuses in the area resumed. Such was the unreliability of many early motorbuses, and the reluctance of the travelling public to accept them, that the Birmingham & Midland Motor Omnibus Co. (BMMO) withdrew its entire fleet from the streets of Birmingham during October 1907 and substituted horse buses (it has been suggested that the local constabulary may have influenced this decision!).

BMMO's newest buses were nine Brush B-type double-deckers with Peter Brotherhood engines (O1283-1291), which had only been placed in service between October 1906 and January 1907. After lying idle for some months six of them were sent to Kent, where they ran for BMMO's Deal & District Motor Services. The other three, O1287/1289/1290, remained out of use until they were hired out to the Leamington & Warwick Electrical Co. (the British Electric Traction Co. (BET) owned this company as well as the BMMO) under an agreement dated 12 March 1908. The Electrical Company, as it was known locally, was to pay BMMO a flat charge of £1 0s 0d per bus per week plus 1d per mile run in service, but

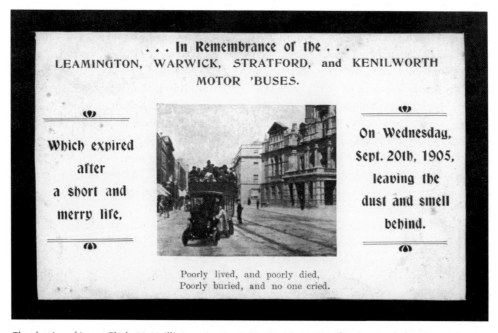

The demise of Lyon, Clark, McNeill's Leamington & District Motor Omnibus Service led to the production of this celebratory postcard. Although their demise was obviously seen as a victory by some, motorbuses were back within three years, this time to stay. The well-loaded double-decker illustrated outside Leamington Town Hall is presumably one of the Milnes-Daimlers (AC2 and AC3) which were initially used on the service along the tramway. Although the tramway reopened after electrification in July, there is no evidence of this in the photograph. (*Warwickshire County Record Office: CR2409/16*)

The Birmingham & Midland Motor Omnibus Co.'s first motorbuses were not a success and were taken off the road in October 1907 and replaced by horse buses! Three of the most recent double-deckers were later hired by the Leamington & Warwick Electrical Co. for use on services around Leamington. One of them, O1290, became a single-decker and is seen here with its crew at Shipston on its regular duty, the service from Leamington. Details of the route were given around the edge of the luggage pen on the roof, while at the front was a prominent advertisement for the Express Parcels Service. The BET's magnet device is visible on the side panels. (*Author's collection*)

reserved the right to renegotiate the terms if the revenue was insufficient to produce an operating profit. Before releasing the vehicles, BMMO were required to put them 'into a state of fair running repair'.

At first the buses were mainly used on services which fed into the tramway in Leamington, but there were also excursions to Stratford at a fare of 3s return from Leamington and 2s 6d from Warwick. These trips were probably many people's first experience of motor travel and proved very popular, although less predictable than many might have wished! On 3 August 1908, the Bank Holiday Monday, O1287 was returning from Kenilworth to Leamington at about 10.15 p.m. when the brakes failed and it ran out of control at Chesford Bridge, crashing into a cottage. As it was a warm night all seventeen passengers were travelling on the open top deck and most were thrown from the vehicle on the impact. Eleven were injured, some seriously, as was the occupant of the cottage, who had been sitting in his front room smoking a pipe. The driver and conductor escaped unhurt.

Fares for the Leamington local services were 2d to the Oak Inn, Cemetery or Binswood Avenue, and 3d to Radford Semele, Whitnash or Lillington. The Whitnash service may have been introduced partly in response to a request from the Leamington Town Improvement Association (LTIA) for a motorbus service to the new golf course. The LTIA had first considered suggesting an extension of the tramway to Whitnash but they felt this would produce objections from residents and traders in Bath Street.

Although this time the motorbus was here to stay, the bus services were not a financial success and there was much debate over whether to continue them during the winter of 1908/1909, and again the following year.

The three Brush buses had arrived from Birmingham with their original open-top double-deck bodies. Later, however, two were fitted with new Birch Bros charabanc bodies (after its accident in the case of O1287), while O1290 became an enclosed single-deck saloon. This was probably achieved by simply removing the top deck from the original body. Another upgrade involved replacing the original wooden wheels with steel ones. In its modified form O1290 was used on a Leamington – Stratford – Shipston-on-Stour service, but the local services in Leamington are thought to have ceased at around this time (a proposal to reintroduce them in the early months of 1912 was rejected).

The Electrical Company bought the Brush buses from BMMO in April 1910, the proposed deal involving three chassis, three omnibus bodies and two charabanc bodies for a total of £375. Also in 1910 came a new Brush 20hp mail van which doubled as a 'public conveyance' (AC1985, registered on 13 August). This was mainly for use on a contract to carry mail to and from Birmingham, but the contract was lost in December and later a normal single-deck bus body was fitted. A further Brush passenger vehicle, U771, is reputed to have come from the Worcester Electric Traction Co., the city's tramway operator.

At the end of 1912 BET sold the Leamington & Warwick Electrical Co. to Balfour Beatty & Co. Ltd. However, the bus operations were retained and transferred to the British Automobile Traction Co. (BAT), BET's fledgling motorbus operator, with effect from 8 November 1912 (but backdated to 1 July). It is recorded that £1,009 15s 7d was paid for the rolling stock, and a further £218 7s 6d for the contents of the stores. BAT agreed to charge a minimum fare of 5d within the boroughs of Warwick and Leamington to avoid competing with the tramway, and in return the Electrical Company agreed not to operate motorbuses again.

BAT re-equipped the fleet during 1913/1914 with four 40hp Daimler single-deckers. AC3612 was the first to arrive, in June 1913, and carried a 'saloon coach' body. Then came AC29 and AC30, which were registered on 12 May 1914, and AC36, registered on 7 September. The latter three, at least, carried a light 'saxon green' livery, with a gold 'British' fleetname on the side, and their registration numbers (unlike AC3612) were in the separate series for 'heavy motor cars'.

Operation by BAT turned out to be short-lived as negotiations were in hand during the second half of 1914 for the Leamington business to be transferred within the BET group to

Two of the trio of Brush B-types, O1287 and O1289, were later fitted with semi-enclosed charabanc bodies, and in this form they are seen outside the Humber works in Coventry, about to set off on an outing to Evesham. Steel wheels had been fitted to replace the wooden originals. By the time this photograph was taken in May 1913, the British Automobile Traction Co. had acquired them, together with the rest of the Electrical Company's motorbus interests. Both have 'British' fleetnames, and the fleet numbers B1 (O1289) and B2 (O1287) are visible on the bonnets. (*National Tramway Museum*)

the Birmingham & Midland Motor Omnibus Co., which in the same year had started a motorbus service from Birmingham to Stratford. The deal included 'three Brush cars, four modern Daimler cars and two light motor cars', as well as the goodwill for the following, as quoted in the letter setting out the agreement:

a) The Stratford & Shipston route which we suggest could be worked as a continuation of your Birmingham & Stratford route;
b) The London & North Western Railway special service contract;
c) The Leamington & Stratford summer service;
d) The private hire connection;
e) The Leamington & Coventry route which is being started and for which licences have already been obtained in Coventry.

The list suggests that the through service from Leamington to Shipston had ceased and that the Leamington – Stratford service was only running in the summer. There was said to be no competition with any of the above services and only a limited amount for private hire business. Takings from 1 January to 9 October 1914 had amounted to £1,670, which equated to just under 1s 3d per mile. BAT's asking price for the vehicles and goodwill was £4,877 6s 10d, although they offered to repurchase the vehicles for £4,033 15s 5d if the War Office had not commandeered them. BMMO would also take over the lease on the corrugated iron shed at the Emscote tram depot which housed the motorbuses, and would honour the agreement not to compete with the tramway by maintaining the 5d minimum fare.

BAT could not offer immediate completion of the deal because their Emscote-based operations were only part of what they termed their 'South Warwick Motor Omnibus Undertaking', the other part being centred on Banbury (in Oxfordshire). Negotiations were said to be underway to transfer the Banbury operations to another company and until this was finalised BAT did not wish to relinquish the Emscote operations. A take-over date of 31 December 1914 was proposed to BMMO but it is believed that the final outcome was a transfer of the Emscote operations on 5 December. BAT's Banbury services continued, and ran for the last time on 29 May 1915; they were then withdrawn without replacement, the proposed sale having come to nothing.

The May 1915 edition of the *Birmingham & District Motor Bus Guide* listed the following services in the Stratford and Leamington areas, all operated by BMMO:

| 23 | Birmingham – Shirley – Monkspath – Hockley Heath – Henley – Stratford-on-Avon – Newbold – Shipston-on-Stour (one journey in each direction ran via Snitterfield) |
| 24a | Leamington – Kenilworth – Coventry |
| 48 | Stratford-on-Avon – Wellesbourne – Warwick – Leamington (renumbered by June 1915 to 23a) |

None of the BAT motorbuses passed to BMMO, who used their own vehicles on the services; they were building up a large fleet of Tilling-Stevens petrol-electrics (thirty 29-seat TS3 model single-deckers were delivered in 1914 alone, with more following during 1915 and 1916). In any case at least some of the BAT Daimlers had been commandeered, AC29/30 serving with the British Expeditionary Force during 1915. They may have returned to BAT as Daimlers carrying registrations AC29/30/36 went to work in Deal in February 1916, subsequently becoming part of the initial fleet of the East Kent Road Car Co. (these may however have been new chassis coupled with the original bodies which retained their registrations). The three Brush vehicles dating from 1906/1907 were by now well past their prime and unlikely to be of much interest to the military authorities, but their fate is not known.

The war had a drastic effect on bus operation throughout the country but BMMO managed to continue running, although forced to experiment with coal gas as an alternative source of power due to the scarcity of petrol. By September 1916 services 23a and 24a had

---

### Services 22 and 23.

**BIRMINGHAM (Bull Ring), SHIRLEY, MONKSPATH, HOCKLEY HEATH, HENLEY, STRATFORD-ON-AVON, NEWBOLD and SHIPSTON-ON-STOUR.**

#### WEEK-DAY SERVICE.

| | a.m. | a.m. | a.m. | a.m. | p.m. | p.m. | p.m. | p.m. | | p.m. | p.m. | p.m. | p.m. | p.m. |
|---|---|---|---|---|---|---|---|---|---|---|---|---|---|---|
| B'ham (Bull Ring) dep. | 5 45 | 7 40 | 9 30 | 1035 | 1235 | 1035 | 3 5 | 3 15 | B'ham (Bull Ring) dep ... | 4 35 | 6 5 | 7 5 | 8 5 | 905 |
| Shirley (Saracen's Head) ... | 6 10 | 8 0 | 9 55 | 11 0 | 1 0 | 20 5 | 3 35 | 3 45 | Shirley (Saracen's Head) ... | 5 5 | 6 35 | 7 35 | 8 35 | 9035 |
| Monkspath (George & Drn.) | 6 15 | 8 5 | 10 0 | 11 5 | 1 5 | 201 | 3 40 | 3 50 | Monkspath (Grge & Dragon) | 5 10 | 6 40 | 7 40 | 8 40 | 9040 |
| Hockley Heath (Nag's Hd.) | 6 25 | — | 1020 | 1120 | 1 20 | — | 4 0 | — | Hockley Heath (Nag's Head) | — | 6M55 | — | 9 00 | — |
| Henley-in-Arden (Bear Htl.) | 6 40 | — | — | 1145 | 1 45 | — | 4 25 | — | Henley-in-Arden (Bear Hotel) | — | — | — | — | — |
| Bearley Cross (Cross Inn) | 6 50 | — | — | 12 0 | 2 0 | — | 4 40 | — | Bearley Cross (Cross Inn) ... | — | — | — | — | — |
| Snitterfield ... | — | — | — | 1215 | — | — | — | — | Stratford-on-Avon (Bridge St.) | •— | — | — | — | — |
| Stratford-on-Avon (Bge.St.) | 7 30 | — | — | 1240 | 2 30 | — | 5 30 | — | | | | | | |
| Newbold ... | 8 0 | — | — | 1 10 | —. | — | 6 0 | — | | | | | | |
| Tredington ... | 8 5 | — | — | 1 15 | — | — | 6 5 | — | | | | | | |
| S'ston-on-Stour (W. Ht.)arr. | 8 15 | — | — | 1 25 | — | — | 6 20 | — | | | | | | |

**SHIPSTON-ON-STOUR, NEWBOLD, STRATFORD-ON-AVON, HENLEY, HOCKLEY HEATH, MONKSPATH, SHIRLEY and BIRMINGHAM (Bull Ring).**

#### WEEK-DAY SERVICE.

| | a.m. | a.m. | a.m. | p.m. | p.m. | p.m. | | p m | p.m. | p.m. | p.m. | p m | p.m. | p.m. |
|---|---|---|---|---|---|---|---|---|---|---|---|---|---|---|
| S'ston-on-Str. (W. H.) dep. | — | 8 30 | — | — | — | 1 40 | S'ston-on-Str. (W.H.) dep. | — | — | — | — | 6 10 | — | — |
| Tredington ... | — | 8 40 | — | — | — | 1 50 | Tredington ... | — | — | — | — | 6 20 | — | — |
| Newbold ... | — | 8 45 | — | — | — | 1 55 | Newbold ... | — | — | — | — | 6 25 | — | — |
| Strat'-on-Avon (Bdge. St.) | — | 9 15 | — | 1235 | — | 2 35 | Strat.-on-Avon (Bdge. St.) | — | — | 5 5 | — | 7 10 | — | — |
| Snitterfield ... | — | — | — | — | — | — | Snitterfield ... | — | — | — | — | 7 30 | — | — |
| Bearley Cross (Cross Inn) | — | — | — | 1255 | — | 3 0 | Bearley Cross (Cross Inn) | — | — | 5 30 | — | 7 45 | — | — |
| Henley-in-Arden (Br. Htl.) | — | — | — | 1 20 | — | 3 20 | Henley-in-Arden (Br. Htl.) | — | — | 5 50 | — | 8 10 | — | — |
| Hockley Hth. (Nag's Hd.) | — | — | 10 40 | 1 40 | 0 | 3 40 | Hockley Hth. (Nag's Hd.) | — | — | 6 15 | 7M5 | 8 30 | 9 05 | 0 |
| Monkspath (Geo. & Drgn) | 8 20 | — | 10 55 | 1 55 | 2 20 | 3 55 | Monkspath (Geo & Drgn) | 4 30 | 5 20 | 6 30 | 7 20 | 8 45 | 9 20 | 10 0 |
| Shirley (Saracen's Head) | 8 25 | — | 11 0 | 2 0 | 2 25 | 4 0 | Shirley (Saracen's Head) | 4 35 | 5 25 | 6 35 | 7 25 | 8 50 | 9 25 | 10 5 |
| B'ham (Bull Ring) arr. | 8 55 | — | 11 30 | 2 30 | 3 0 | 4 30 | B'ham (Bull Ring) arr. | 5 5 | 5 55 | 7 • | 7 55 | 8 55 | 9 20 | 1040 |

**BIRMINGHAM (Bull Ring), SHIRLEY, MONKSPATH, HOCKLEY HEATH, HENLEY, STRATFORD-ON-AVON, NEWBOLD, SHIPSTON-ON-STOUR.**

#### SUNDAY SERVICE.

| | | | | a.m. | a.m. | p.m. | p.m. | p.m. | p.m. | p.m. | p.m. | p.m. | p.m. |
|---|---|---|---|---|---|---|---|---|---|---|---|---|---|---|
| Birmingham (Bull Ring) ... | ... | ... | dep. | 10-35 | 11-5 | 2-5 | 3-0 | 3-5 | 4-5 | 5-5 | 6-5 | 7-5 | 8-5 |
| Shirley (Saracen's Head) | ... | ... | ... | 11-5 | 11-35 | 2-35 | 3-30 | 3-35 | 4-35 | 5-35 | 6-35 | 7-35 | 8-35 |
| Monkspath (George & Dragon) | ... | ... | ... | 11-10 | 11-40 | 2-40 | 3-35 | 3-40 | 4-40 | 5-40 | 6-40 | 7-40 | 8-40 |
| Hockley Heath (Nag's Head) | ... | ... | ... | 11-30 | — | — | — | 4-0 | 5-0 | — | 7-0 | — | 9-0 |
| Henley-in-Arden (Bear Hotel) | ... | ... | ... | 11-55 | — | — | — | 4-25 | — | — | — | — | — |
| Bearley Cross (Cross Inn) | ... | ... | ... | 12-10 | — | — | — | 4-40 | — | — | — | — | — |
| Snitterfield | ... | ... | ... | — | — | — | — | 4-55 | — | — | — | — | — |
| Stratford-on-Avon (Bridge Street) | ... | ... | arr. | 12-30 | — | — | — | 5-10 | — | — | — | — | — |

**SHIPSTON-ON-STOUR, NEWBOLD, STRATFORD-ON-AVON, HENLEY, HOCKLEY HEATH, MONKSPATH, SHIRLEY, BIRMINGHAM (Bull Ring).**

| | | | | p.m. | p.m. | p.m. | p.m. | p.m. | p.m. | p.m. | p.m. | p.m. | p.m. |
|---|---|---|---|---|---|---|---|---|---|---|---|---|---|---|
| Stratford-on-Avon (Bridge Street) | ... | ... | dep. | — | 12-35 | — | — | — | — | — | — | 7-0 | — |
| Snitterfield | ... | ... | ... | — | — | — | — | — | — | — | — | 7-20 | — |
| Bearley Cross (Cross Inn) | ... | ... | ... | — | 12-55 | — | — | — | — | — | — | 7-35 | — |
| Henley-in-Arden (Bear Hotel) | ... | ... | ... | — | 1-20 | — | — | — | — | — | — | 8-0 | — |
| Hockley Heath (Nag's Head) | ... | ... | ... | — | 1-40 | — | — | 5-5 | — | 7-5 | — | 8-20 | 9-5 |
| Monkspath (George & Dragon) | ... | ... | ... | 1-0 | 1-55 | 3-20 | 4-20 | 5-20 | 6-20 | 7-20 | 8-20 | 8-35 | 9-20 |
| Shirley (Saracen's Head) | ... | ... | ... | 1-5 | 2-0 | 3-25 | 4-25 | 5-25 | 6-25 | 7-25 | 8-25 | 8-40 | 9-25 |
| Birmingham (Bull Ring) | ... | ... | arr. | 1-40 | 2-30 | 3-55 | 4-55 | 5-55 | 6-55 | 8-0 | 8-55 | 9-10 | 9-50 |

M—Mondays, Thursdays and Saturdays only.   O—Saturdays only.

**FARES**—Bull Ring and Hockley Heath, 9d.   Bull Ring and Henley-in-Arden, 1/2.   Bull Ring and Bearley, 1/6.
Bull Ring and Stratford, 1/9.   Bull Ring and Newbold, 2/5.   Bull Ring and Shipston-on-Stour, 2/9.

---

After acquiring the BAT's Leamington area motorbus interests at the end of 1914, BMMO extended their Birmingham – Stratford service through to Shipston. This timetable comes from the *Birmingham and District Motor Bus Guide* of May 1915, and shows four round trips from Birmingham to Stratford on weekdays, with three journeys each way between Stratford and Shipston.

## Service No. **77.**
### BANBURY, WARMINGTON, KINETON & STRATFORD.

| | | | THURS. | | TUESDAYS & FRIDAYS. |
|---|---|---|---|---|---|
| | | | a.m. | p.m. | a.m. |
| Banbury (Town Hall) | ... | dep. | 10–30 | 5–10 | 7–45 |
| Warmington (Church) | ... | ,, | 10–55 | 5–35 | 8–10 |
| Gaydon (Post Office) | ... | ,, | 11–20 | 6–0 | 8–35 |
| Kineton (Church) ... | ... | ,, | 11–35 | 6–15 | 9–0 |
| Butlers Marston | ... | ,, | — | — | 9–7 |
| Pillerton Priors | ... | ,, | — | — | 9–15 |
| Ettington ... | ... | ,, | — | — | 9–30 |
| Stratford-on-Avon | ... | arr. | — | — | 9–55 |

| | | | THURS. | | TUESDAYS & FRIDAYS. |
|---|---|---|---|---|---|
| | | | a.m. | p.m. | p.m. |
| Stratford-on-Avon | ... | dep. | — | — | 5–30 |
| Ettington ... | ... | ,, | — | — | 5–55 |
| Pillerton Priors | ... | ,, | — | — | 6–10 |
| Butlers Marston | ... | ,, | — | — | 6–18 |
| Kineton (Church) ... | ... | ,, | 11–40 | 6–30 | 6–30 |
| Gaydon (Post Office) | ... | ,, | 11–55 | 6–45 | 6–45 |
| Warmington (Church) | ... | ,, | 12–20 | 7–10 | 7–10 |
| Banbury (Town Hall) | ... | ,, | 12–45 | 7–35 | 7–35 |

## Service No. **77c.**
### STRATFORD, MICKLETON, ASTON SUBEDGE, SAINTBURY and BROADWAY.

#### TUESDAYS & FRIDAYS ONLY.

| | | a.m. | p.m. | | | | a.m. | p.m. |
|---|---|---|---|---|---|---|---|---|
| Stratford (B'dge St.) | dep. | 10–0 | 3–0 | Broadway | ... ... | dep. | 11–15 | 4–15 |
| Clifford Chambers | ,, | 10–10 | 3–10 | Willersley | ... ... | ,, | 11–22 | 4–22 |
| Quinton Turn | ,, | 10–30 | 3–30 | Saintbury | ... ... | ,, | 11–30 | 4–30 |
| Mickleton ... | ,, | 10–42 | 3–42 | Weston Subedge | ... | ,, | 11–35 | 4–35 |
| Aston Subedge | ,, | 10–47 | 3–47 | Aston Subedge | ... | ,, | 11–40 | 4–40 |
| Weston Subedge | ,, | 10–52 | 3–52 | Mickleton | ... ... | ,, | 11–50 | 4–50 |
| Saintbury | ,, | 10–56 | 3–56 | Quinton Turn | ... ... | ,, | 12–5 | 5–5 |
| Willersley | ,, | 11–3 | 4–3 | Clifford Chambers | ,, | 12–22 | 5–22 |
| Broadway | ... arr. | 11–10 | 4–10 | Stratford | ... ... | ,, | 12–30 | 5–30 |

These timetables from the Winter 1922/1923 BMMO timetable show the services from Banbury to Stratford (77) and from Stratford to Broadway (77c), which ran on Tuesdays and Fridays. They were operated by a Banbury-based single-decker, and effectively ran as a through service, the journey from Banbury to Broadway taking three hours twenty-five minutes, with only a five-minute break in Stratford. The ascent of Warmington Hill on the return journey to Banbury would have been a laborious task for Midland Red's early vehicles.

been merged into a new service 22, running from Coventry to Shipston via Leamington, Warwick and Stratford, but the 23 was still running between Birmingham and Shipston. These were the only routes to serve Stratford at this time, and remained so for some time to come.

The end of the war in 1918 permitted a gradual return to normal, and the supply of new vehicles resumed in 1919 with the delivery of another thirty-four Tilling-Stevens TS3s, followed by over eighty in 1920, plus some second-hand 'de-mobbed' vehicles from the War Department. However, most of these were put to use well away from the area which this book covers, and post-war expansion around Stratford was slow at first; until 1920 the only services to reach Stratford were the 22 and 23.

By the summer of 1924, the list of services to and from Stratford had expanded to include the following:

| | |
|---|---|
| 17e | Stratford – Bidford – Evesham ('temporarily suspended') |
| 22 | Coventry – Leamington – Warwick – Stratford – Shipston |
| 22a | Stratford – Snitterfield |
| 23 | Birmingham – Hockley Heath – Henley – Stratford – Newbold – Shipston |
| 74 | Stratford – Shipston – Cherington – Brailes – Swalcliffe – Banbury |
| 77 | Stratford – Kineton – Warmington – Banbury |
| 77c | Stratford – Mickleton – Aston Subedge – Saintbury – Broadway |
| 124 | Stratford – Bidford – Alcester – Studley – Redditch – Bromsgrove |
| 128 | Stratford – Droitwich – Worcester |

Dates of introduction for the new services from 1920 were November 1920 (22a), January 1921 (124), May 1921 (74 and 74a, a Stratford – Ettington service later replaced by service 77), June 1921 (17e and 128) and August 1922 (77 and 77c).

Letter suffixes could denote either variations of the main route, or services which were operated by the same vehicle (the 77c being an example of the latter). This system lasted until 1925 when all services were renumbered into a new series starting at 100, reflecting the massive expansion which had already taken place, but allowing room for a lot more (not enough as it turned out; all services had to be renumbered again in 1928, but this time they got it right and achieved a stability which was to last for several decades, some vestiges of the 1928 series even surviving into the twenty-first century). The Stratford – Evesham service (17e) did not feature in the 1925 renumbering, the suspension having become more than temporary, but the other services listed above became respectively the 382, 385, 128, 351, 350, 386, 237 and 260, and in June 1926 these were still the only services which reached Stratford.

Some further expansion around Stratford took place in August 1926 with the introduction of services to Shottery (387) on the 4th, followed by others to Aston Cantlow (388) and

Although Midland Red expanded rapidly during the 1920s the days of the local carriers were not yet over, and in the early post-war years many converted from horse to mechanical traction. Mr Johnson of Henley-in-Arden was one of the carriers who ran regular passenger and goods services, and his first purpose-built passenger vehicle was this Birmingham-made Garner 'Patent Bus Van' with twenty seats, supplied in August 1923. The terminal point for carriers' services was very often a public house, and Mr Johnson's Stratford 'depot' is shown on the side as the Plymouth Arms in Wood Street. Notable features of the 'Bus Van' are the rear doors and hinged platform, and the rail for carrying goods on the roof. It ran on solid tyres – a far cry from the low-floor buses operated by Johnsons on behalf of Warwickshire County Council at the start of the twenty-first century. (*Johnsons of Henley*)

By the time Stratford-on-Avon Motor Services began operations in April 1927 the 'Midland Red' had already been running buses in the area for well over ten years. Typical of the early vehicles was OA7081, a 1915 petrol-electric Tilling-Stevens which lasted until 1927, carrying four different 29-seat Tilling bodies during this time. In its early days during the First World War it ran on coal gas and carried a massive bag on its roof, but later reverted to petrol as the source of power for the electric motor which propelled the rear wheels. This view shows it in Shipston High Street, outside the Olde White Bear, the starting point for the service to Coventry via Leamington. (*Author's collection*)

Hampton Lucy (384) on the 27th. The Shottery service initially ran each weekday, but after a time was reduced to operate on Tuesdays and Fridays only. The Aston Cantlow service also ran on Tuesdays and Fridays, but the Hampton Lucy service was Friday–only.

The title carried on the side of the bright red BMMO buses was simply 'Midland', and from the 1920s the company was almost universally known by the popular name of 'Midland Red'. By this time they had a network of services stretching from the Welsh borders in the west across to Leicester and Northampton in the east, with relatively few gaps in between except where the municipal tramways held sway. The expansion of the company was rapid and ensured that few other operators entered the market in a significant way, and many of those who did gain a foothold were soon taken over. Around Stratford there were no challengers to the dominance of the Midland Red until 1927, when George Grail and Stanley Joiner decided to start their service to Shottery and set up Stratford-on-Avon Motor Services (SoAMS).

# 2

# An Eventful Start
# 1927–1929

Friday 1 April 1927 will not spring to mind as a significant date in the history of Stratford-on-Avon. However, that morning Stratford-on-Avon Motor Services began its first bus service, using a blue Chevrolet 14-seater which modestly carried the title 'Stratford-on-Avon' on the sides and paving the way for something which was to become an integral part of the town's fabric for most of the next seventy-five years or more – Stratford Blue. The new service linked the town with Shottery and Alveston, and the very first journey was the 8.15 a.m. to Shottery, driven by Mr Frank Hirons.

Stratford-on-Avon Motor Services was founded by George Grail and Stanley Joiner, who were both from the Forest of Dean area but were working in Stratford. Mr Grail was with the Prudential Assurance Co. and Mr Joiner was supervising a sewerage contract for the family business, the Dean Forest Contracting Co. (James Joiner & Sons Ltd). The two men got to know each other and one day discussed the inadequacy of the bus service for visitors to Anne Hathaway's Cottage at Shottery, a mile or so from the town centre (Midland Red's 387 service had started running between Stratford and Shottery in August 1926, but was soon reduced to Tuesdays and Fridays). Before the First World War the Dean Forest Contracting Co. had run a wagonette service between Cinderford and Soudley so Stanley Joiner had some relevant experience, and he and George Grail quickly decided to buy a bus and start up in business. Following some advice from John Watts, who ran a number of bus services in the Forest of Dean and South Wales and was also able to supply Albion and Chevrolet buses, an order was placed for one of the very popular lightweight Chevrolet LM models, fitted with a 14-seater body built by Frank Allen Ltd of Brigg, Lincolnshire. Blue paintwork was specified to make the bus stand out from the Midland Red buses, which had already been a familiar sight in and around Stratford for more than ten years. The bus (UE3403) was delivered during March and registered by Warwickshire County Council on the 25th.

The timetable drawn up by Stanley Joiner involved the bus running from Stratford along Evesham Road to Shottery, back into town along Alcester Road then via Clopton Bridge, Loxley Road and Knights Lane to Tiddington and Alveston, returning the way it had come. The service ran six days a week (not Sundays) from 8.15 a.m. to 7.45 p.m., with a basic frequency of every ninety minutes. This gave thirteen journeys a day to Shottery and eight to Alveston, but on Thursdays and Saturdays the service was extended through the evening, finishing with a 9.50 p.m. cinema bus to Alveston. Two gaps in the timetable when the bus would otherwise have run to Shottery provided a break for Mr Hirons and his conductor.

---

**Commencing April 1st, 1927, and until Further Notice (Sundays Excepted).**

# Stratford-on-Avon Motor Services.

SHOTTERY—ALVESTON, via ALCESTER ROAD, G.W.R. STATION, BRIDGE STREET, LOXLEY ROAD, and KNIGHTS LANE.

| | | A.M. | A.M. | A.M. 10.0 | A.M. 11.30 | P.M. 1.0 | P.M. 2.30 | P.M. 4.0 | P.M. 5.30 | P.M. 7.0 | Thur. & Sat. | Sat. only 8.30 | Thur. & Sat. Cinema |
|---|---|---|---|---|---|---|---|---|---|---|---|---|---|
| Shottery | Dep. | | | 10.0 | 11.30 | 1.0 | 2.30 | 4.0 | 5.30 | 7.0 | | 8.30 | |
| Stratford | ,, | | 8 40 | 10.10 | 11.40 | 1.10 | 2.40 | 4.10 | 5.40 | 7.10 | | 8.40 | 9.50 |
| Knights Lane Crossing | | | 8.47 | 10.17 | 10.47 | 1.17 | 2.47 | 4.17 | 5.47 | 7.17 | | 8.47 | 9.57 |
| Tiddington | ,, | | 8.50 | 10.20 | 11.50 | 1.20 | 2.50 | 4.20 | 5.50 | 7.20 | | 8.50 | 10.0 |
| Alveston | Arr. | | 8.55 | 10.25 | 11.55 | 1.25 | 2.55 | 4.25 | 5.55 | 7.25 | | 8.55 | 10.5 |
| Alveston | Dep. | | 9.0 | 10.30 | 12 0 | 1 30 | 3.0 | 4.30 | 6.0 | 7.30 | | 9.0 | 10.5 |
| Tiddington | Dep. | | 9.5 | 10.35 | 12.5 | 1.35 | 3.5 | 4.35 | 6.5 | 7.35 | | 9.5 | 10.10 |
| Knights Lane Crossing | | | 9.8 | 10.38 | 12.8 | 1.38 | 3.8 | 4.38 | 6.8 | 7.38 | | 9.8 | —— |
| Stratford | ,, | 8.15 | 9.15 | 10.45 | 12.15 | 1.45 STOP | 3.15 | 4.45 | 6.15 STOP | 7.45 STOP | 7.45 | 9.15 | 10.15 STOP |
| Shottery | Arr. | 8.25 | 9.25 | 10.55 | 12.25 | | 3.25 | 4.55 | | | 7.55 | 9.25 | |

### SHOTTERY and STRATFORD, via EVESHAM ROAD.

| | | | | | | | | | | | | |
|---|---|---|---|---|---|---|---|---|---|---|---|---|
| Shottery | Dep. | 8.30 | 9.30 | 11.0 | 12.30 | | 3.30 | 5.0 | | 8.0 | 9.30 |
| Stratford | Arr. | 8.40 | 9.40 | 11.10 | 12.40 | | 3.40 | 5.10 | | 8.10 Sat. only | 9.40 |
| Stratford | Dep. | | 9.50 | 11.20 | 12.50 | 2.20 | 3.50 | 5.20 | 6.50 | 8.20 | |
| Shottery | Arr. | | 10 0 | 11.30 | 1.0 | 2.30 | 4.0 | 5.30 | 7.0 | 8.30 | |

We will use every endeavour to maintain these Services, but we do not hold ourselves responsible for any delays, as punctuality is not guaranteed.

For further particulars, parcels service, &c., apply Manager, 22, EVESHAM PLACE, STRATFORD-ON-AVON.

KEEP YOUR TICKET, IT MAY BE THE WINNER.

Passengers are asked to retain their tickets, as a Free Pass will be given each week enabling the holder of a selected numbered ticket to travel over the whole of the Company's Service for one week, free of charge.

The number of the Winning Ticket will be posted in the Company's 'Buses each Monday.

---

The timetable which launched Stratford-on-Avon Motor Services on 1 April 1927, reproduced from the same day's *Stratford-upon-Avon Herald*. The bus and its crew were on the road six days a week from 8.15 a.m. until 7.45 p.m., with two thirty-five-minute breaks, but on Thursdays and Saturdays they worked until the late cinema bus returned from Alveston at 10.15 p.m. The weekly draw for a free pass illustrates Stanley Joiner's entrepreneurial skills.

The service quickly flourished and after only a week the *Herald* reported that an improved timetable was being drawn up. Grail and Joiner were delighted to see their investment paying off so quickly and ordered a second Chevrolet, similar to the first. This was registered on 5 May as UE3897 and enabled a service to be introduced to Clifford Chambers, two miles south of Stratford off the main road to Broadway and Cheltenham (Clifford Chambers was then in Gloucestershire, being transferred to Warwickshire with the boundary changes of 1931, which also saw Shipston-on-Stour transferred from Worcestershire to Warwickshire). Also during May local evening tours were introduced, with tickets available either from conductors or from 'the Misses Bennett's Stores', and by the beginning of June the Chevrolets were running to destinations as far away as Weston-Super-Mare, the Wye Valley and Oxford when they were not needed for the bus services. These excursions competed with the Warwickshire County Garage, a long-established operator of charabanc tours who were based on the Waterside in Stratford.

Midland Red were not prepared to sit back as SoAMS expanded, and on 12 May they started two new services in competition with the newcomer, the 411 to Alveston and the 413 to Clifford Chambers, and probably at the same time the 387 to Shottery reverted to weekday operation instead of operating only on Tuesdays and Fridays.

SoAMS placed a third 14-seat Chevrolet (No.3, UE4189) on the road at the beginning of June and a service was started to Preston-on-Stour and Wimpstone, off the Shipston road.

Stanley Joiner, who served as SoAMS's manager while continuing with his other work, was a true entrepreneur and never short of ideas to attract passengers. As an example, Thursday was advertised as Children's Day, when 'a child's toy balloon will be given to every passenger upon the Blue Cars', and at the end of June he organised an excursion to Bordon Hill (off the Evesham Road) to witness an eclipse of the sun. This was a complete sell-out and all three buses were needed.

Other operators were also keen to respond to the increasing demand for bus travel and on 18 July the Reliance Bus Co. of Bidford-on-Avon began operations with a service between Stratford and Evesham. This ran via Welford-on-Avon, Barton, Bidford-on-Avon, Salford Priors, Harvington and Norton. The proprietors, George Crompton and William Longford, also chose the Chevrolet LM, but theirs had bodywork by Willowbrook of Loughborough. UE4618, which carried a brown livery, was registered on 14 July.

Exactly a week after Reliance started, Stratford-on-Avon Motor Services also began a Stratford to Evesham service, but with a slightly different route from the Reliance, taking in Luddington but running north of the Avon via Cranhill instead of via Welford and Barton. This marked a change in policy as only three months earlier Grail and Joiner had said that the Shottery service was to cater for those who had no alternative services, and that there was 'no intention of Stratford Motor Services competing'. The SoAMS service ran every three hours, with four trips each way on Mondays to Fridays and five on Saturdays, when an evening bus

### RELIANCE 'BUS CO.

#### STRATFORD - ON - AVON TO EVESHAM.
BUSES will run on the above service, commencing MONDAY, JULY 18th, *via* Welford-on-Avon, Barton, Bidford-on-Avon, Salford Priors, Harvington, Norton, and Evesham.

First 'bus leaves Fountain at 9.30, and will run every two hours, until further notice.

The Reliance Bus Co.'s first advertisement, placed in the *Herald* of 15 July 1927 to announce the bus service to start the following Monday, was almost lost amongst the classified advertisements. Details of the timetable were very sketchy – when was the last bus each day?

Stratford-on-Avon Motor Services started their Stratford – Evesham service a week after the Reliance, on Monday 25 July, allowing a more realistic three hours for the round trip. SoAMS's 'Blue Safety Saloon Cars' followed a different route, taking in Luddington but running direct between Binton Corner and Bidford, where Reliance ran south of the Avon through Welford and Barton.

## STRATFORD-ON-AVON MOTOR SERVICES.
### Blue Safety Saloon Cars.

COMMENCING MONDAY, JULY 25th, a NEW SERVICE as follows:
**STRATFORD—BIDFORD—EVESHAM SERVICE No. 5.**
(Via Luddington, Binton Corner, Salford Priors, Harvington, Golden Cross, &c.).

|  | a.m. | a.m. | p.m. | p.m. | p.m. | p.m. | p.m. |
|---|---|---|---|---|---|---|---|
|  |  |  |  |  | Sats. only | Sundays only | |
| Leave Stratford (Fountain) | 8.0 | 11.0 | 2.0 | 5.0 | 8.0 | 2.0 | 5.0 |
| ,, Bidford | 8.35 | 11.35 | 2.35 | 5.35 | 8.35 | 2.35 | 5.35 |
| Arr. Evesham (approx.) | 9.10 | 12.10 | 3.10 | 6.10 | 9.10 | 3.10 | 6.10 |
| Leave Evesham | 9.30 | 12.30 | 3.30 | 6.30 | 9.30 | 3.30 | 6.30 |
| ,, Bidford | 10.5 | 1.5 | 4.5 | 7.5 | 10.5 | 4.5 | 7.5 |
| Arr. Stratford (approx.) | 10.40 | 1.40 | 4.40 | 7.40 | 10.40 | 4.40 | 7.40 |

We will use every endeavour to maintain these services, but we do not hold ourselves responsible for any delays, as punctuality is not guaranteed. We reserve the right to suspend or alter any time-table as circumstances may demand.

For further particulars apply the Manager.

Offices : 22, Evesham Place, Stratford-on-Avon.          S. H. JOINER, Manager.

### TRAVEL BLUE.

left Stratford at 8.00 p.m., returning from Evesham at 9.30 p.m. On Sundays there were two journeys each way. The service only needed one bus, but another two 14-seat Chevrolets (Nos 4 and 5; UE4664/4665) were added to the fleet in late July.

The new service was described as service 5, the first one to have a number, following the general practice among larger bus companies. Although the numbers were probably not shown on the buses, it seems that the Shottery and Alveston services must have been referred to as 1 and 2, the Clifford Chambers service as number 3, and the Preston-on-Stour and Wimpstone service as number 4. These early service numbers were not used for long, but the Evesham service became the 5 again in the post-war period and this number was used, along with a 5A variant, until the 1970s.

---

# RELIANCE 'BUS CO.

## The Daily 'Bus Service

Running between

### EVESHAM, BIDFORD, AND STRATFORD,

Via

Norton, Harvington, Salford, Barton, Welford-on-Avon, and Binton Bridges.

| Leaves Evesham Merstow Green. | Bidford | Welford | Arrive Stratford The Fountain |
|---|---|---|---|
| — | 9.30 a.m. | 9.50 a.m. | 10.15 a.m. |
| 12.55 p.m. | 1.30 p.m. | 1.50 p.m. | 2.15 p.m. |
| 4.15 ,, | 4.50 p.m. | 5.10 p.m. | 5.45 p.m. |

| Leaves Stratford Fountain | Welford | Bidford | Arrive Evesham Merstow Green |
|---|---|---|---|
| 10.20 a.m. | 10.40 a.m. | 11.0 a.m. | 11.40 a.m. |
| 2.50 p.m. | 3.10 p.m. | 3.30 p.m. | 4.10 p.m. |
| 6.0 p.m. | 6.20 p.m. | 6.50 p.m. | — |

MONDAYS, WEDNESDAYS, AND SATURDAYS.

Early 'Bus leaves Bidford Bridge at 8.25 a.m., arrive Evesham 9 a.m. First 'Bus leaves Evesham on usual route to Stratford at 9.5 a.m. A Late Service will run between Evesham, Bidford, and Stratford, leaving Evesham 10 p.m. on usual route to Stratford, and leaves Stratford for Bidford only at 11 p.m. during the Festival. Travel in Comfort. Travel Reliance. Special Terms for Theatre Parties, &c.

Apply Manager :—G. CROMPTON, Reliance Garage, Bidford-on-Avon. 'Phone 50.

---

## STRATFORD-ON-AVON MOTOR SERVICES.

### Blue Safety Saloon Cars.

REVISED TIME TABLE.

COMMENCING MONDAY, AUGUST 1st, a NEW SERVICE as follows :—

### STRATFORD—BIDFORD—EVESHAM SERVICE No. 5.

(Via Luddington, Binton Corner, Salford Priors, Harvington, Golden Cross, &c.).

**DAILY.**

| | a.m. | a.m. | a.m. | p.m. | p.m. | p.m. | p.m. | p.m. |
|---|---|---|---|---|---|---|---|---|
| Leave Stratford (Fountain) | 8.0 | 9.30 | 11.0 | 12.30 | 2.0 | 3.30 | 5.0 | 6.30 |
| ,, Bidford | 8.35 | 10.5 | 11.35 | 1.5 | 2.35 | 4.5 | 5.35 | 7.5 |
| Arr. Evesham (Vine-street) | 9.10 | 10.40 | 12.10 | 1.40 | 3.10 | 4.40 | 6.10 | 7.40 |

| | Saturdays only. | | Sundays only. | |
|---|---|---|---|---|
| | | Cinema | p.m. | p.m. |
| Leave Stratford (Fountain) | 8.0 | 9.50 | 2.0 | 5.0 |
| ,, Bidford | 8.35 | 10.25 | 2.35 | 5.35 |
| Arr. Evesham (Vine-street) | 9.10 | STOP | 3.10 | 6.10 |

**DAILY.**

| | a.m. | a.m. | p.m. | p.m. | p.m. | p.m. | p.m. | p.m. |
|---|---|---|---|---|---|---|---|---|
| Leave Evesham (Vine-street) | 9.30 | 11.0 | 12.30 | 2.0 | 3.30 | 5.0 | 6.30 | 8.0 |
| ,, Bidford | 10.5 | 11.35 | 1.5 | 2.35 | 4.5 | 5.35 | 7.5 | 8.35 |
| Arr. Stratford (Fountain) | 10.40 | 12.10 | 1.40 | 3.10 | 4.40 | 6.10 | 7.40 | 9.10 |

| | Saturdays only. | | Sundays only. | |
|---|---|---|---|---|
| | p.m. | p.m. | p.m. | p.m. |
| Leave Evesham (Vine-street) | 9.30 | | 3.30 | 6.30 |
| ,, Bidford | 10.5 | 10.30 | 4.5 | 7.5 |
| Arr. Stratford (Fountain) | 10.40 | 11.5 | 4.40 | 7.40 |

AUGUST BANK HOLIDAY AND TUESDAY as on Saturdays.

We will use every endeavour to maintain these services, but we do not hold ourselves responsible for any delays, as punctuality is not guaranteed. We reserve the right to suspend or alter any time-table as circumstances may demand.

For further particulars apply the Manager.

Offices : 22, Evesham Place, Stratford-on-Avon. S. H. JOINER, Manager.

## TRAVEL BLUE.

Reliance and SoAMS both advertised their Stratford – Evesham services in the *Herald* of 29 July 1927. Whereas the Reliance timetable had fewer journeys than two weeks earlier, SoAMS had already put a second bus on after only a week, doubling the frequency to every hour and a half.

After only a week, on 1 August the frequency of service 5 was doubled to every ninety minutes. The journey from Stratford to the Vine Street terminus in Evesham took an hour and ten minutes, and a second bus was now needed on the service. This meant that all five Chevrolets were now in daily use, leaving no spare to cover for the inevitable breakdowns and other mishaps.

The Reliance also introduced a new timetable in August, with the journey time increased to an hour and twenty minutes; George Crompton, the manager, had probably found by experience that one bus could not realistically maintain a two-hourly service. The service was reduced to two round trips a day between Stratford and Evesham with an extra journey each way between Stratford and Bidford, but an earlier start on Mondays, Wednesdays and Saturdays gave a third Evesham – Stratford journey. Like SoAMS, Reliance started from the American Fountain (Rother Street) in Stratford, but their Evesham terminus was at Merstow Green. Reliance's second Chevrolet/Willowbrook 14-seater (UE4601) arrived in September.

On 2 September a third Stratford – Evesham operator appeared on the scene when Midland Red re-introduced a service after an absence of about five years. This was a rather limited operation and probably began by running on Fridays only, but was soon increased.

The next major development was on 12 September, when Stratford-on-Avon Motor Services extended the Preston and Wimpstone service to Shipston-on-Stour, via Alderminster, Newbold-on-Stour and Tredington. The Midland Red were already running between Stratford and Shipston, and Stanley Joiner's advert in the *Herald* asserted that 'You have long asked for this service, your sure way to retain it is to travel Blue!' SoAMS were no longer afraid of taking on the Midland Red, yet the service was omitted from a new timetable published in October, so it may not have lasted long.

A lot of goodwill had been built up in the few months since April, but not without questions in the local press about inconsistencies in fares and the apparent lack of timetables (or more likely lack of adherence to them). Nevertheless by September it was reported that faretables were displayed at least on the Bidford route.

In late September a final pair of Chevrolets (Nos 6 and 7; UE4933/4934) were licensed, bringing the total to seven, and it soon emerged that they had been bought for expansion towards Leamington. This in itself came as no surprise, but Stanley Joiner's intentions caused consternation in some quarters; he had applied to the municipal authorities in Leamington and Warwick to operate between the two towns in direct competition with the trams of the Leamington & Warwick Electrical Co. The applications were submitted in September and granted in October, allowing any of the seven vehicles to ply for hire along the route.

The decision of Leamington Town Council's Watch Committee to grant the licences for twelve months was conditional on the buses being approved by their engineer before the service started and again after six months of operation. Everything was in order and the service started shortly afterwards, running between Warwick Market Place and a terminus at Regent Grove in Leamington. The timetable leaflet dated 13 October 1927 showed a much-expanded operation with a Stratford – Kenilworth service running via Wellesbourne, Charlecote, Barford and Warwick, then along the tram route to Leamington, continuing via Lillington and Chesford Bridge to the terminus at Kenilworth (Clock). Some journeys ran direct between Warwick and Kenilworth via Leek Wootton and there were also a few between Warwick and Leamington only. In a thinly veiled reference to the Midland Red, this timetable warned that

## STRATFORD-ON-AVON.
# MOTOR SERVICES,
### REVISED AND EXTENDED SERVICES.

#### Commencing Thursday, October 13th, 1927.
Temporary Time Table, subject to alteration without notice.

**STRATFORD—WARWICK—LEAMINGTON—KENILWORTH**
Week Days Only.

| | | a.m. | a.m. | a.m. | a.m. | a.m. | p.m. | p.m. | p.m. | p.m. | p.m. | p.m. | p.m. | N.S. p.m. | Sats. p.m. | Extra. p.m. |
|---|---|---|---|---|---|---|---|---|---|---|---|---|---|---|---|---|
| Stratford (Bridge St.) | dep. | 8 10 | 9 10 | 10 25 | | | 1 45 | 3 0 | | | 5 30 | 7 15 | 0 | 8 25 | 9 50 | |
| Wellesbourne | ,, | 8 25 | 9 30 | 10 37 | | | 2 0 | | | | 5 45 | 0 | | | Closes | |
| Charlecote | ,, | 8 30 | | 10 45 | | | 2 5 | 3 20 | | | 5 50 | 5 | 7 20 | 8 45 | 10 15 | |
| Barford | ,, | 8 40 | 9 40 | 10 55 | | | 2 15 | 3 30 | | | 6 0 | | 7 20 | | | |
| Warwick (Square) | ,, | 8 50 | 9 50 | 11 10 | 11 15 | 12 25 | 2 25 | 3 40 | 4 45 | 5 20 | 6 15 | | 7 40 | 8 50 | | |
| Leam'ton R'gt Gr. | ,, | 9 5 | 10 10 | 11 30 | L | 12 40 | 2 45 | 3 55 | L | 4 55 | 5 40 | 6 25 | | 8 0 | L | |
| Lillington (Church Lane) | ,, | 9 10 | 10 20 | 11 40 | | 12 50 | 2 55 | 4 0 | | | | | 8 5 | | | |
| Kenilworth (Clock) | ,, | 9 25 | 10 35 | 11 55 | 11 35 | 1 0 | 3 5 | 4 15 | 4 0 | | ·. | | 8 20 | 9 10 | | |

**KENILWORTH—LEAMINGTON—WARWICK—STRATFORD**

| | | a.m. | a.m. | a.m. | a.m. | a.m. | p.m. | p.m. | p.m. | p.m. | p.m. | p.m. | p.m. | p.m. | p.m. | p.m. |
|---|---|---|---|---|---|---|---|---|---|---|---|---|---|---|---|---|
| Kenilworth (Clock) | dep. | | 9 30 | 10 40 | 11 40 | 12 0 | 1 5 | 3 10 | 4 20 | | | | 8 25 | 9 15 | | |
| Lillington Church Lane | ,, | | 9 45 | L | 11 55 | L | 1 20 | L | 4 15 | L | | L | 9 30 | | | |
| Leam'ton R'gt Gr. | ,, | | 9 55 | | 12 10 | | 1 25 | | 4 30 | | 5 5 | 5 45 | 7 0 | | 9 35 | 10 0 | |
| Warwick (Square) | ,, | | 10 10 | 11 | 12 25 | 12 20 | 1 40 | 3 30 | 4 40 | 4 40 | 5 15 | 6 10 | 7 10 | 8 45 | | 10 15 |
| Barford | ,, | | 10 20 | | 12 35 | | 1 50 | | 4 50 | | | 6 20 | 7 20 | | | 10 25 |
| Charlecote | ,, | 7 50 | 10 30 | | 12 45 | 2 0 | | 5 0 | | | 6 30 | 7 30 | | 8 50 | 10 35 | |
| Wellesbourne | ,, | | 10 35 | | 12 50 | | | 5 5 | | | 6 35 | | | | | |
| Stratford | arr. | 8 5 | 10 50 | | 1 10 | | 2 20 | | 5 20 | | | 6 50 | 7 50 | | 9 15 | 10 50 |

L. Direct Route. N.S. Not Saturdays

We will use every endeavour to maintain these services, but do not hold ourselves responsible for any delay as punctuality is not guaranteed.

#### "OUR SERVICE IS YOUR SERVICE."

This Time-Table is arranged by the Stratford-on-Avon Motor Service Company. All their buses are **BLUE**. The **Monopolists** are endeavouring to keep us off the roads and retain their services to you without competition.

If you are not in favour of a **Monopoly** of public service omnibuses you will, whenever possible

# TRAVEL BLUE!

A **Monopoly** Bus will probably be running just in front of this time-table. The remedy for freedom of service is entirely **IN YOUR HANDS.**

Season Tickets are issued to regular travellers and School children, on all Routes, upon application.

#### KEEP YOUR TICKET, IT MAY BE THE WINNER.

Offices: | Manager:
22 Evesham Place, Stratford-on-Avon. | S. H. JOINER.

A. J. Stanley, Printer, Tudor Press, Ely Street, Stratford-on-Avon.

This handbill dated 13 October 1927 announced the ambitious expansion which took Stratford-on-Avon Motor Services to Leamington, Warwick and Kenilworth, competing both with Midland Red and the Leamington & Warwick Electrical Co.'s trams. Note the various references to the 'monopolists' and their activities, and the exhortation to 'Travel Blue'. Operation between Leamington and Kenilworth was short-lived and had ceased by December.

A map of Stratford-on-Avon Motor Services' bus routes as at 13 October 1927. The section from Wimpstone Turn to Shipston is shown, but although this was introduced on 12 September it may have been discontinued by October.

'the monopolists are endeavouring to keep us off the roads and retain their services to you without competition. A monopoly bus will probably be running just in front of this timetable. The remedy for freedom of service is entirely in your hands.' One immediate result of the competition was that on 15 October the Leamington & Warwick Electrical Co. dropped the tram fare between the two towns from 4*d* to the pre-war fare of 3*d*.

For a time, Stratford-on-Avon Motor Services ran a half-hourly service along the tramway, but from December this was increased to every fifteen minutes. This was partly at the expense of the Kenilworth service, which was reduced to two journeys a day to and from Warwick, although extended to terminate at Kenilworth Castle; journeys between Leamington and Kenilworth were discontinued. Between Stratford and Warwick some journeys now ran via Snitterfield and Norton Lindsey, to the west of the main road, instead of via Wellesbourne.

Midland Red had been operating between Stratford and Coventry via Leamington and Kenilworth for more than ten years, and the appearance of the Blue buses led them to take steps to safeguard their revenue. Without naming either party, a letter in the *Leamington Spa Courier* in November 1927 referred to 'an enterprising proprietor' who had started to provide three or four buses a day from Leek Wootton to Kenilworth and Warwick, but found his efforts thwarted by 'a well-established firm of bus owners' running two minutes in front. The writer questioned whether, if the newcomer was driven off the road, it was right for the local residents 'to be left quite at the mercy of those who regard our roads merely as a site for a commercial battle, with no thought for the public whose support has enabled them to defeat their rivals'.

The first of a new generation of SoAMS buses joined the fleet in the last few weeks of 1927. This was No.8 (UE5283), a Thornycroft A2-Long model fitted with a 20-seat saloon body by Hall, Lewis & Co. of Park Royal, London. It was registered on 5 December and immediately became the pride of the fleet. Two days before Christmas a photograph of it appeared in the *Herald*, where it was described in glowing terms with its low entrance step, pneumatic tyres, special springs, 'sociable rear' (smoking area), blue leather upholstery and blue and white linoleum floor. There were also 'special balanced windows which permit of conversion into

SoAMS bought seven Chevrolets in their first six months, and the final pair was acquired for the major expansion into the Leamington area in October 1927. No.7 (UE4934) was registered on 30 September, and is shown here at the Regent Grove terminus in Leamington while employed on the Stratford – Kenilworth service. The notice placed in the small upper window at the rear urges passengers to 'Travel Blue'. The crew are both well wrapped up in their winter uniforms on this wet day. (*Author's collection*)

an open bus'. What this meant is not entirely clear, but at the time the fashion for charabancs had not completely died, and although service buses were normally fully enclosed, vehicles used for touring usually left the passengers in closer contact with the elements. Folding or sliding canvas roofs were particularly popular, and it was probably with excursions in mind that the 'open bus' option was specified. The Thornycroft was certainly a far more refined vehicle than the preceding Chevrolets. The *Herald* article also commented that 'few towns of the size of Stratford can boast so efficient a bus service. The growth of the Company has been phenomenal. Coming into existence last April, buses have been put on the road at the rate of one per month. That they have proved a boon to local residents cannot be doubted.'

Towards the end of the year a town-centre office was established at 28 Wood Street, business having previously been carried out from George Grail's house at 22 Evesham Place. The Wood Street address was used for the press announcement that services would be suspended on Christmas Day, normal services resuming at noon on Boxing Day.

At the start of 1928 SoAMS was locked in intense rivalry with the Leamington & Warwick trams and, closer to home, facing increased competition from the Midland Red around Stratford. Although Midland Red had no base in Stratford, they did have garages in Birmingham and several other surrounding towns – Banbury (opened 1919), Bromsgrove (1920), Leamington (1922) and Worcester (1914) – and these were used to maintain the Stratford services. Midland Red published a new timetable on 11 February 1928 when all services were again renumbered, and this listed the following services from Stratford:

| | |
|---|---|
| 150 | Stratford – Birmingham |
| 324 | Stratford – Bromsgrove |
| 353 | Stratford – Worcester |
| 517 | Coventry – Stratford – Shipston |
| 521 | Stratford – Hampton Lucy |
| 522 | Stratford – Snitterfield |
| 523 | Stratford – Broadway |
| 524 | Stratford – Shottery |
| 526 | Stratford – Aston Cantlow |
| 527 | Stratford – Alveston Turn |
| 528 | Stratford – Clifford Chambers |
| 529 | Stratford – Moreton Morrell |
| 530 | Stratford – Evesham |
| 531 | Stratford – Ardens Grafton |
| 532 | Stratford – Chipping Campden |
| 533 | Stratford – Ilmington |
| 534 | Stratford – Shipston – Banbury |
| 559 | Stratford – Norton Lindsey – Wolverton – Leamington |
| 590 | Stratford – Warwick – Coventry |

Some of these had been introduced in the preceding year to meet the competition from Stratford-on-Avon Motor Services (and, in the case of the Evesham service, which had already been increased to operate six days a week, with Reliance as well). Among the vehicles

After the Chevrolets came a quartet of Thornycroft 20-seaters, the first of which was No.8 (UE5283), registered in December 1927. This photograph shows it when brand new, probably at the London premises of the coachbuilders, Hall, Lewis & Co. The small lettering behind the rear wheel shows the contemporary maximum speed of 12mph – a limit which was widely ignored by bus operators, who timetabled services on the basis of much higher operating speeds. These buses were a big improvement on the relatively basic Chevrolets, and much better suited for runs such as the Stratford – Kenilworth service, which for a time was extended at either end to operate Evesham – Coventry, taking 2½ hours. (*The Omnibus Society*)

Soon after delivery in December 1927, No.8 was posed outside Anne Hathaway's Cottage, with appropriate destination blind and slipboard below the side windows. Note that the fleetname read 'Stratford-*upon*-Avon', unlike the Chevrolets. (*Author's collection*)

used were early examples of the home-built Midland Red 'SOS'. These highly successful machines were the brainchild of Midland Red's Chief Engineer, Mr L.G. Wyndham Shire (the letters SOS are said to have stood for Shire's Own Specification) and were a match for any bus of the time – more than a match for most. The lively performance of the SOSs must have given Stanley Joiner's nippy little Chevrolets and the sturdier Thornycrofts a good run for their money, yet they could carry twice as many passengers as the Chevrolets.

Over in Leamington, the Blue buses were having a serious impact on the performance of the tramway. Having assessed the situation, the Electrical Company concluded that the only way to beat them was to resume motorbus operation themselves, and in February four 1927 Tilling-Stevens (RA4002-4005) with 30-seat bodies were acquired from the Midland General Omnibus Co. in Derbyshire. Midland General and the Leamington & Warwick Electrical Co. were both controlled by the Balfour Beatty group and used the group's standard green and cream colours, so the buses would have looked quite at home alongside the trams.

Licences were obtained and the buses were put to work along the tramway on 4 February, thereby further reducing takings on the trams, whose future began to look distinctly bleak. Originally the buses ran to the Avenue Road tram terminus in Leamington, but following a request from the Chief Constable a loop via York Road was instigated. The additional time required for this was used as a pretext to introduce an extra bus onto the service, exceeding the number authorised, but this was challenged by the authorities and stopped.

Three more 20-seat Thornycrofts joined the SoAMS fleet in the early months of 1928. No.9 (UE5749) was registered in February and Nos 10/11 (UE6494/6734) followed in May and June; these two having a dual-door layout with the extra door at the rear of the saloon. Prior to the delivery of the latter pair, two Italian Lancia buses were borrowed from Hall Lewis for a short time.

During March one vehicle was badly damaged when it skidded in a blizzard and hit a tree at Milverton, between Warwick and Leamington. It was reported that the side of the bus was

By 1928 virtually everywhere the 'Blue' went, the 'Red' went also, but Midland Red had a much more extensive network which stretched to Banbury, Birmingham, Broadway, Coventry and Worcester. This advertisement was placed in the first edition of the *Shakespeare Pictorial and Visitors' Weekly Guide*, published on 23 May 1928, and shows the extent of the services from Stratford. Midland Red had parcels and enquiry agents in Bridge Street, but the telephone number given for information is Leamington 194. The bus appears to be an early example of Midland Red's own-built 'FS' (Forward Steering) type, the first in which the driver sat beside rather than behind the engine.

smashed and the steering column broken. Although several passengers were cut by broken glass there were no serious injuries and the driver escaped shaken but unhurt. The bus had been carrying passengers to a cross-country race at Leamington. Another bus was damaged in April as it rounded a bend at Charlecote and collided with an oncoming car whose chauffeur was returning his lady passenger from Warwick. One bus passenger was hurt. With the fleet now standing at eleven these temporary losses could perhaps be sustained without any disruption to services – in any case one bus missing from the combined frequency between Leamington and Warwick may not have been noticed.

As the summer approached, the buses had to work harder, handling not only the seasonal influx of visitors but also the programme of excursions. On Whit Sunday an all-day tour to the Wye Valley was offered for a fare of 10s 6d, leaving Stratford at 10.00 a.m. This was probably inspired by Stanley Joiner's knowledge of Gloucestershire, and ran via Malvern, Ross-on-Wye, Symonds Yat and Tintern Abbey to Chepstow, returning through Newnham-on-Severn, Gloucester and Cheltenham. Other tours and excursions were operated, although the programme was less extensive than that of the Warwickshire County Garage, which had bought two new charabancs for the 1928 season: UE6159, an 18-seater Morris, and UE6520, a Guy.

The Wood Street office was now taking bookings for the long-distance coach services which had started to spring up, including those from Chester and Liverpool to London via Stratford and Oxford. Until 1928 coaches were restricted to 12mph, although this was quite openly disregarded, even to the extent of publishing timetables which could not be operated legally. The new limit from October 1928 was 20mph, but it was not unknown for charabancs and coaches to travel at much greater speeds. Contemporary press reports referred to 40 or even 50mph being recorded, and later in the year one of the drivers on the Liverpool run was fined for speeding.

Reverting to the local buses, an innovation during July was a special all-day ticket for unlimited travel on the Blue buses. This cost 3s and could either be bought from conductors or in advance from the office. Midland Red were already offering 'Day Anywhere' tickets from their offices in Birmingham and elsewhere, but clearly felt there was a need to respond to the SoAMS ticket. Within three weeks they were advertising a more restricted (and cheaper) version of their 'Anywhere' ticket, valid on 'most of the routes to and from Stratford-on-Avon' including to Kenilworth, which SoAMS now reached five times a day (on Sundays there were only three journeys). Midland Red's 'Anywhere' ticket cost 2s 6d, undercutting SoAMS by 6d, but apparently could only be bought from the local 'Red' bus inspector in Bridge Street, and not from conductors. Although most Midland Red buses carried on to Coventry the tickets were not valid beyond Kenilworth, which was the limit of SoAMS's operations.

Stanley Joiner had applied to run through to Coventry but the city's Watch Committee had refused the application, so Midland Red continued to have the road between Kenilworth and Coventry to themselves. Undaunted, he lodged an appeal with the Ministry of Transport, and a hearing was held in Coventry in July. SoAMS was represented by Mr G.W. Moore and the Watch Committee by Mr Fred Smith, the Town Clerk. George Grail and Stanley Joiner were also present at the hearing, together with Coventry Corporation's Tramway Manager, the Chief of Police, and three Midland Red representatives, including Mr O.C. Power, the Traffic Manager.

## STRATFORD-UPON-AVON BLUE MOTOR SERVICES.

To See Nature's Pictures

TRAVEL BLUE.

BLUE SALOON BUS AT ANNE HATHAWAY'S COTTAGE

Daily Services to all parts of Shakespeare's Country.

FOR A PLEASANT OUTING TRY OUR COMBINED ROAD AND RIVER TRIP by any Blue 'Bus to BIDFORD-ON-AVON and Holland's River Boats on the Avon to CLEVE.

**RETURN FARE, 2/3 inclusive.**

By June 1928, when this advertisement was placed, the word 'Blue' had been incorporated into the company's title. Note the use of the posed photograph of Thornycroft No.8 (UE5283) at Anne Hathaway's cottage. The combined road and river trip to Cleeve Prior, about two miles downriver from Bidford, must have been a perfect way to spend a hot summer afternoon.

In support of the SoAMS application it was claimed that services between Evesham, Stratford and Coventry were inadequate and needed improving, but the Town Clerk was opposed to licensing any further buses on the grounds of congestion. The press report quoted the Watch Committee's view that 'the town was already served by the Midland Red' and stated that since the application from SoAMS had first been rejected another ten licences had been issued to the Midland Red. This brought their total up to seventy, on top of which the Corporation had thirty buses licensed.

Mr Smith stated that the Blue buses had run as far as Kenilworth some time previously but the service had been withdrawn and only resumed a few days before the inquiry. The reason for the erratic operation was said to be Midland Red's practice of running a bus just in front of the Blue one, to no fixed timetable. When he heard this Mr Atkinson, who conducted the hearing, pronounced 'it is a perfect scandal that Town Councils allow omnibus companies to have monopolies, and run about as though roads were race tracks'. He then granted Joiner's application, overturning the Watch Committee's decision. Whilst this was an undoubted victory for SoAMS, the Coventry service proved to be short lived. Although four journeys each way were shown in the January 1929 timetable (most of which ran through to/from Evesham), the service was truncated at Kenilworth again before the June 1929 agreement with Midland Red was negotiated.

During August there was a court case in Leamington as a result of an incident in York Road on 31 July (SoAMS were presumably now running as far as York Road to match the 'Green' buses, having originally run only to Regent Grove). Reginald Paget, a Leamington & Warwick Green bus driver, had attempted to overtake a Blue bus while a Miss Matthews was driving in the opposite direction. In his evidence, William Barnes, the Blue bus driver, said that there was no doubt that the driver of the Green bus was racing him. As a result Paget, of Castle Street, Warwick, was fined £1 0s 0d for 'driving to the danger of the public'.

In an incident of a different kind, SoAMS driver Mr F.A. Orchard was driving his bus along Shipston Road in Stratford one day in September when he encountered a burning charabanc belonging to the South Midland company of Oxford, but despite his efforts with a 'patent extinguisher' the chara was completely destroyed.

The rivalry around Stratford continued, but with less intensity than in Leamington and Warwick, and Stratford Town Council were carefully watching events. In July SoAMS had been asked not to allow their larger buses (the Thornycrofts) to use Knights Lane or Loxley Road, and in October the Sanitary & Highways Committee discussed the question of bus competition. Concern about competitive tactics was mounting, and Alderman Smith proposed that all bus licences should be endorsed 'This licence is issued solely on the condition that the bus runs at such a time and in such a direction as approved by the Council'. In support of his motion the Alderman commented that buses were running in twos and chasing each other, without enough passengers to fill even one bus. He claimed they were ruining the roads, costing the Council thousands of pounds in maintenance. However, he was careful to stress that his criticisms applied equally to the Red and Blue buses. After listening to this and to Alderman Bullard, who said that buses ran in duplicate all the time on his local route, the Town Clerk pointed out that the companies had already been asked to submit timetables and to give an undertaking to stick to them, which they had done; the problem for the Council was to ensure that the undertaking was honoured. Alderman Winter asked if the Council had powers to curtail licences prematurely, but the Town Clerk replied that the procedure was simply not to renew the licences of offending companies. Alderman Smith's motion was passed, but the problems were not resolved overnight.

Early in November SoAMS introduced a regular Thursday excursion to Birmingham, which was already well served by Midland Red's service 150 and by the Great Western Railway. No doubt this further aggravated relations between Red and Blue. The excursion bus left from outside the Wood Street office at 2.00 p.m. and returned from Birmingham at 9.00 p.m. Seats could be pre-booked at 3s 6d return, although after two weeks this was reduced to 3s.

The hostility between the operators was illustrated by a case before Warwick County Police Court on 17 November which resulted in Midland Red driver Joseph Mansill being bound over for threatening behaviour. This arose from an altercation in Wellesbourne between Mansill and William Skidmore, a SoAMS driver. The *Herald* reported that Skidmore had been driving from Warwick to Stratford but twice pulled out into the middle of the road to prevent Mansill from overtaking. Eventually Mansill did get past, and on reaching Wellesbourne Skidmore found him standing in the road and had to brake sharply to avoid hitting him. Mansill then walked across to Skidmore's bus, stepped inside and threatened to punch him between the eyes, vowing that in future he would cut up every Blue bus that he passed. The conductor and a passenger corroborated this. When he announced the bench's decision, Sir Michael Lakin said that any future cases of this nature would be treated more severely.

Although violent clashes between bus drivers were not a daily occurrence in the fiercely competitive days of the late 1920s, Stanley Baldwin's Conservative government was aware of similar rivalry up and down the country and had set up a Royal Commission on Transport, which amongst other things was charged with drafting legislation to curb the worst excesses of competition.

An unexpected development in December was Stratford Town Council's decision to license the Great Western Railway to run two motorbuses between Shipston and Stratford. The GWR had been one of the pioneers of motorbus operation, having started its first service, between Helston and the Lizard in Cornwall, in August 1903. Services had later been developed throughout the GWR's territory, and by 1928 around 300 buses were in operation. These were used on a wide variety of work from local feeder routes to grandly styled 'Land Cruises', the forerunners of today's luxury coach touring holidays. The Railway (Road Transport) Acts of 1928 paved the way for a major expansion of the railway companies' bus service operations, mainly through buying shares in the established 'territorial' bus companies. However, direct railway operation was envisaged for Stratford, using buses in the GWR's well-known 'chocolate and cream' livery. This was welcomed by a *Herald* reporter, who scathingly wrote 'At the present time, Shipston's railway facilities are almost beneath contempt ... the trip from Shipston to Stratford (ten road miles) occupies approximately two-and-a-half hours! With the inauguration of the Great Western Railway bus services it would be little loss to Shipston if the passenger station were to be closed'. The lengthy rail journey was explained by the fact that a passenger from Shipston first had to travel south via stations at Longdon Road (Darlingscott) and Stretton-on-Fosse to Moreton-in-Marsh, and then change onto a less than direct train via Honeybourne to Stratford. Despite the grant of the licences it was to be some months before the GWR started bus operations in the district, and then it was not in the form proposed.

At the end of 1928 matters in Leamington were rapidly coming to a head. The Leamington & Warwick Electrical Co. realised that it was unable to compete on equal terms with its rivals. Running a tramway was an expensive business, made worse by some of the statutory obligations such as maintaining parts of the highway. Alternative strategies were examined, and the company decided in favour of replacing the tramway with a trolleybus system. This was to include an additional route between the towns, via Old Warwick Road and Myton, and the company had already started a motorbus service on this route during September with three brand new 20-seat Reos (UE7085-7087).

The trolleybus proposals were included in a bill which was prepared in the latter half of 1928. As well as seeking powers to abandon the tramway and substitute trolleybuses, the Leamington and Warwick Traction Bill sought a restriction on competition in return for the imposition of a statutory duty 'to provide a reasonable service, including workmen's services'. Opposition to the Bill was fierce, with the proposal to introduce trolleybuses proving to be the most controversial. Warwick Town Council objected strongly, protesting that 'the trackless tramcars [a common term for trolleybuses at the time], combined with the erection of ugly standards and overhead wiring, will ruin Warwick's beauty'. The prospect of trolley-buses passing Lord Leycester's Hospital, St Mary's Church and the castle entrance was bad enough for the Council, but the final straw was the 'desecration of the castle view' which would be caused by installing wiring over Castle Bridge on the Myton route. The Council for the Protection of Rural England joined the protest, as did Leamington Town Council and Warwickshire County Council.

Apart from the aesthetic concerns, fears were also expressed about the attempts to secure monopoly powers. Not surprisingly this is what most concerned SoAMS, who opposed the Bill. Their concern was quite naturally to protect their own interests, but they had the

## 5

### PASSENGER REGULATIONS.

1. Every endeavour will be made to maintain the services as given in this Time Table, but the Company do not guarantee punctuality, and reserve the right to cancel or alter any service as circumstances may demand. The Company cannot accept any liability for any loss or damage sustained thereby.

2. Children under 3 years free; 3 to 14 years half ordinary full fare, if not occupying a seat.

3. Passengers are warned not to attempt to enter or alight from the Bus while in motion.

4. Intending passengers are requested to signal the driver if it is desired to stop the Bus.

5. All passengers must obtain tickets properly punched, to the value of the fare paid, which must be retained for production to any of the Company's officials for inspection.

6. Passenger's parcels under 21lbs carried free; above 21lbs. according to weight. The Company reserve the right to refuse to carry any parcel or package.

Any suggestions for the Improvement of these services, complaint as to irregularity, or incivility on the part of any of the Company's staff will receive attention..

'Phone 307

OFFICES: 28 WOOD STREET, STRATFORD-ON-AVON.

MANAGER: S. H. JOINER.

### TRAVEL BLUE.

---

## 11

### STRATFORD-ON-AVON
# BLUE MOTOR SERVICES.

Services to all parts of

# SHAKESPEARE'S COUNTRY

| | |
|---|---|
| WARWICK. | SHIPSTON-ON-STOUR, |
| LEAMINGTON SPA. | BIDFORD-ON-AVON. |
| SNITTERFIELD | EVESHAM. |
| SHOTTERY | ALVESTON. |
| GUY'S CLIFFE, | KENILWORTH. Etc. |

COVENTRY.

Time Tables will be posted to any address upon application.

Head Enquiry Office:     Manager:
28 WOOD STREET,    **S. H. Joiner.**
STRATFORD.
'Phone 307.

### TRAVEL BLUE.

---

**STRATFORD, WARWICK, LEAMINGTON, KENILWORTH & COVENTRY.**

| | | Week Days | | | | | | | S.O. | Sundays. | | |
|---|---|---|---|---|---|---|---|---|---|---|---|---|
| | | a.m. | a.m. | a.m. | a.m. | p.m. | p.m. | p.m. | p.m. | p.m. | p.m. | p.m. |
| Evesham | dep. | | | | | 10 0 | 1 30 | 4 30 | 7 0 | | | |
| Bidford | ,, | | | | | 10 30 | 2 10 | 5 10 | 7 40 | | | |
| Stratford | ,, | 7 30 | 7 50 | 8 0 | 9 30 | 11 20 | 2 50 | 5 45 | 8 15 | 2 0 | 5 0 | 7 20 |
| Snitterfield | ,, | 7 45 | | | 9 45 | | 3 5 | 6 0 | 8 30 | 2 15 | | |
| Wolverton | ,, | 7 50 | | | 9 50 | | 3 10 | 6 5 | | 2 20 | | |
| Norton Lindsey | ,, | 7 55 | | | 9 55 | | 3 15 | 6 10 | 8 40 | 2 25 | | |
| Hampton-on-the-Hill | ,, | 8 0 | | | 10 0 | | 3 20 | 6 15 | 8 45 | 2 30 | | |
| Wellesbourne | ,, | | 8 15 | | | 11 35 | | | | 5 15 | 7 35 | |
| Charlecote | ,, | | 8 20 | | | 11 40 | | | | 5 30 | 7 30 | |
| Barford | ,, | | 8 30 | | | 11 50 | | | | 5 30 | 7 30 | |
| Warwick (Square) | ,, | 8 15 | 8 25 | 8 40 | 10 15 | 12 20 | 3 35 | 6 25 | 9 0 | 2 40 | 5 45 | 7 55 |
| Leamington | arr. | 8 25 | | 8 50 | 10 30 | 12 20 | 3 50 | 6 35 | 9 15 | 2 55 | 6 0 | 8 20 |
| Guy's Cliff | dep. | | 8 30 | | | 12 30 | 3 40 | 6 30 | | | | |
| Leek Wootton (P.O.) | ,, | | 8 35 | | | 12 35 | 3 45 | 6 35 | | | | |
| Kenilworth (Clock) | ,, | | 8 40 | | | 12 40 | 3 50 | 6 40 | | | | |
| Coventry | arr. | | 8 55 | | | 1 5 | 4 5 | 7 50 | | | | |

# HATTON'S FOR BOY'S AND MEN'S CLOTHING.

Market Place, WARWICK.
**Blue Motors stop at the door.**

---

**STRATFORD—NEWBOLD—SHIPSTON-ON-STOUR.**

| | | Week Days | | | | | | | | S.O. | |
|---|---|---|---|---|---|---|---|---|---|---|---|
| | | a.m. | a.m. | a.m. | p.m. | p.m. | p.m. | p.m. | p.m. | p.m. | |
| | | | | XX | | | | | | | |
| Stratford (Bridge St.) | dep. | ... | 8 50 | ... | 12 30 | 2 20 | 4 30 | 7 15 | ... | 9 50 | EVERY Thursday a BLUE BUS |
| Preston Turn | ,, | ... | 9 0 | ... | 12 40 | 2 30 | 4 40 | 7 25 | ... | 10 5 | leaves Shipston for |
| Whimpstone Turn | ,, | ... | 9 5 | ... | 12 45 | 2 35 | 4 45 | 7 30 | ... | 10 10 | BIRMINGHAM at 1.30 |
| Alderminster | ,, | ... | 9 10 | ... | 12 50 | 2 40 | 4 50 | 7 35 | ... | 10 15 | Returning from |
| Newbold | ,, | ... | | ... | 12 55 | 2 45 | 4 55 | 7 40 | ... | 10 20 | BIRMINGHAM at 9. |
| Tredington | ,, | 7 50 | 9 20 | ... | 1 0 | 2 50 | 5 0 | 7 45 | ... | STOP | |
| Shipston | arr. | 8 55 | | ... | 1 10 | 3 0 | 5 10 | 7 50 | ... | | |

**SHIPSTON-ON-STOUR—NEWBOLD—STRATFORD.**

| | | | | | XX | | | | | | |
|---|---|---|---|---|---|---|---|---|---|---|---|
| Shipston | dep. | 8 10 | 10 0 | ... | 1 30 | 5 15 | 7 50 | s o | ... | ... | You can get in a |
| Tredington | ,, | 8 15 | 10 10 | ... | 1 40 | 5 25 | 8 0 | ... | ... | ... | first house perfor- |
| Newbold | ,, | 8 25 | 10 15 | ... | 1 45 | 5 30 | 8 5 | ... | ... | ... | mance at a |
| Alderminster | ,, | 8 30 | 10 20 | ... | 1 50 | 5 35 | 8 10 | ... | ... | ... | B'mingham Theatre |
| Whimpstone Turn | ,, | 8 35 | 10 25 | ... | 1 55 | 5 40 | 9 15 | ... | ... | ... | on our Thursday |
| Preston Turn | ,, | 8 40 | 10 30 | ... | 2 0 | 5 45 | 9 20 | ... | ... | ... | afternoon trips. |
| Stratford | ,, | 8 50 | 10 45 | ... | 2 10 | 5 55 | 9 30 | ... | ... | ... | |
| Stratford G.W.St. | arr. | ... | ... | ... | 3 45 | ... | ... | ... | ... | ... | |

XX Not Thursdays.     S.O. Sat. only.

Extracts from a timetable booklet published in January 1929, showing part of the timetable for the short-lived Evesham – Coventry service.

---

## 23

### TRAVEL BLUE !

## *Special Road and River Trip*

daily by Blue Buses to

# Bidford-on-Avon and Cleeve Hills

FROM

### Stratford-on-Avon or Evesham.

**For Times see Page 9.**

**14 Miles by Road**
**6 Miles by River**    **2/3** per person

## HOLLAND'S TEA GARDENS,
PARTIES CATERED FOR.

**Enquiries to the Candy Shop, Evesham or 28 Wood Street, Stratford-on-Avon.**

Parcels for delivery on route can be accepted at either of the above Enquiry Offices.

support of the travelling public, who feared a return to the fares charged by the Electrical Company before the Blue buses started running.

Recognising the strength of the opposition, the Electrical Company eventually decided to propose conventional motorbuses, which would not require overhead wiring, instead of trolleybuses. This went a long way towards satisfying the majority of the Bill's opponents, but a lively debate took place when the Bill went before the House of Commons in March 1929.

Mr Wrottesley KC, who represented the promoters of the Bill, described in some detail the history of the tramway, particularly since September 1927 when Grail and Joiner had applied for the licences allowing them to compete. Included in Mr Wrottesley's evidence was the following damning attack on SoAMS:

> ... *Stratford-on-Avon Motor Services applied to the Corporation to run omnibuses on the following route: Stratford, Warwick, Leamington and Kenilworth. Seven licences were granted unconditionally to that firm, and the result was that in October 1927 there commenced what was at first a somewhat spasmodic service from Stratford to Warwick and Leamington. So far as we are aware, the buses went rarely, if at all, to Kenilworth. That was not the worst of it. The operators in question soon afterwards dropped out Stratford on many journeys and ran an intense service along the Leamington – Warwick route. I don't say they never went to Stratford, but that was not their regular service. Here you see a firm applying for licences for a particular route which from the beginning right down to date has not observed the conditions under which the licences were granted. In the circumstances it seemed rather a hardship to a statutory undertaking like this company – which after all does provide an established service, charge workmen's fares, and keeps up a large portion of the tramway at its own expense and pays rates, besides employing local labour – whereas the Blue bus company does not run a proper timetable service, does not run workmen's trams, does not keep up any portion of the highway, and, so far as we know, does not pay local rates or employ local labour. It seems hard on a company which does all these things to have competitors licensed – almost encouraged – to run on its route. Evidence can be given to show how partial and intermittent was the service of the Blue bus company. It bears no sort of relationship to the sort of service which the statutory company has to give, and give under penalty if necessary.*

Mr G.B. Crowder, representing SoAMS, was given the opportunity to question Sir Joseph Nall, Chairman of the Electrical Company. Parts of this cross-examination, after Mr Crowder had asked Sir Joseph whether he was claiming that the Blue bus service was inefficient, went as follows:

| | |
|---|---|
| SIR JOSEPH | Well, 168 journeys were missed in four weeks. |
| MR CROWDER | But they provide a service which caters for a public need? |
| SIR JOSEPH | I say it is not necessarily in the public service. |
| MR CROWDER | The public are served and with some small profit to my client? |
| SIR JOSEPH | I presume so. |
| MR CROWDER | I suggest that you are dealing hardly with my company in coming to parliament and seeking powers to exclude us altogether from trading along your route. |

| | |
|---|---|
| SIR JOSEPH | No. |
| MR CROWDER | We feel that your company has failed in open competition with us, and that you are therefore seeking these exclusive powers. |
| SIR JOSEPH | On the contrary we have not competed with them. They have gone on to Kenilworth and Stratford. |

On 14 March 1929, Sir John Ganzoni MP, the Chairman of the Select Committee, announced that it had decided to allow some protection of the Electrical Company's interests, but that four Blue buses would remain licensed to run over the tram route. At this point it was mentioned that the Electrical Company had made an offer to purchase SoAMS but although it had been turned down the offer remained open. What the offer amounted to is not known, but faced with the prospect of having to cut back their operations the proprietors were obviously tempted. Some quick thinking followed, and after further discussion a deal was struck. This involved the Electrical Company paying £2,120 for two Chevrolet buses together with 'the interest and goodwill in that portion of their business which consists of plying for public hire between and within the Boroughs of Warwick and Royal Leamington Spa'. The two buses, Nos 4 and 5 (UE4664/4665), were delivered to the Electrical Company on 25 March, leaving SoAMS with a fleet of nine.

After operation on Saturday 23rd, SoAMS withdrew its service along the familiar battleground of the tramway and left the doomed tramcars to soldier on alongside the Electrical Company's small fleet of motorbuses. The following Friday the *Courier* was moved to comment in its editorial columns that 'the Blue buses ... indulged in a very vigorous farewell "kick" against their rivals. Blue buses seemed to pass us every minute in Warwick Street, and not one of them seemed prepared to take us to Stratford. So ended that phase of a memorable struggle'.

Stanley Joiner clearly felt that this report was less than fair and wrote to the paper to put the record straight. In doing so he explained much of the philosophy behind SoAMS, and for this reason it is reproduced below as a fitting conclusion to this chapter:

> SIR – *Your remarks in the* Courier *of the 29th ult., in which you refer to the Blue buses indulging in a farewell "kick", are apt to mislead some of our patrons into thinking that all services other than those between Leamington and Warwick were dropped, and that every available Blue bus was used to give what you term a "vigorous farewell kick" on that final Saturday.*
>
> *We can only conclude that you were misinformed or, if you stood in Warwick Street for many minutes and saw Blue buses passing at the rate of one a minute, that it was an optical illusion on your part.*
>
> *No, sir, such was not the case. Whatever your opinion as to the recent struggle by the authorities concerned may be, you must admit that the Blue buses were helpful in getting rid of your trams and overhead gear.*
>
> *We do not claim any credit for the final result but so far as what you term "a memorable struggle" was concerned, we met the competition in a fair competitive manner, and were willing at all times to operate to a timetable. An agreement was made between us and the tramway*

company, under which we were to continue on the route between Leamington and Warwick until Saturday March 23rd.

We did not have a "last vigorous kick" as you suggest, we ran our usual service as before. This, we think, our late competitors will agree is correct, and your suggestions might easily lead them to think that we had not ended the "memorable struggle" in a creditable and honourable manner. If you and the general public of Leamington and Warwick are satisfied with the result, we are content to leave it at that, but we do contend, sir, in all seriousness, that your remarks are uncalled for, and not in accordance with the facts.

Much was said before the Select Committee about the Blue buses, but we can assure you that the Leamington to Stratford service has been running to a schedule. Obviously with a service running between Leamington and Warwick every 20 minutes you could not get on any and all of these and expect to get straight through to Stratford.

We could say much as to what was said concerning the Blue buses before the Select Committee, but for obvious reasons prefer to abstain. The writer was ready and willing to go in as a witness, but as you know not one single witness was called for the petitioners against the Bill, and that is sufficient proof, in our opinion, of the soundness of the case against the Bill, and the way it was handled by those concerned.

Much has been said about omnibuses running without any control over them, but we can assure you that the small omnibus owners will not object to any control which protects the large companies from the unfair competition of the small owner, provided that the small owner gets a similar protection from the large companies.

We have always desired to run our services to published timetables, but if a competing bus is allowed to run in front of the time scheduled for ours, what can you expect but a certain amount of pirating in self-protection?

We have every wish to serve the public. More than half the routes we serve had no regular services prior to the Blue bus company coming their way. That in itself will be sufficient evidence that we do not wish to "pinch other people's routes". The first Blue bus to be put on the road was run to a timetable on a route not previously served, which timetable was pirated by a large company putting on a bus exactly five minutes in front of our own.

We shall be glad if you will enquire further into your remarks, when we think you will agree that they were somewhat hasty, and leave you to your own method to correct the view expressed.

*S.H. JOINER*

# 3

# Consolidation and Takeover
# 1929–1931

By the end of March 1929 the battle with the Leamington & Warwick trams was over and the proprietors of Stratford-on-Avon Motor Services could concentrate on their home town again.

The Midland Red had stepped up their activities and both companies were now running at the same time on several services, but SoAMS had achieved considerable customer loyalty and many Midland Red buses were said to be running around completely empty because the villagers refused to use them. This was obviously not profitable and, probably at Midland Red's instigation, talks were held. The outcome was an agreement dated 6 June 1929 which aimed to reduce competition by carving up the services between the operators and by fixing the times and fares on stretches of road which would still be covered by both. Before this the competition had been so intense that Midland Red's local inspector had found it necessary to take his timetable cases down every night to prevent them from disappearing!

Under the June agreement, part of which at least had actually been implemented from mid-May, Stratford – Leamington via Snitterfield became a Stratford Blue operation and the route via Wellesbourne became the sole preserve of the Midland Red, but either could still operate the main road route via Black Hill. Midland Red ceded the Stratford – Shottery services, but took over all journeys to Clifford Chambers, while Stratford – Shipston became another shared service. SoAMS also retained the right to run to Kenilworth, via Leamington or Leek Wootton, so long as a minimum fare of 7d (10d return) applied between Leamington and Kenilworth. Similarly Midland Red could operate four journeys a day between Stratford and Evesham at a minimum fare of 1s 6d single or 2s 6d return; these were to form part of the through Leicester/Leamington – Cheltenham service (X92) which started in 1930 but ran for only a few months. Midland Red's service 530 from Stratford to Evesham and the 531 to Temple Grafton also ceased.

Throughout the summer of 1929, Stratford Blue offered a range of excursions and tours, as in the previous two summers, competing with the Warwickshire County Garage. By now the enquiry office had also become a booking agency for Greyhound Motors of Bristol, who ran two coaches a day between Stratford and Bristol. The growth of long-distance coach services in the late 1920s was rapid, and other services through Stratford included those from Birmingham to Bournemouth run by the Link Safety Coach Co. and by Elliott Brothers (Bournemouth) Ltd, who were better known by their 'Royal Blue' trading name. Mr Southam, the tobacconist at 8 Bridge Street, sold tickets for the Link service, while Guyvers' garage handled Royal Blue bookings. Black & White Motorways also operated through Stratford, on a service between Leicester and Cheltenham, where connections were available to points throughout the South West, and W.H. Smith's took bookings for this.

In early July, the long-awaited Great Western Railway bus services were introduced, running from Shipston to Moreton-in-Marsh, Ilmington and Great Wolford. The plan to operate to Stratford had been dropped as the Midland Red and Stratford Blue services were now considered adequate. The Great Wolford service only ran on Saturdays, but from September it was replaced by a Saturday service to Chipping Norton which lasted until January 1930. The Moreton-in-Marsh service replaced the passenger train service between Shipston and Moreton, although the line remained open until 1960, in a neglected state and used only by a very limited number of goods trains. The bus services did not perform as the GWR had hoped and by May 1930 it was in discussion with Midland Red about the possibility of handing them over (earlier in the year the GWR had acquired a 20 per cent stake in Midland Red, with the London, Midland & Scottish Railway taking 30 per cent), together with other GWR bus services in Midland Red's area. Apart from the operation based at Cradley Heath in the Black Country, Mr Power seemed none too keen and reported that they would have to take over a varied fleet of small vehicles, 'all various makes and types, and run them from isolated "barns", mostly as one man 'buses, which will be very awkward under the Midland "Red" regime'. He even considered suggesting that the GWR offer the Shipston services to the 'Stratford Blue' or 'Evesham Reliance', but felt that it would be unwise to strengthen the position of either operator even if this had been acceptable to the GWR.

# GREAT WESTERN RAILWAY.

## ROAD MOTOR SERVICE

# MORETON-IN-MARSH & SHIPSTON-ON-STOUR DISTRICTS.

### On and from Monday, September 23rd, 1929, and until further notice.

## SHIPSTON-ON-STOUR and MORETON-IN-MARSH
#### in connection with trains at Moreton-in-Marsh Station.

WEEK DAYS ONLY.

| | | a.m. | noon | p.m. |
|---|---|---|---|---|
| ROAD. | Shipston-on-Stour Station .. .. .. .. dep. | 9 0 | 12 0 | 6 20 |
| | | | p.m. | |
| | Shipston-on-Stour (Rectory Corner) .. .. " | 9 2 | 12 2 | 6 22 |
| | Stretton-on-Fosse Turn .. .. .. " | 9 15 | 12 15 | 6 35 |
| | Todenham Turn (on " Fosse Way ") .. .. " | 9 19 | 12 19 | 6 39 |
| | Lower Lemington Turn .. .. .. " | 9 26 | 12 26 | 6 46 |
| | Moreton-in-Marsh Station .. .. .. arr. | 9 30 | 12 30 | 6 50 |

| | | a.m. | p.m. | p.m. |
|---|---|---|---|---|
| RAIL. | Moreton-in-Marsh .. .. .. dep. | 9 33 | 1 3 | 6 56 |
| | Oxford .. .. .. .. .. arr. | 10 4 | 1 44 | 7 35 |
| | London (Paddington) .. .. .. " | 11 15 | 3 5 | 9 20 |
| | | a.m. | p.m. | p.m. |
| | Moreton-in-Marsh .. .. .. dep. | 11 58 | 12 42 | 7 17 |
| | Evesham .. .. .. .. arr. | 12 25 | 1 20 | 7 54 |
| | Worcester .. .. .. .. " | 12 43 | 1 52 | 8 19 |

WEEK DAYS ONLY.

| | | a.m. | a.m. a.m. | p.m. |
|---|---|---|---|---|
| RAIL. | London (Paddington) .. .. .. .. dep. | 5 30 | 9 45 — | 4C45 |
| | Oxford .. .. .. .. .. " | 7 32 | — 11 35 | 6C 2 |
| | Moreton-in-Marsh .. .. .. .. arr. | 8 47 | 11 58 12 42 | 6C34 |
| | | a.m. | p.m. | p.m. |
| | Worcester .. .. .. .. .. dep. | 9 2 | 12 10 | 6 5 |
| | Evesham .. .. .. .. .. " | 9 24 | 12 33 | 6 27 |
| | Moreton-in-Marsh .. .. .. .. arr. | 9 55 | 1 3 | 6 51 |

| | | a.m. | p.m. | p.m. |
|---|---|---|---|---|
| ROAD. | Moreton-in-Marsh .. .. .. .. dep. | 10 0 | 1 10 | 6 55 |
| | Lower Lemington Turn .. .. .. " | 10 4 | 1 14 | 6 59 |
| | Stretton-on-Fosse Turn .. .. .. " | 10 11 | 1 21 | 7 6 |
| | Todenham Turn (on " Fosse Way ") .. .. " | 10 15 | 1 25 | 7 10 |
| | Shipston-on-Stour (Rectory Corner) .. .. arr. | 10 28 | 1 38 | 7 23 |
| | Shipston-on-Stour Station .. .. .. " | 10 30 | 1 40 | 7 25 |

C—Slip Carriage.

The original proposal for the Great Western Railway to run a bus service between Stratford and Shipston did not come about, but from July 1929 to December 1930 the GWR did run a small number of services from Shipston to other destinations. The service to Moreton-in-Marsh replaced the passenger train service but was designed to ensure that Shipston still had a connection at Moreton with GWR trains to and from London and Worcester. This timetable was issued in September 1929 when a Shipston – Chipping Norton service was started, replacing the short-lived service to Great Wolford.

At this time the Shipston services, together with those from Chipping Norton to Banbury and Bledington, were operated by three 20-seater Guys (Nos 1652/1653/1658; UU9607/9608 and UV9123) and a 14-seat Morris Commercial (No.1662; UU5009) all of which were new in 1929.

In the event Midland Red decided not to replace the two remaining services from Shipston, to Moreton-in-Marsh and Ilmington, and they ceased at the end of 1930, resulting in the closure of the GWR's Shipston depot.

Three further 20-seat Thornycroft saloons joined the SoAMS fleet during 1929, but unlike the previous four these were second-hand and of the earlier A1 model with only two-wheel braking. They probably replaced a similar number of Chevrolets. No.12 (TX1498) had been supplied new to a member of the Barry Associated Motors consortium in South Wales in 1926 but its original Hall Lewis body is thought to have been destroyed by fire, and when acquired it had a body by Northern Counties. Nos 13 (UT411) and 14 (NR9527) had previously belonged to V.J. Wheeler (Castle Motors) of Kirby Muxloe, Leicestershire, who had sold out to Midland Red in January. They dated from 1927 and 1926 respectively and had bodywork by Vickers (No.13) and Challands Ross (No.14).

With the Midland Red agreement now in place, a period of stability followed. Apart from the Midland Red, Stratford Blue, as it was now generally known, was comfortably the biggest operator in the area. Although there were several small operators, most of them were content to carry on as they were and seemed unlikely to expand significantly. The only exception was the Reliance Garage at Bidford, but most of their new routes were to the west of Evesham, well away from Stratford Blue territory.

However, Stanley Joiner was keen to extend the Stratford – Evesham service through to Cheltenham and made an application to Cheltenham Corporation during November 1929. Not surprisingly Frank Martin, who had been running between Cheltenham and Evesham since gaining a licence in 1924, lodged an objection. George Grail and Stanley Joiner went to Cheltenham to discuss the application with the Council, but Martin's objection was upheld and the road to Cheltenham remained barred to Stratford Blue.

Another two former Barry Associated Motors Thornycroft A1s were bought during 1930, and given numbers following on from the previous acquisitions. Nos 15/16 (TX598/647) also dated from 1926 but retained their original Hall Lewis 20-seat bodywork. There were now nine 20-seat Thornycrofts in the fleet, and it is thought that the final Chevrolet (No.1) was sold in the latter half of 1930.

The pattern of operation during 1930 was very similar to that of 1929, with a programme of excursions complementing the local services during the summer months. However, negotiations were taking place behind the scenes and in early November it was announced that Grail and Joiner had acquired Frank Martin's eight-bus business, thereby gaining the coveted Evesham – Cheltenham service and another between Cheltenham and Malvern.

Martin's bus services dated back at least five years, and possibly longer. In June 1921 a Daimler Y-type 32-seater had been registered in his name, but this was probably a charabanc rather than a bus. However in November 1924 Cheltenham Corporation's General Purposes and Watch Committee granted him a licence to run a 30-seater on three journeys each way (two on Sundays) between Cheltenham and Evesham. During April 1926 the Bristol Tramways & Carriage Co. had also applied for licences to run between Cheltenham and

Evesham, with seven journeys each way per day. Martin objected, and the objection was upheld on the unusual condition that he obtained a second bus within two weeks to increase the frequency of his own service. This was done, although possibly not within a fortnight as it was November before a formal application was made to run the second vehicle.

Martin's other service, between Cheltenham and Malvern, only started in 1929, the application being submitted in February and approved in April.

Although Martin had eight buses at the time of takeover, only four of them were allocated numbers for use in the Stratford Blue fleet, becoming Nos 17-20. No.17 (DF4771) was a 1928

## MARTIN'S MOTOR BUS SERVICE.
## CHELTENHAM & EVESHAM.

### From The Lamp, Clarence Street.

| Fare | | | a.m. | a.m. | p.m. | p.m. | p.m. | p.m. (e) | p.m. (d) | p.m. | Sunday Service a.m. | p.m. | p.m. | p.m. | p.m. |
|---|---|---|---|---|---|---|---|---|---|---|---|---|---|---|---|
| | | CHELTENHAM Clarence Street | 8 0 | 9 30 | 12 55 | 2 0 | 4 30 | 6 0 | 8 45 | 9 45 | 10 0 | 2- 0 | 2-30 | 6 0 | 8 45 |
| 2d. | 2d. | Marle Hill Court Rd. | 8 5 | 9 35 | 1 0 | 2 5 | 4 35 | 6 5 | 8 50 | 9 50 | 10 5 | 2 5 | 2 35 | 6 5 | 8 50 |
| 3d. | 3d. | Newlands | 8 10 | 9 40 | 1 5 | 2 10 | 4 40 | 6 10 | 8 55 | 9 55 | 10 10 | 2 10 | 2 40 | 6 10 | 8 55 |
| 4d. | 4d. | Bishop's Cleeve | 8 15 | 9 45 | 1 10 | 2 15 | 4 45 | 6 15 | 9 0 | 10 0 | 10 15 | 2 15 | 2 45 | 6 15 | 9 0 |
| 5d. | 5d. | Gotherington Road | 8 20 | 9 50 | 1 20 | 2 20 | 4 50 | 6 20 | 9 5 | 10 5 | 10 20 | 2 20 | 2 50 | 6 20 | 9 5 |
| 6d. | 6d. | Woolstone Turn | 8 23 | 9 53 | 1 23 | 2 23 | 4 53 | 6 23 | 9 8 | 10 8 | 10 25 | 2 23 | 2 53 | 6 23 | 9 8 |
| 7d. | 7d. | Oxenton | 8 26 | 9 56 | 1 26 | 2 26 | 4 56 | 6 26 | 9 11 | 10 11 | 10 26 | 2 26 | 2 56 | 6 26 | 9 11 |
| 7d. | 7d. | Poplar Row | 8 28 | 9 58 | 1 28 | 2 28 | 4 58 | 6 28 | 9 13 | 10 13 | 10 28 | 2 28 | 2 58 | 6 28 | 9 13 |
| 9d. | | Teddington C. Hands | 8 35 | | | 2 35 | | 6 35 | | 10 20 | | 2 35 | | 6 35 | |
| | 8d. | Aston Cross | | 10 5 | 1 30 | | 5 5 | | 9 15 | | 10 33 | | 3 5 | | 9 15 |
| | 10d. | Kemerton | | 10 15 | 1 35 | | 5 15 | | 9 25 | | 10 35 | | 3 15 | | 9 25 |
| | 11d. | Overbury | | 10 20 | 1 38 | | 5 20 | | 9 30 | | 10 40 | | 3 20 | | 9 30 |
| 1/- | 1/- | Beckford Hotel | 8 45 | 10a30 | 1 45 | 2a40 | 5 30 | 6a40 | 9 40 | 10 30 | 10 45 | 2 40 | 3 30 | 6 40 | 9 40 |
| 1/1 | 1/1 | Ashton-under-Hill | 8 55 | 10 40 | 1 50 | 2 50 | 5 40 | 6 50 | 9 45 | | 10 55 | 2 50 | 3 40 | 6 50 | 9 45 |
| 1/2 | 1/2 | Sedgeberrow | 9 3 | 10 48 | 1 55 | 2 55 | 5 48 | 6 58 | 9 50 | | 11 3 | 2 55 | 3 48 | 6 58 | 9 50 |
| 1/3 | 1/3 | Hinton Cross | 9 6 | 10 50 | 1 58 | 3 0 | 5 50 | 7 3 | 9 52 | | 11 8 | 3 0 | 3 50 | 7 3 | 9 52 |
| 1/5 | 1/5 | Hampton Mill Lane | 9 8 | 10 52 | 2 3 | 3 5 | 5 51 | 7 5 | 9 55 | | 11 14 | 3 5 | 3 51 | 7 5 | 9 55 |
| 1/6 | 1/6 | EVESHAM | 9 10 | 10 55 | 2 10 | 3 10 | 5 55 | 7 10 | 10 0 | | 11 20 | 3 10 | 3 55 | 7 10 | 10 0 |

### From Vine Street

| Fare | | | a.m. | a.m. | a.m. | p.m. | p.m. | p.m. | p.m. (c) | p.m. (d) | Sunday Service a.m. | p.m. | p.m. | p.m. |
|---|---|---|---|---|---|---|---|---|---|---|---|---|---|---|
| | | EVESHAM Vine Street | 8 0 | 10 10 | 11 20 | 2 20 | 4 10 | 6 20 | 8 10 | 9 0 | 11 30 | 4 10 | 6 20 | 8 10 |
| 2d. | 2d. | Hampton Mill Lane | 8 3 | 10 13 | 11 23 | 2 23 | 4 13 | 6 23 | 8 13 | 9 6 | 11 36 | 4 13 | 6 23 | 8 13 |
| 3d. | 3d. | Hinton Cross | 8 5 | 10 16 | 11 26 | 2 26 | 4 16 | 6 26 | 8 16 | 9 12 | 11 42 | 4 16 | 6 26 | 8 16 |
| 4d. | 4d. | Sedgeberrow | 8 10 | 10 20 | 11 30 | 2 30 | 4 20 | 6 30 | 8 20 | 9 16 | 11 47 | 4 20 | 6 30 | 8 20 |
| 5d. | 5d. | Ashton-under-Hill | 8 15 | 10 25 | 11 35 | 2 35 | 4 25 | 6 35 | 8 25 | 9 25 | 11 55 | 4 25 | 6 35 | 8 25 |
| 6d. | 6d. | Beckford Hotel | 8 25 | 10 35 | 11 45 | 2a45 | 4 35 | 6a45 | 8 35 | 9 35 | 12 5 | 4 35 | 6 45 | 8 35 |
| 9d. | | Teddington C. Hands | | | 10 45 | | | 4 45 | 8 45 | 9 45 | | 4 45 | | 8 45 |
| | 9d. | Overbury | 8 35 | | 11 55 | 2 55 | | 6 55 | | | 12 15 | | 6 55 | |
| | 10d. | Kemerton | 8 40 | | 12 0 | 3 0 | | 7 0 | | | 12 20 | | 7 0 | |
| | 1/- | Ashton Cross. | 8 50 | | 12 10 | 3 10 | | 7 10 | | | 12 30 | | 7 10 | |
| 1/- | 1/- | Poplar Row | 8 57 | 10 51 | 12 17 | 3 17 | 4 51 | 7 17 | 8 51 | 9 51 | 12 33 | 4 51 | 7 17 | 8 51 |
| 1/- | 1/- | Oxenton | 8 59 | 10 53 | 12 19 | 3 19 | 4 53 | 7 19 | 8 53 | 9 53 | 12 36 | 4 53 | 7 19 | 8 53 |
| 1/1 | 1/1 | Woolstone Turn | 9 2 | 10 56 | 12 22 | 3 22 | 4 56 | 7 22 | 8 56 | 9 56 | 12 39 | 4 56 | 7 22 | 8 56 |
| 1/2 | 1/2 | Gotherington Rd. | 9 5 | 10 59 | 12 25 | 3 25 | 4 59 | 7 25 | 8 59 | 9 59 | 12 41 | 4 59 | 7 25 | 8 59 |
| 1/3 | 1/3 | Bishop's Cleeve | 9 10 | 11 4 | 12 30 | 3 30 | 5 4 | 7 30 | 9 4 | 10 4 | 12 45 | 5 4 | 7 30 | 9 4 |
| 1/4 | 1/4 | Newlands | 9 15 | 11 10 | 12 35 | 3 35 | 5 10 | 7 35 | 9 10 | 10 10 | 12 48 | 5 10 | 7 35 | 9 10 |
| 1/5 | 1/5 | Marle Hill Court Rd | 9 20 | 11 15 | 12 40 | 3 40 | 5 15 | 7 40 | 9 15 | 10 15 | 12 50 | 5 15 | 7 40 | 9 15 |
| 1/6 | 1/6 | CHELTENHAM | 9 25 | 11 20 | 12 45 | 3 45 | 5 20 | 7 45 | 9 20 | 10 20 | 12 55 | 5 20 | 7 45 | 9 20 |

**a** Connects at BECKFORD for CHELTENHAM.    **c** NOT SATURDAYS    **d** SATURDAYS ONLY

**e** Through Service THURSDAYS, FRIDAYS, SATURDAYS and SUNDAYS ONLY.

In November 1930 Frank Martin's bus services from Cheltenham to Evesham and Malvern were acquired, together with several vehicles. Stratford-on-Avon Motor Services had previously had its application to run to Cheltenham rejected, and acquiring Martin's seemed to be the only way to reach the town. This timetable dates from December 1928 (the Malvern service did not start until 1929) and shows the alternative routes via Kemerton and Overbury, or direct via Teddington Hands, a pattern which Stratford Blue perpetuated for many years.

Thornycroft A2 with 20-seater Hall Lewis bodywork, No.18 (TR1866) a 1926 Thornycroft A1 with a 20-seat Wadham body, No.19 (RU1931) a 1925 Morris with a 14-seat Kiddle body, and No.20 (DG127) a 1930 14-seater Ford AA. Martin had bought DF4771 and DG127 new, but the other two had been acquired from Hants & Dorset Motor Services, TR1866 having originated with Godfrey (Greyhound Motor Coaches) of Southampton. The four unnumbered vehicles included a 1924 Thornycroft BT with a 26-seat Bartle body (HO6332), also ex Hants & Dorset, a 1927 Graham-Dodge A-type 20-seater (DF2319) and former SoAMS Chevrolet No.6 (UE4933). The fourth has not been positively identified.

Only the two 20-seater Thornycrofts, Nos 17 and 18, lasted for any length of time with Stratford Blue. The unnumbered vehicles were possibly not used at all and the Morris (No.19) and Ford (No.20) were sold after very short periods (despite the fact that the Ford was the newest bus in the Stratford Blue fleet, only seven months old when acquired). On 2 December a Mr Marfell of Ruardean Woodside came to Martin's premises to inspect the former SoAMS Chevrolet, UE4933, and he bought it the following day. It appears that the body was removed and placed on a new Chevrolet chassis registered DG1847, after which the original chassis saw no further use.

As soon as the takeover was completed Stratford Blue asked the authorities at Cheltenham to license former Castle Motors Thornycrofts Nos 13/14 for use on the Cheltenham – Evesham service, instead of DF2319 and RU1931.

Martin's premises at London Road, Cheltenham, did not form part of the deal, and instead Stratford Blue ran the services from a yard in Hanover Street.

In the same month that SoAMS acquired Martin's business, Bristol Tramways made a further application for a Cheltenham – Evesham service. This time four licences were sought and granted. This was bad news for Stratford Blue, who immediately faced competition from their much larger neighbour to the south west.

By the end of the year, bus company managers throughout the country were preoccupied with the 1930 Road Traffic Act, which stemmed from the work of the Royal Commission and was to bring about fundamental changes to the régime under which bus services operated. For the first time, a comprehensive licensing system was introduced, covering not only the buses, which would require 'Certificates of Fitness', but also drivers, conductors and services. Bus drivers would now have to pass a driving test! The Act replaced a hotchpotch of previous legislation covering the provision of road public transport, principally the 1832 Stage Carriage Act and the Town Police Clauses Acts of 1847 and 1889, all of which well pre-dated the motorbus. Whereas previously any controls which had been exercised had been in the hands of the local authorities (and some did not see the need to have any), the new legislation was to be enforced by Traffic Commissioners. The Act divided England into eleven Traffic Areas, each controlled by its own Commissioners. Warwickshire and Worcestershire fell into the West Midland Traffic Area, while Gloucestershire became part of the Western area.

After 1 April 1931 a bus service could not be operated without a Road Service Licence, and these could only be granted for services which had started by 9 February (services started after this could not continue beyond 31 March). However the Commissioners were unable to meet this deadline so all services for which licence applications had been made were allowed to continue until the applications were considered. Once a Road Service Licence was granted the timetable and fares for the service became fixed and could not then be altered without the Traffic Commissioners' approval.

Stratford Blue applied for eight Road Service Licences 'to continue the services of stage carriages operated by them during the past year' (note the continued use of the antiquated term 'stage carriages' perpetuated by the 1930 Act). These are listed below, quoting the Traffic Commissioners' reference numbers:

| | |
|---|---|
| D951 | Stratford – Shottery |
| D952 | Stratford – Alveston |
| D953 | Stratford – Shipston |
| D954 | Leamington – Cheltenham via Stratford and Evesham |
| D955 | Stratford – Evesham via the Graftons and Dunnington |
| D956 | Stratford – Alcester direct, and via Haselor and Great Alne |
| D957 | Stratford – Loxley |
| D958 | Malvern – Cheltenham |

The West Midland Traffic Commissioners published the applications on 22 April 1931, and a week later announced that seven of them would be heard during May. The exception, D954, was adjourned. No doubt this was the most controversial since although all parts of the route were already covered, it was essentially an application for a new service, parts of which were also covered by other operators.

This was a crucial time for Stratford-on-Avon Motor Services, whose very survival depended on the Road Service Licences being granted. It was also a period of further behind-the-scenes negotiation, and in May it emerged that after four years of building the company up George Grail and Stanley Joiner had sold it to the Balfour Beatty group, owners of the Leamington & Warwick Electrical Co. and many other transport and electricity under-takings throughout the country. The agreement for sale was dated 21 April 1931, and the price of £10,500 included the goodwill, the eleven Thornycroft buses, freehold property described as the 'Bridgetown Service Station' at the junction of the Banbury and Shipston roads, and all tools, equipment and stock. As a result a new company, Stratford-upon-Avon Blue Motors Ltd, was registered on 4 May 1931.

Balfour Beatty had a complex structure and Stratford Blue was wholly owned by the Derbyshire-based Midland General Omnibus Co. Ltd, which in turn was owned by the Midland Counties Electric Supply Co. Ltd.

The limited company commenced trading on 8 May and at the first board meeting, held that day at Stratford Town Hall, Joiner became Chairman and G.A. Thorpe Secretary, while George Grail was also appointed a director. Three further directors were appointed on 16 June, including Sir Joseph Nall DSO, who had already served as Chairman of the Leamington & Warwick Electrical Co. Sir Joseph became Chairman of Stratford Blue in place of Stanley Joiner on 22 July, and on the same day the board resolved to transfer the registered office from 28 Wood Street, Stratford, to 66 Queen Street, London EC4.

Thus the independent existence of Stratford-on-Avon Motor Services came to an end, after barely four years, although fortunately the new owners decided to maintain the company's separate identity and there was no obvious sign of change.

# 4

# The Balfour Beatty Years
# 1931–1935

One of the first events to shape the future of Stratford-upon-Avon Blue Motors was the sixth sitting of the West Midland Traffic Commissioners, at Warwick Court House on 15 May 1931. Six of Stratford Blue's applications for Road Service Licences were heard and granted; the exceptions were those for the Leamington – Cheltenham and Cheltenham – Malvern services, which were deferred because of objections.

On 23 May a new timetable was published, which included the following services:

| | |
|---|---|
| Stratford – Shottery | Daily |
| Stratford – Tiddington – Alveston | Daily |
| Stratford – Snitterfield – Warwick – Leamington | Daily |
| Stratford – Newbold – Shipston | Monday to Saturday |
| Stratford – Bidford – Evesham | Daily |
| Stratford – Binton – Ardens Grafton – Evesham | Friday to Monday |
| Stratford – Billesley – Alcester | Friday only |
| Stratford – Loxley | Friday only |

These coincided to a large extent with the six licences granted by the Traffic Commissioners, although the Stratford – Leamington and Stratford – Bidford – Evesham services formed part of the contested application D954. Also shown were special Thursday evening buses to the 'talkies' at Alcester, with a combined bus/cinema ticket with balcony seat costing 2s 6d. The Cheltenham-area services (to Evesham and Malvern) were presumably shown in a separate leaflet.

Midland Red and Stratford Blue had both applied for through Leamington – Cheltenham services, but other companies had applied for services over parts of the forty-mile route. At the western end the Bristol Tramways & Carriage Co. made two applications for Cheltenham – Evesham services, which drew objections from Stratford Blue, so Bristol Tramways then objected to Stratford Blue's application. At the Leamington end the Red House Garage Co., which had begun services from Coventry to Leamington and Warwick in 1929, applied to extend these to Stratford, one via Wellesbourne and one direct via Black Hill. As well as the predictable objections from Stratford Blue and Midland Red, there were others from Coventry Corporation, the Great Western Railway and the London, Midland & Scottish Railway. In the event Red House were granted licences only for their existing routes.

Stratford Blue and Midland Red eventually withdrew their applications for the through service (Midland Red's X92 had ceased to operate at the end of 1930; this had started in February 1930 as a Leicester – Cheltenham service but in April was cut back to run only between Leamington and Cheltenham, surviving in this form until December). Stratford Blue substituted four new applications, as follows:

| | |
|---|---|
| D4146 | Stratford – Norton Lindsey – Leamington |
| D4147 | Stratford – Bidford – Evesham |
| D4148 | Evesham – Cheltenham direct |
| D4149 | Evesham – Kemerton – Cheltenham |

In the meantime, the future of the Evesham – Cheltenham service had been the subject of discussions between Stratford Blue and Bristol Tramways. It was recognised that Frank Martin had started this, but it was less clear who had the most valid claim to a licence for the Cheltenham – Malvern service. After some debate a way forward was agreed: Bristol Tramways would pay Stratford Blue £2,000, in return for which Stratford Blue would withdraw from the Malvern run and Cheltenham – Evesham would become a joint operation with Stratford Blue running two thirds of the mileage and Bristol Tramways one third. It is thought that Stratford Blue withdrew from Malvern in July 1931 and that joint operation on the Cheltenham – Evesham service began in late September or early October. The reduced

The first additions to the Stratford Blue fleet after acquisition by Balfour Beatty were five 1927 Tilling-Stevens, transferred from Midland General during 1931. No.19 (RA3869) was one of them and is seen here in Clarence Street, Cheltenham, at the start of a journey to Evesham. As well as the Flowers' brewery advertisement ('Palex', the new light ale at 3s for a dozen bottles), there is a 'Bisto' advert on the rear, which may have come with the bus from Derbyshire. These buses may well have introduced the 'Stratford Blue' fleetname style which remained familiar until the 1960s. (*Author's collection*)

The former Midland General buses were sturdy machines and began a long association with the Tilling-Stevens Express model; no less than forty-four forward-control versions were later acquired from the North Western, Trent and West Yorkshire Road Car fleets. No.22 (RA3959) lasted until 1936 and is shown here in George Street, Leamington, outside the premises of Mr Rouse, 'the practical chimney sweep'. Behind it is a Red House Garage Maudslay (WK9708) which became Stratford Blue No.23 in 1936. (*National Tramway Museum*)

level of operation from Cheltenham led to the closure of Stratford Blue's small operating base at Hanover Street, and all buses were then based at Stratford again.

Following a hearing on 29 December at Birmingham Council House Stratford Blue's four new applications were granted, as were Bristol Tramways' applications to run to Evesham. Thoughts of the through Leamington – Cheltenham service were then abandoned, leaving passengers between the two spa towns to change buses in Evesham and Stratford (although the same Stratford Blue bus often ran through from Stratford to Cheltenham, Stratford – Evesham and Evesham – Cheltenham were always treated as separate services). For a time Stratford Blue and Bristol Tramways offered Leamington – Cheltenham fares at 3s 9d single and 6s 6d return, but these were later withdrawn.

Stratford-upon-Avon Blue Motors Ltd had started with the eleven Thornycrofts inherited from its predecessor (Nos 8-18), but during the summer four additional vehicles were acquired from Midland General, at a total cost of £1,160. These were 1927 Tilling-Stevens Express 30-seaters, the first of this make for the fleet and the largest buses yet operated. They had forward-entrance bodies probably built by Strachan & Brown, and became Stratford Blue Nos 19, 21, 22 and 24 (RA3869/3870/3959/3958). Soon afterwards, they were joined by similar RA3538, which became No.20 at Stratford (it is unclear why there was no No.23). Repainting may not have been necessary as Midland General had adopted a blue and cream livery during 1930 to replace the earlier green and cream, and the shade of blue used by Stratford Blue was possibly the same as Midland General's in an effort to standardise within the Balfour Beatty group.

Also of major significance during 1931 was the appointment of Walter Agg as Local Superintendent from 1 August. Mr Agg came from the Cheltenham District Traction Co. (CDT), another Balfour Beatty subsidiary, and was to lead Stratford Blue for many years. He had joined CDT in May 1910 at the age of fourteen, and his starting salary at Stratford was £300 a year.

To round off a dramatic year, George Grail and Stanley Joiner resigned from the board during December, bringing their involvement with the company they had founded to an end.

Earlier in 1931, and independently of Stratford Blue, Joiner had applied for a Road Service Licence for a service between Gloucester and Malvern via Staunton, Welland and Hanley Swan. This had probably started in about September 1930 and ran under the title 'Malvern Green', using a 14-seater Chevrolet drafted in from Stratford and presumably repainted. The application was made from Joiner's address at Soudley, Gloucestershire. Midland Red and Bristol Tramways objected, and the Traffic Commissioners refused the application. Undeterred, Joiner appealed to the Minister of Transport, but the decision was upheld in September 1931 and costs were awarded against him. By 1932, C.H. Lewis Ltd of Littledean were operating on the Gloucester – Malvern service and it is understood that in about 1933 Stanley Joiner bought this company, but it was sold again to Bristol Tramways in 1935.

Despite his other activities Stanley Joiner's involvement with bus operation in Warwickshire ceased with his departure from Stratford Blue, although his mark on local transport around Stratford was to survive for another forty years or more. George Grail, however, remained in Stratford and represented Market Hall ward on the town council for many years.

Many smaller operators in the area were probably put off by the 'red tape' of the new licensing system and decided to call it a day at about this time. Benjamin Burton of Snitterfield was one such operator, one of forty-five carriers to and from Stratford listed in *Kelly's Directory* for 1927. In 1926 he had bought a small Ford (UE127) which was licensed to carry passengers and goods, but he did not apply for a Road Service Licence. Even so, many local carriers did successfully apply for licences. Amongst them were:

- Samuel Bennett of Ilmington (Ilmington to Shipston and Stratford)
- Francis Edward Bloxham of Tysoe (Tysoe to Banbury, Leamington and Stratford)
- William Brandish of Ettington (Ettington to Stratford)
- George Henry Burrow Jnr of Stourton (Stourton to Banbury, and Whichford to Stratford)
- S. Chown of Banbury (Banbury to Edgehill)
- William Ernest Raw of Avon Dassett (Avon Dassett to Banbury and Leamington)
- Willoughby Ernest Rouse of Oxhill (Oxhill to Banbury, Stratford and Stretton-on-Fosse)

Most of these services operated only once or twice a week, mainly on local market days, and continued the tradition of generations by terminating at one of the inns in the towns served. However, some of the operators above also ran a number of other services away from the Stratford area, and two bigger operators who also gained licences were Kineton Green and Reliance of Bidford, whose activities are described in more detail later.

The requirements of the new Act were not universally understood, and some who should have applied for Road Service Licences failed to do so. Richard Webb, a haulier from Tredington, fell into this category and one evening in December 1931 a police constable observed him picking up Shipston-bound passengers in Halford with a 14-seat bus. He was later fined 10s at Shipston Police Court for using the bus as a stage carriage vehicle without an appropriate licence.

As intended, the Act led to greater stability and Road Service Licence holders were now safe from the unwelcome prospect of fresh competition. One way for the more ambitious companies to expand was by buying out the smaller operators, who had something of value to sell after obtaining a Road Service Licence. Although the licences could not be sold the Traffic Commissioners normally allowed their transfer when businesses changed hands, so the buyer paid for the goodwill attached to the licence rather than for the licence itself.

Even excursions were regulated by the Road Traffic Act, and Stratford Blue applied for a licence to run day tours to twenty-three destinations as far away as Barry Island, Cheddar Gorge, and Whipsnade Zoo, with Cheltenham and Woodstock amongst the destinations for half-day tours. Race meetings were also popular destinations, and trips to Ascot, Cheltenham, Epsom, Warwick and Worcester were listed. Midland Red and the GWR opposed the application, but apart from the proposed half-day tours to Birmingham and to Warwick, it was granted. The number of vehicles to be used on any one day was restricted to four. By contrast, the Warwickshire County Garage application for an Excursion and Tour Licence listed only ten destinations, all half-day tours.

For Stratford Blue excursions had been little more than a profitable sideline, and no purpose-built charabancs or coaches had been bought. All trips were run with the usual service buses, which were somewhat lacking in creature comforts, especially when compared with the vehicles of the Warwickshire County Garage, the other main excursion operator in Stratford. Recognising this, a magnificent new Albion was obtained for the 1932 season. This was the first vehicle in the fleet to have the modern 'forward-control' layout, in which the driver sat alongside the engine in a 'half-cab'. It was registered as WD3338 on 15 April and was probably allocated fleet number 23, at least on paper (it may well have run without a number). Within days the regular advertisements in the *Herald* were boasting of 'the latest super sunshine coaches' in an attempt to attract business from the County Garage's 'Yellow

The Albion Valiant with Cowieson bodywork was placed in service in April 1932, and immediately put to good use promoting Stratford Blue's activities, this advertisement appearing in a souvenir supplement to the *Stratford-upon-Avon Herald*. Unfortunately it was returned to the manufacturer on completion of a six-month trial. This had been in vain as far as Albion Motors were concerned as no orders were forthcoming, and no other Albions ever ran for Stratford Blue.

FOR BUSINESS OR PLEASURE
TRAVEL BY

Frequent Daily Services to Warwick, Leamington, Evesham Cheltenham, Shipston-on-Stour, Shottery, Anne Hathaway's Cottage, etc    Delightful Tours operated during the Season to all Places of Interest
LET US QUOTE YOU FOR YOUR PARTY OR OUTING.  ANYWHERE.  ANYTIME.
THE STRATFORD-UPON-AVON BLUE MOTORS, LTD., 20a Wood St., Tel. 307

During its stay the Albion was used mainly on excursions and private hire work, the folding canvas roof earning it the description 'Super Sunshine Coach' in contemporary Stratford Blue advertising. In reality the style of bodywork was quite functional and WD3338 could have been equally at home as a service bus. This view was probably taken before delivery from Glasgow, where both Albion and body manufacturer Cowieson were based, and shows it in pristine condition. No fleet number is visible and it may well have run without one. (*The Omnibus Society*)

Coaches'. The new vehicle also appeared in advertisements for the chassis manufacturer although there it was described as a bus rather than a coach; in fact it was an early example of what later became widely known as a dual-purpose vehicle.

WD3338 was not owned by Stratford Blue, although prepared in full livery, but was hired for a six-month period at the rate of 3*d* per mile, with an option to purchase when the six months was up. The 32-seat body was by Cowieson, making the whole vehicle of Scottish manufacture. According to the records of Albion Motors Ltd the chassis, a Valiant PV70 model, was originally ordered by the Midland General Omnibus Co. on 20 August 1931. However, it is thought that Midland General cancelled the order, the vehicle instead being retained by Albion Motors for demonstration purposes. Albion's job sheet shows a number of special features, including an EN70-type engine with serial number 1, suggesting that the chassis was possibly a pre-production version of the new Valiant series.

Sadly, WD3338 was returned after its hire period ended in October, and hopes that its appearance had heralded the establishment of a separate luxury coach fleet were dashed. By the following spring the Albion was operating for Kingswood Queen of Bristol, in which city it was to remain for several years.

Another remarkable coach was to be seen in Stratford from April 1932, although having no direct connection with Stratford Blue. This was UR7924, a Karrier owned by the LMS Railway, which was used to carry guests between the Welcombe Hotel, off Warwick Road, and Blisworth, near Northampton, where connections were made with trains to and from

London. Its unique claim to fame was that after travelling from the Welcombe into Stratford the 'Road-Railer', which looked much like most contemporary coaches, quickly switched to its other set of wheels and proceeded by rail from Old Town station to Blisworth! Unfortunately after less than three months it suffered a major mechanical failure, and the service was discontinued.

Undoubtedly the biggest event of 1932 was Stratford Blue's acquisition of the bus opera-tions of the Reliance Garage of Bidford, for a sum of £4,550 (the car side of the business was not involved, and the Reliance Garage survived in the hands of the Crompton family into the 1990s, latterly as a Rover dealership). The takeover date was 6 June 1932, although discussions had been going on since at least October 1931, when a small payment had been made to George Crompton, and an agreement to sell was confirmed in February. The June date was probably intended to allow time for the transfer of the Road Service Licences and for discussions with Midland Red about the longer-term future of some of the routes.

Competition between Reliance and Stratford Blue on the Stratford – Evesham route had started in 1927, and in the intervening five years Reliance had flourished in similar fashion to Stratford Blue. An extensive network of services had been developed around Evesham, and

Soon after the GWR bus services based on Shipston finished, a coach owned by the LMS Railway became a regular sight in Stratford. However, UR7924 was no ordinary coach, having a set of standard-gauge railway wheels in addition to its road wheels! In April 1932 it began a daily service between the Welcombe Hotel and Blisworth (Northamptonshire), where London trains were met. From the hotel it travelled into Stratford along Warwick Road and then to the station in Old Town where it joined the rails of the former East & West Junction Railway for the thirty-three-mile journey to Blisworth. The most obvious clues to the unique flexibility of the 'Road-Railer' were the offside door, the supplementary railway lighting at the front, and the wheel arch design which allowed the road wheels to be raised. There was a similar door on the nearside and two passenger compartments, one with fourteen seats ahead of the doors and a smaller smoking section at the rear. This view shows it at the Welcombe, which the LMS had opened as a hotel during 1931. Unfortunately a serious mechanical problem led to withdrawal of the service after little over two months. (*Colin Maggs collection*)

there had been a corresponding increase in the fleet. After the two Chevrolets mentioned in Chapter Two (UE4601/4618) further new vehicles were bought on a regular basis; another 14-seat Chevrolet (UE5447) and a 20-seat Star Flyer (UE6467) arrived in 1928. A larger 26-seat Star (UE7973) and a 20-seat Guy (UE9319) followed in 1929, while 1930 produced a second Guy 20-seater (UE9816) and a 14-seat Ford (WD1171). Willowbrook bodies were fitted to the Chevrolets and Stars. Other buses were bought second-hand during this period.

The development of the route network led to Reliance making ten applications for Road Service Licences, more than Stratford Blue. These applications, which were all granted by the West Midland Traffic Commissioners, are listed below:

| | | |
|---|---|---|
| D1868 | Stratford – Bidford – Evesham | (service 1) |
| D1869 | Stratford – Pebworth – Evesham | (service 2) |
| D1870 | Evesham – The Lenches | (service 3) |
| D1871 | Evesham – Bishampton | (service 4) |
| D1872 | Evesham – Pershore | (service 5) |
| D1873 | Evesham – Bricklehampton | (service 6) |
| D1874 | Broom – Stratford | (service 7) |
| D1875 | Bidford – Alcester | (service 8) |
| D1876 | Evesham – Pershore – Tewkesbury | (service 10) |
| D1877 | Evesham – Pershore – Cheltenham | (service 9) |

The service numbers were not quoted on the applications, but are shown in a Reliance timetable which is believed to date from 1931. The frequencies varied from several journeys daily on service 1 to a single round trip to Alcester Picture House on Wednesday evenings on service 8. Seven buses were needed to maintain the full timetable. A notable feature was the number of extra journeys on Saturday evenings. During the week only one bus was on the road after 8.00 p.m., and this finished with a 9.00 p.m. service 1 journey from Evesham back to Bidford. By contrast, Saturdays saw seven buses working throughout the evening, the last buses from Evesham taking revellers home at 10.30 p.m. to Harvington and the Lenches (service 3) and to Throckmorton and Bishampton (service 4) as well as back to Bidford via Harvington on service 1.

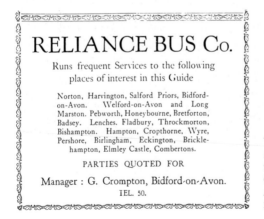

This advertisement placed in the 1930 edition of *Evesham & the Neighbourhood Illustrated* shows the extensive network of services which George Crompton had built up in only three years. Although Bidford and Welford get a mention, Stratford does not.

The Reliance Garage sold their bus services to Stratford Blue in 1932, after five years of operation. The first Reliance bus was UE4618, a 14-seat Chevrolet of the type also favoured by Stratford-on-Avon Motor Services, but with bodywork by Willowbrook. It was registered on 14 July 1927 in readiness for the start of the Stratford – Evesham service four days later. Behind it in this view in Rother Street, Stratford (near the American Fountain) is SoAMS's second Thornycroft (No.9; UE5749), which joined the fleet in February 1928. This quiet scene gives no impression of rivalry between the two companies. (*The Reliance Garage*)

This more stylish Reliance machine, posed here when brand new, was almost certainly UE7973, a Willowbrook-bodied Star Flyer delivered in March 1929. Separate passenger doors were fitted at the front and rear of the saloon, and the lettering behind the front wing shows the maximum authorised speed of 20mph. This could be exceeded by a very comfortable margin. After the takeover, UE7973 became Stratford Blue No.18, surviving until the early months of 1936. (*The Reliance Garage*)

Eight vehicles passed to Stratford Blue (Chevrolet UE5447, Ford WD1171, the two 20-seat Guys, the two Stars and two second-hand vehicles, UY6470 and YF8295). UY6470 was a Bean 20-seater which had been supplied new to John Hays of Redditch in 1929, while YF8295 was a former Great Western Railway Guy FBB with a 32-seat Vickers body. Fifty-five FBBs entered service with the GWR in the first half of 1927, but they were found to be excessively heavy and reliability problems ensued. YF8295 (GWR No.1272) was one of twenty which in 1929 passed with the GWR's bus services in South and West Wales to the Western Welsh Omnibus Co., and from there it found its way to Bidford.

Several staff also transferred to the new owners, amongst them Reg Careless, who was later well known as a Stratford Blue inspector.

The impact on Stratford Blue's sphere of operations was not as great as it might have been because most of the Reliance routes centred on Evesham were immediately sold on to Midland Red, who had conveniently opened a garage in Evesham in August 1931. Under an agreement dated 10 September 1932 Midland Red paid £1,000 for the goodwill of services 3-6, 9 and 10, all of which they took over direct from Reliance in June (service 9 was by now curtailed to run only to Aston Cross, some eight miles short of Cheltenham, because the application for a Road Service Licence in the Western Traffic Area had been refused, despite the grant of a licence by the West Midland Commissioners).

As a result of the sale of these services Stratford Blue did not need most of the Reliance vehicles and they were quickly disposed of, all but the Stars having gone by September. These became Nos 7 and 18 (UE6467/7973), the latter taking the number of one of the former Martin Thornycrofts (TR1866) which along with similar No.13 (UT411) left the fleet at

**Service No. 1.    Stratford, Welford, Bidford, Harvington, Norton, Evesham.**

| | a.m. | a.m. | a.m. | p.m. | p.m. | | p.m. | Fridays Extra p.m. | p.m. | p.m. | p.m. | Saturdays Extra a.m. | p.m. | p.m. | p.m. | p.m. | Sundays | p.m. | p.m. |
|---|---|---|---|---|---|---|---|---|---|---|---|---|---|---|---|---|---|---|---|
| Stratford dep ... | | 8 50 | 10 30 | 1 15 | 4 30 | 7 15 | | 12 20 | 2 15 | 3 45 | 5 0 | 3 30 | 6 15 | | | 10 0 | | 3 30 | 6 45 |
| Welford ... | | 9 5 | 10 50 | 1 30 | 4 50 | 7 30 | | 12 35 | 2 30 | 4 0 | 5 15 | 3 50 | 6 30 | | | 10 15 | | 3 50 | 7 0 |
| Bidford ... | 7 30 | 9 20 | 11 0 | 1 45 | 5 5 | 7 50 | | 12 50 | | | 5 30 | 4 0 | 6 45 | 7 50 | | 10 35 | 1 30 | 4 5 | 7 15 |
| Harvington ... | 7 40 | | 11 15 | 2 0 | 5 20 | | | | | | | 11 15 | 4 15 | 7 0 | 8 5 | 8 15 | | 1 45 | 4 20 | 7 30 |
| Norton ... | 7 45 | | 11 20 | 2 5 | 5 25 | | | | | | | 11 20 | 4 20 | 7 5 | 8 10 | 8 20 | | 1 50 | 4 25 | 7 35 |
| Evesham arr ... | 8 0 | | 11 30 | 2 10 | 5 30 | | | | | | | 11 30 | 4 30 | 7 15 | 8 15 | 8 30 | | 2 0 | 4 30 | 7 45 |

| | a.m. | a.m | p.m. | p.m. | p.m. | p.m. | * | p.m | p.m p.m | 0 | a.m. | p.m. | p.m. | p.m. | p.m. | p.m. | p.m. | p.m. | p.m. | p.m. |
|---|---|---|---|---|---|---|---|---|---|---|---|---|---|---|---|---|---|---|---|---|
| Evesham dep ... | | | 12 0 | 2 30 | 5 45 | 6 15 | 7 30 | 9 0 | | | 11 0 | 2 0 | 5 0 | 8 0 | 8 15 | 10. 5 | 10 30 | 2 0 | 5 30 | 10 0 |
| Norton ... | | | 12 10 | 2 40 | 5 55 | 6 25 | 7 40 | 9 10 | | | 11 10 | 2 10 | 5 10 | 8 10 | 8 25 | 10 15 | 10 40 | 2 10 | 5 40 | 10 10 |
| Harvington ... | | | 12 15 | 2 45 | 6 0 | 6 30 | 7 45 | 9 15 | | | 11 15 | 2 15 | 5 15 | 8 15 | 8 30 | 10 20 | 10 45 | 2 15 | 5 45 | 10 15 |
| Bidford ... | 8 10 | 9 20 | 12 35 | 3 0 | 6 20 | 6 45 | 8 0 | 9 30 | 10 30 | 1 15 | | 2 35 | 5 35 | | 8 50 | 10 35 | 11 5 | 2 35 | 6 5 | 10 35 |
| Welford ... | 8 30 | 9 35 | 12 50 | 3 15 | 6 35 | | | | 10 45 | 1 30 | 2 45 | 4 0 | | 2 50 | 5 50 | | 9 5 | | 2 50 | 6 20 |
| Stratford arr ... | 8 50 | 9 55 | 1 10 | 3 35 | 6 50 | | | | 11 5 | 1 45 | 3 0 | 4 15 | 3 10 | 6 10 | | 9 25 | | 3 5 | 6 35 |

† Monday and Thursday          * Saturdays excepted

**Service No. 2.    Stratford, Welford, Long Marston, Pebworth,**
**Honeybourne, Bretforton, Badsey, Evesham.**

| | a m | * | p m | p m | | | p m | p m | p m | p m |
|---|---|---|---|---|---|---|---|---|---|---|
| Stratford dep ... | | 1 35 | | 5 0 | Evesham dep ... | 12 0 | 3 30 | s8 30 | s10 0 |
| Welford ... | | 1 50 | | 5 15 | Badsey... | 12 10 | 3 40 | s8 40 | s10 10 |
| Long Marston... | | 2 0 | | 5 25 | Bretforton ... | 12 15 | 3 45 | s8 45 | s10 15 |
| Pebworth arr ... | | 2 10 | | 5 35 | Honeybourne ... | 12 25 | 3 55 | s8 55 | s10 25 |
| Pebworth dep... | 8 30 | 2 10 | t1 0 | s5 35 | Pebworth arr ... | 12 35 | 4 5 | s9 5 | s10 30 |
| Honeybourne ... | 8 40 | 2 20 | t1 10 | s5 45 | Pebworth dep... | 1 0 | *4 5 |
| Bretforton ... | 8 50 | 2 30 | t1 20 | s5 55 | Long Marston... | 1 10 | *4 15 |
| Badsey... | 8 55 | 2 40 | s1 30 | s6 0 | Welford ... | 1 20 | *4 20 |
| Evesham arr ... | 9 5 | 2 45 | s1 35 | s6 10 | Stratford arr ... | 1 35 | *4 40 |

    * Wednesdays and Thursdays excepted.          t Thursdays only.
               s Saturdays only.

**Service No. 7.**
**Broom, Bidford, Welford,**
**Stratford.**
**Fridays Only.**

| | | a m | p m |
|---|---|---|---|
| Broom | approx. | 9 10 | 12 55 |
| Bidford | ,, | 9 20 | 1 15 |
| Welford | ,, | 9 35 | 1 30 |
| Stratford | ,, | 9 55 | 1 45 |
| | | a m | |
| Stratford | ,, | | 12 20 |
| Welford | ,, | | 12 35 |
| Bidford | ,, | 9 0 | 12 50 |
| Broom | ,, | 9 5 | 12 55 |

Extracts from a Reliance timetable which probably dates from 1931. Shown here are the three services which ran into Stratford (1, Evesham via Bidford; 2, Evesham via Pebworth, and 7, Broom).

A line-up of Reliance staff (plus a dog!) posed outside the garage at Bidford-on-Avon. PSV drivers and conductors were licensed under the 1930 Road Traffic Act, and the driver with the uniform cap is wearing what appears to be his PSV badge to show his status. The bus is UE7973 again, now looking less than immaculate and having gained a destination box at the front. Towards the rear the folding canvas roof is visible. (*The Reliance Garage*)

around this lime, the first Thornycrofts to go. The two 20-seat Guys went to the Cheltenham District Traction Co., where they fitted in well with other vehicles in the fleet.

The agreement with Midland Red over the purchase of the Reliance business led to a wider territorial agreement between the two companies, replacing the 1929 agreement, and was also signed on 10 September. The Stratford company was now allocated fifteen routes, including the remaining former Reliance services, as detailed below (the numbers are from the schedule attached to the agreement, but were not service numbers):

1. Stratford – Shottery
2. Stratford – Leamington via Snitterfield, Wolverton, Norton Lindsey and Warwick
3. Stratford – Evesham via Luddington, Binton, Bidford, Harvington and Norton
4. Stratford – Loxley via Loxley Road
5. Stratford – Tiddington – Alveston via Loxley Lane
6. Stratford – Shipston-on-Stour via Alderminster, Newbold and Tredington
7. Stratford – Grafton via Luddington and Bidford
8. Stratford – Alcester via Billesley, Haselor and Great Alne or direct via the main road
9. Stratford – Evesham via Binton or Luddington, Temple Grafton, Ardens Grafton, Broom and Dunnington
10. Evesham – Cheltenham via Beckford, Overbury, Kemerton, Aston Cross and Bishops Cleeve
11. Evesham – Cheltenham via Beckford Hotel, Teddington Hands and Bishops Cleeve

12. Stratford – Evesham via Welford Turn, Welford-on-Avon, Welford Pasture, Barton, Bidford-on-Avon, Salford Priors, Abbots Salford, Harvington, Norton and Greenhill

13. Stratford – Evesham via Welford Turn, Welford-on-Avon, Long Marston, Pebworth, Honeybourne Grove, Church Honeybourne, Cow Honeybourne, Bretforton, Badsey and Bengeworth

14. Broom – Stratford via Bidford-on-Avon, Barton, Welford Pasture and Welford-on-Avon

15. Alcester – Bidford-on-Avon via Arrow, Wixford and Broom

Apart from the obvious expansion since 1929 resulting from the purchase of Martin and Reliance, there were other notable changes. Stratford Blue were now excluded from the direct Stratford – Warwick route via Black Hill, apart from certain duplicates and school journeys, and Midland Red were no longer able to run between Stratford and Evesham, except for two journeys a day as part of the very long X91 Leicester – Hereford service. Stratford Blue were permitted to link their services together to create a through Leamington – Cheltenham service, but perversely they now chose not to. Finally, Midland Red agreed to Stratford Blue and the Leamington & Warwick Electrical Co. operating each other's services, so long as the latter did not run in their own right outside the boroughs of Leamington and Warwick.

This flexibility of working was particularly important as the Electrical Company had assumed overall management responsibility for Stratford Blue in June 1932, and their manager, Mr Percy Olver, had been appointed to the Stratford Blue board. Mr Agg remained in charge of day-to-day operations at Stratford, but all future maintenance and overhaul work on the Stratford Blue fleet was to be undertaken at Emscote. Mr Agg also now benefited from a company car, a second-hand 1928 Standard saloon which was bought for £48.

Back on 16 June 1931 the board had approved a proposal to build a bus garage for ten vehicles on the land at Bridgetown, but work had not started because of the possibility of a more suitable site coming up. This turned out to be the bowling green at the corner of Warwick Road and Guild Street, which was put up for sale by the Charity Commissioners.

The Bell at Abbots Salford was one of many picturesque country inns passed by the early Stratford Blue buses on the Stratford – Evesham service. Inclusion of this photograph is justified by the timetable display boards on the wall to the right of the inn sign, for Reliance, Stratford-on-Avon Motor Services and Midland Red. Only the Reliance board appears to have no information, so the photograph may have been taken just after they ceased operating. (*Author's collection*)

It was ideal for the new garage as it was just across Warwick Road from the Red Lion Inn, where a piece of land had been leased from Flowers' brewery for use as a bus terminus. The lease was signed in August 1932 and the Red Lion Bus Park came into use shortly afterwards, later evolving into the familiar bus station which remained in use until the 1980s. Stratford Blue's offer of £2,200 for the bowling green site was accepted and it was decided to use the Bridgetown site for a petrol filling station.

There was a close relationship between Stratford Blue and Flower & Sons Ltd, who by this time had been brewing in Stratford for over 100 years, and it has even been suggested that the brewers may have provided some financial backing when Stratford-on-Avon Motor Services was founded. The visible evidence of this co-operation was Flowers' use of virtually all external advertising space on the buses. In the early years these advertisements were semi-permanent features, being hand-painted using standard blue and cream fleet colours.

At the Red Lion site a parcels office and the Bridge Café were built, both backing onto the canal (the town centre office was then transferred from 28 to 20a Wood Street, where it remained until completion of the new garage). The lease allowed Stratford Blue to park up to eight buses at a time on the area to the Bridgefoot side of the Red Lion, which was reached by turning off Warwick Road beyond the inn and using a private roadway to the rear. In 1934 Midland Red struck a similar deal with Flowers, allowing up to four buses to use the Red Lion Bus Park for a fee of £30 a year. The Kineton Green Bus Service also used the Red Lion as its terminus, but this was a local arrangement between Mrs Hunt and the licensee, rather than with the brewery, and the fee was 3s a week. The Red Lion also served as a parcels agency for Kineton Green.

During January 1933 one of the Tilling-Stevens (RA3538) was returned to Midland General in exchange for a new No.20, a 32-seat Commer F4 with registration FG5227. This vehicle had an interesting history, having been supplied new to the General Motor Carrying Co. of Kirkcaldy, Fife, in July 1929. This company was controlled by the Wemyss & District Tramways Co., another Balfour Beatty subsidiary, which in part explains how it reached Midland General. It was described as having bodywork of the 'sun-saloon' type, but for some reason it lasted only a few months in Stratford, the only Commer ever to be operated.

Another fleet addition in early 1933 was a superb AEC Regal coach (AMD739) with streamlined coachwork by Thomas Harrington of Hove. Like the previous year's Albion, which would have looked positively plain beside it, it was probably hired from the chassis manufacturer. The hiring rate was 2¼d per mile at a guaranteed average of 600 miles per week, and after the six-month hire period there was an option to purchase for £1,364 10s less hiring charges already paid. No.23, as it became, was a 32-seater and vastly superior in virtually every respect to anything else in the fleet, but did not produce an order for AEC. Indeed, despite the companies' efforts, Stratford Blue never purchased a single new vehicle from either Albion or AEC, and it was to be five years before another true luxury coach appeared in the fleet. It can only be assumed that the company felt that the short summer season did not justify the investment; a great pity, as the Regal enhanced Stratford Blue's image enormously during the period of the loan.

Departures from the fleet in 1933 were three more Thornycrofts, Nos 14-16 (NR9527 and TX598/647), which were struck off and sold during the summer, apparently without replacement.

Although the option given by the 1932 agreement to run through buses between Leamington and Cheltenham was never taken up, for a time some journeys on the Leamington service ran through to Shipston. A timetable dated 29 July 1933 shows four through journeys from the Leamington end, but only two from Shipston and since one of these spent half an hour in Stratford between the two legs of the journey, the through journeys were probably a consequence of the way the schedules were drawn up rather than a serious attempt to attract through passengers.

Also introduced at about this time were two new services not covered by the 1932 agreement, which must have raised no objections from the Midland Red. These were both local services within Stratford, one running to the Mission on Banbury Road with four return trips on weekdays (five on Saturdays) and the other serving the new council housing development at Justins Avenue, off the Birmingham Road. This operated hourly, starting at the 'Market Cross' (Bridge Street) and running out along Arden Street past the Hospital and back via Birmingham Road to what was grandiosely termed the Coach Station (in fact the Red Lion Bus Park). The other principal change since 1932 was the expansion and consolidation of services towards Alcester, either via Haselor and Great Alne or via the Graftons and Broom. These revisions incorporated the former Reliance service 7, but operations were still mostly confined to Fridays and Saturdays. The Wednesday evening cinema bus which Reliance had run no longer featured.

Ten buses were required to operate the journeys shown in the July 1933 timetable, although others were of course needed for duties such as excursions.

Proof of the close ties between the two companies was the regular appearance of Leamington & Warwick vehicles operating on hire to Stratford Blue, a practice which invariably aroused the suspicions of the watchful Midland Red staff at Leamington. Whilst some of these were one-off occurrences, for example to cover breakdowns, at least two were of a more lasting nature. One was UE9916, a 1930 Daimler CF6 which was transferred to Stratford Blue during 1933 and repainted blue ('camouflaged' was the term used by the cynical Midland Red, convinced that this was a cover for some sort of sharp practice!). The real explanation probably lay in the 1929 Leamington and Warwick Traction Act. Under the Act, operation of the Leamington & Warwick company's vehicles outside the two boroughs, even on private hires, was of dubious legality and ways were sought to get round the problem. The favoured solution was for Leamington & Warwick to take private hire bookings and then subcontract the work to Stratford Blue, who had no legal constraints on this type of operation. Many such jobs were carried out by Leamington & Warwick green buses, with labels or sometimes painted boards reading 'On hire to Stratford Blue'. This was perhaps a shade too close to the fringes of the law, and the transfer of UE9916 to Stratford Blue on a more permanent footing was felt to be a better solution. Despite this, it may well have remained based at Leamington & Warwick's Emscote depot, as Midland Red's vigilant staff noted it carrying a private party from Warwick Liberal Club to Wellesbourne and back on 20 January 1934. The Stratford Blue driver travelled as a passenger from Stratford to pick the bus up at Emscote and returned the same way to Stratford when the job was done. UE9916 is thought to have remained with Stratford Blue until early 1935, mainly for use on coach duties despite the complete lack of luxury features. Although one contemporary Midland Red report refers to it as a 30-seater there is no other evidence to suggest that it was modified

MOTORS **S**TRATFORD **D** LIMITED
**BLUE**

BRIDGETOWN FILLING STATION :
Junction of Banbury and Shipston Roads,
Stratford-upon-Avon.

# ELECTRIC PETROL SERVICE

AIR AND WATER.

All the leading brands of Petrol and Lubricating Oils
kept in stock.

CAR PARK.

Cloak Room Accommodation for Ladies and
Gentlemen.

*Above*: A 1933 advert for the filling station at Bridgetown, which Stratford Blue maintained until 1970. There is still a filling station at this prime site although not offering a choice of brands of petrol.

*Right*: A July 1934 advertisement from the *Herald* announcing the land and sea cruise to Barry Island, as well as a more sedate 'afternoon circular drive' around Kineton and Edgehill and an evening 'mystery run', all on the 29th. Bookings were also being taken for Shrewsbury Flower Show, probably another job for the Daimler drafted in from Leamington & Warwick.

*Below*: Stratford's annual mop fair in October is a long-standing tradition which for centuries has drawn people in from the surrounding villages. This 1935 handbill was aimed at visitors from Cheltenham, who would have to change buses in Evesham, the journey generally taking about two hours. Because the fair took over many of the town-centre streets, Chestnut Walk was temporarily in use as the departure point for the Evesham service.

**S**TRATFORD **D**
**BLUE**
MOTORS LIMITED.

LUXURIOUS MOTOR COACH TOURS.

SUNDAY, JULY 29.
LAND AND SEA CRUISE TO
BARRY ISLAND.
Return Fare 12/6.
Depart 6.30 a.m.      Home 11 o'clock approx.
Intending Passengers must book their Seats before
7 p.m. SATURDAY, JULY 28th.
See small handbills for full information, obtainable from Red Lion Coach Station; Central Café, Rother-street; L. Howell, High-street, Welford-on-Avon, and Reliance Garage, Bidford-on-Avon.

AFTERNOON CIRCULAR DRIVE.
KINETON AND EDGE HILLS.
Depart 2.30.    Return Fare 2/3    Home 6.15

EVENING MYSTERY RUN.
Depart 6.30.    Return Fare 1/6    Home 9.15
Reserved seats, for which no ticket has been issued, must be claimed and paid for half-an-hour before the advertised time of departure.

SHREWSBURY FLOWER SHOW,
WEDNESDAY & THURSDAY, AUG. 15 & 16.
Coach will leave Stratford-on-Avon each day.
Return Fare 7/6.
Stratford-upon-Avon Blue Motors, Ltd., Warwick-road. 'Phone 307.

---

MOTORS **S**TRATFORD **D** LIMITED
**BLUE**

# STRATFORD MOP

### Saturday, October 12th, 1935.

## CHELTENHAM & STRATFORD

### RETURN 3/9 FARE
(CHILDREN 1/3 SINGLE)

'BUSES LEAVE CLARENCE STREET AT

B        B            B
7.35 a.m.,  10 a.m.,  11.0 a.m.,  12.0 noon,  1.10 p.m.,
2.30 p.m.   4.30 p.m.   6.50 p.m.   9.10 p.m.

RETURNING FROM STRATFORD-ON-AVON
(CHESTNUT WALK)

V          M            V          M          V
9.50 a.m.,  11.0 a.m.,  12.0 noon,  1.0 p.m.,  2.0 p.m,
V          V            V
4.0 p.m.,  7.0 p.m.,  9.0 p.m.

V.—Via Evesham, Beckford and Kemerton. M.—Via Evesham, Beckford and
Teddington Hands. B.—Bristol Tramways 'Buses from Cheltenham to Evesham.

Every endeavour will be made to maintain these Services, but the Company
do not hold themselves responsible for any Loss, Damage, or Delay arising
from the failure to maintain them.

Head Offices : Warwick Road, Stratford-on-Avon.     'Phone 307.

HERALD PRINTING WORKS, STRATFORD-ON-AVON.

---

### Stratford-on-Avon Blue Motors Ltd.
#### SHOTTERY——ALVESTON
### FARE SCHEDULE.

| STAGE | SHOTTERY | | | | | | | |
|---|---|---|---|---|---|---|---|---|
| 1 Church Lane<br>Hathaway Lane | 1d | Church Lane<br>Hathaway Lane | | | | | NO RETURN TICKETS ISSUED OR<br>ACCEPTED ON BANK HOLIDAYS. | |
| 2 Clarence Road<br>Bordon Place | 1½d | 1d | Clarence Road<br>Borden Place | | | | | |
| 3 Stratford (Bridge Foot) | 2d | 2d | 1d | Stratford (Bridge Foot) | | | | |
| 4 Manor Road<br>(Loxley Road) | 3d | 3d | 2d | 1d | Manor Rd. (Loxley Rd.) | | | |
| 5 Knights' Lane | 3½d | 3½d | 2½d | 1½d | 1d | Knights' Lane | | |
| 6 Tiddington | 4d | 4d | 3d | 2d | 2d | 1d | Tiddington | |
| 7 Alveston | 5d | 5d | 4d | 3d | 3d | 2d | 2d | Alveston |

Stratford (Bridge Foot)
and Alveston
**5**d. Return

The figures in Larger Type are the Return Fares.
CHILDREN under 14 years of age HALF-FARES.     Fractions of 1d. counted as 1d.
SMALL DOGS may be carried at the Owner's Risk only.     Fares : **1**d. for any stage up to
**6**d. and an additional **1**d. for each **6**d. stage or portion thereof paid by a single passenger for the
same journey.     *The Company reserve the right to refuse any Dog.*

*Above*: A 1930s faretable, showing a charge of 2*d* single to either Shottery or Tiddington, and 3*d* to Alveston (5*d* return). Fares remained unchanged until the early 1950s but after that rose increasingly frequently.

in any way from its original 32-seat service bus form. During its stay it continued to carry L&W fleet number 20, which had previously been used by Stratford Blue on the short-lived Commer. In February 1935 it was repainted green again.

An earlier sighting, probably an isolated occurrence, was another Daimler CF6 (UE9326), which on 4 November 1933 operated the 11.45 a.m. from Stratford to Shipston and back. An 'on hire' sticker was carried and the crew was made up of a 'Blue' conductor and a 'Green' driver.

During 1934, UE9916 was joined at Stratford by UE9323, another Leamington & Warwick Daimler CF6. Unlike UE9916, this vehicle was extensively modified for its new role. Work carried out during May included the fitting of thirty moquette-covered coach seats, luggage racks, a sliding sunroof and a 'Philco' radio. The body panels were also extended in order to give 'a more fashionable low-loading appearance'. It was probably repainted blue at the same time; this was certainly done at some stage. Fleet number 23, allocated the previous year to the AEC Regal, was now given to UE9323, which succeeded it as the 'luxury coach' for the 1934 season. In addition to private hire work, No.23 was no doubt used on excursions. Amongst these was a 'Land and Sea Cruise' on 29 July, which involved travelling by coach from Stratford to Bristol to join P&A Campbell's saloon paddle steamer for the sailing to Barry Island, arriving at 12.35 p.m. On the return journey, the steamer left Barry at 6.15 p.m., reaching Bristol at 9.50 p.m. for the coach journey back to Stratford. The fare was 12s 6d for adults and 7s 6d for children.

The exact date of opening of the Warwick Road bus garage is not known, but it was probably towards the end of 1933 as notice was given to vacate the office at 20a Wood Street on 30 November. Once open, all buses were kept under cover, a great improvement over the previous arrangement whereby buses were kept in the old sale yard at Bridgefoot.

The filling station at Bridgetown was completed during 1934 but petrol sales had started earlier, using temporary accommodation described as a tent, which was later replaced by a second-hand tramcar body! A manually operated pump was installed initially, but electric pumps soon replaced this.

The stabilising effect of the 1932 'area agreement' with Midland Red, together with the 1930 Road Traffic Act, was now very much apparent and the bus services changed little during 1933 and 1934. The timetable introduced on 12 April 1934 was much the same as the previous July's, although the Saturday journeys to Alcester and Loxley were discontinued, both services now running only on Fridays.

A further new timetable, which came into operation on 7 June, introduced several improvements, especially on the Stratford local routes, with Banbury Road now hourly and the Shottery service every thirty minutes, alternately via Alcester Road and Evesham Road. Other innovations were the cinema buses on Sunday evenings, leaving at 10.00 p.m. for Alveston, Bidford, Shottery and Snitterfield. These were prompted by the fact that the Picture House in Greenhill Street, which had recently been completely refurbished, had begun Sunday performances on 3 June, starting with *The White Sister*, which featured Clark Gable and Helen Hayes. Sunday opening proved very controversial, and a poll showed only 712 local residents in favour, with 1,775 against. Reporting on the poll the *Herald* rather pompously commented, 'It is noteworthy that the only districts to give a majority in favour of opening comprised the Council houses in Justins-avenue and Lodge-road.'

Later in the year a Friday-only run to Claverdon was introduced, probably replacing a Midland Red service. There were two round trips, the first running from Stratford the same way as the Leamington service through Snitterfield to Wolverton and then in a clockwise loop via Langley to Claverdon and back to Wolverton and Stratford. The afternoon journey followed the loop in the opposite direction, going to Claverdon before Langley.

The fleet was updated during the autumn of 1934 by the acquisition of four 1930 Guy Conquests from the associated Cheltenham District Traction Company, at a cost of £475 each. These were of the 'normal-control' layout, with a six-cylinder engine housed under a massive bonnet in front of the driver, and had 28-seat forward-entrance bodies also made by Guy Motors at Wolverhampton. They were numbered 14-16 and 20 (DG1312/1317/1316/1310).

More Thornycrofts were displaced, Nos 10 and 11 (UE6494/6734) being transferred to Leamington & Warwick and leaving only five of the smaller 20-seat buses in stock.

The reduced winter timetable came into operation on Thursday 18 October 1934 but alterations were few, mostly involving frequency reductions on the Stratford town services on Sundays. The journeys involved were reinstated with the summer 1935 timetable, introduced on 30 May. This also showed quite significant changes on the Stratford – Evesham service.

The winter of 1934/1935 had been uneventful, with the local services supplemented by excursions to Birmingham for the pantomimes and on 17 January to see Gracie Fields at the Hippodrome, with Grand Circle seats at an all-inclusive price of 5s 5d. As summer approached, a wider variety of excursions was once again offered, the destinations including Whipsnade Zoo and Ascot (for the Gold Cup) as well as mystery trips and runs to local favourites such as Upton House.

During 1935 there were no changes to the fleet, but if the year had seemed uneventful that was to change suddenly in December when it was revealed that the company had once again changed hands. In an agreement dated 28 June 1935 the whole of the issued share capital was purchased from Midland General by the rival Midland Red, for a price of £15,000. By another agreement of the same date, Midland Red also acquired the transport interests of the Leamington & Warwick Electrical Co.

Although the agreement was dated June it was not until December that the takeover of Stratford Blue was formally effected and became public knowledge. As soon as this had happened, on Friday 13 December Mr O.C. Power and Mr F.B. Watts from the BMMO visited Stratford and concluded the formalities, thereby further strengthening the Midland Red monopoly of bus services in mid and south Warwickshire.

# 5

# Under New Ownership
# 1935-1937

Midland Red's usual policy with acquired operators was to eliminate all trace of their existence as quickly as possible. Vehicles were rarely included in takeover agreements, and in most cases they were replaced from the outset by standard SOS buses. To those who knew this the prospects for Stratford Blue must have looked bleak, but it soon became clear that the normal policy would not apply; not only would the company be allowed to retain its separate identity, but the fleet would be acquired too.

On the day of the takeover, 12 December 1935, Mr Power, Midland Red's Traffic Manager, attended a board meeting in London at which he and Mr R.J. Howley CBE were appointed directors of Stratford Blue and Mr Howley replaced Sir Joseph Nall as Chairman. The other Balfour Beatty directors, including Mr Olver, resigned. One of the decisions taken at this meeting was to move the company's registered office to 88 Kingsway, London WC2, the headquarters of the British Electric Traction group (BET), which owned Midland Red and now Stratford Blue.

The next day Mr Power was in Stratford with his colleague Mr Watts to meet Mr Agg and conclude the formalities of the takeover, and on the 16 December he wrote in an internal memo that 'it is proposed to carry on the business entirely separate from the BMMO Company, and Mr Agg will continue in his position as Local Manager'. The Midland Red staff were asked to treat the Stratford company as if it was a branch of the Midland Red and to help them wherever possible. Shortly afterwards, in his speech at the annual Christmas dinner at the Falcon Hotel, Mr Power said that he had looked at Stratford Blue with admiring eyes for many years. Mr Power was a forceful character, but why Stratford Blue was retained and not merged into Midland Red for another thirty-five years has never been fully explained.

Fourteen Stratford Blue buses passed into BET ownership, all but two of them second-hand. The vehicles concerned, which would have been thoroughly out of place in the parent Midland Red fleet, were as follows:

| | |
|---|---|
| Two former Reliance Star Flyers: | 7, 18 (UE6467/7973) |
| Two Thornycrofts bought new by SoAMS: | 8, 9 (UE5283/5749) |
| One former Barry Associated Motors Thornycroft: | 12 (TX1498) |
| Four former Cheltenham District Guys: | 14-16, 20 |
| | (DG1312/1317/1316/1310) |
| One former Martin Thornycroft: | 17 (DF4771) |

Four former Midland General Tilling-Stevens:     19, 21/22/24
                                                 (RA3869/3870/3959/3958)

In addition, the Leamington & Warwick Daimler CF6 which had been upgraded to serve as a coach (No.23; UE9323) was still on hire to Stratford Blue, and being painted blue was effectively a fifteenth member of the fleet.

Also transferred were sixteen Road Service Licences, one for excursions and tours from Stratford and the others for stage carriage services. There was obvious scope for rationalising the two companies' services around Stratford, particularly in view of Midland Red's lack of a garage in the town, and rationalisation of the fleet also seemed likely. Perhaps Midland Red would introduce some of its own-built SOS vehicles to replace the many elderly machines in the Stratford Blue fleet?

As it turned out, the next buses did come from Midland Red, but they were not SOSs. The Red House Garage's services from Coventry to Leamington and Warwick had been a thorn in Midland Red's side since 1929, but Midland Red took them over from 1 March 1936 and promptly absorbed them into their own services. Midland Red had no use for the Red House buses but chose to acquire five locally built Maudslays for use in the Leamington & Warwick and Stratford Blue fleets; within days WK9631/9708 and VC7801 were with Stratford Blue and VC1619/2476 at Emscote. The Stratford trio cost the company £100 each and were to Maudslay's ML3 specification (WK9631 had been converted from a normal-control ML4), with 32-seat bodies by Willowbrook of Loughborough. The first two dated from 1929 but had replacement 1932 bodies, while VC7801 was new in 1931. They were recorded as Stratford Blue Nos 17, 23 and 18 respectively, and displaced the hired Daimler (No.23) and the Star Flyers (Nos 7 and 18). However, it seems likely that WK9631 became No.7 rather than 17 as Thornycroft No.17 (DF4771) survived in service until the autumn.

The Daimler was not returned immediately to Leamington & Warwick as it was decided to adapt one of the Maudslays to replace it, but the extent of the alterations, if indeed they went ahead, is not known. It was May before it went back to Emscote, although in early June it made a brief return to Stratford to meet further private hire requirements.

The expected rationalisation of services with Midland Red took place on 25 May 1936 when return tickets became valid on either company's buses on the most common sections of route, and the Blue buses returned to several villages which they had been absent from since the 'area agreement' of 1932, including Clifford Chambers and Wimpstone. Stratford Blue gained (or regained) the services to Clifford Chambers, Hampton Lucy (including a Sunday evening church bus), Ilmington and Long Compton (journeys via Shipston to King Edward VI School in Stratford). Losses were the Friday-only Alcester service and the Saturday journeys to Evesham via Pebworth, the last vestige in the Stratford Blue timetable of Reliance service 2. The through journeys between Leamington and Shipston also ceased.

A weekly traffic return from April 1936 suggests that Mr Agg would not have been too sorry about the services he lost; the Pebworth run was the company's worst performer, producing only £2 6s 3d in revenue for 110.4 miles operated, a fraction over 5d a mile. The Alcester service was little better at 5.79d a mile, but in contrast the Leamington service returned 8.8d a mile. Other figures in this report confirm that there were fifteen buses in the

**Stratford=upon=Avon Blue Motors Limited.**

Frequent DAILY SERVICES between Stratford, Warwick
Leamington, Shipston-on-Stour, Bidford, Evesham, Cheltenham, etc.

*Directors:*

SIR JOSEPH NALL, D.S.O.
R. J. HOWLEY, C.B.E.
O. C. POWER, J.P.

RELIABLE PRIVATE HIRE SERVICE
SUPER TOURS AND EXCURSIONS.

TELEPHONE No.
STRATFORD 2307.

**WARWICK ROAD, STRATFORD-UPON-AVON.**

A letterhead from 1936, showing the board of directors appointed in December 1935 when Stratford Blue passed into Midland Red ownership. The illustration shows the Albion Valiant which, although long gone by this time, was comfortably newer than any of the current fleet.

fleet, although only ten were needed for service at any one time, and that on average each bus covered 559.4 miles a week, generating revenue of £16 4*s* 6*d*.

On 8 July, the management of Stratford Blue and Leamington & Warwick met at Stratford to discuss future vehicle policy. Stratford Blue was represented by Mr Agg and Mr Hirons, who had been the first SoAMS driver back in 1927 and was now Garage Superintendent. For Stratford Blue the Thornycrofts and the former Midland General Tillings were the immediate problem. Mr Hirons indicated that the four Thornycrofts would cost around £75 each to bring up to Certificate of Fitness standard, mostly because of the poor state of the bodywork, but as they were eight to ten years old he felt the expense could not be justified. The Tilling-Stevens had even more serious bodywork problems and he recommended that they were sold when the certificates expired in November and December (because they had proved economical to run and easy to maintain rebodying was seriously looked at, but it was found that this would probably cost more than buying second-hand replacement buses). It was also decided in the meeting that Leamington & Warwick should standardise on Maudslays for future acquisitions, and this included the three then with Stratford Blue. This meant that eleven Stratford Blue buses were earmarked for disposal, and to replace them it was proposed to buy ten Tilling-Stevens Expresses from the Derby-based Trent Motor Traction Co. (a member of the Tilling and British Automobile Traction group, which was closely associated with BET). Finally, it was decided that complete standardisation should be the goal so the only other buses in the Stratford Blue fleet, the Guys, would only be kept until another four Tillings were found to replace them. The result would be a fleet of fourteen Tilling-Stevens, three more than the peak service requirement during the summer. So much for the prospect of brand new SOS buses!

This drastic replacement programme was put in hand during September 1936 when the first two TSMs, as they were often known, arrived from Trent. They cost £60 each (excluding tyres) and were 32-seaters based on the forward-control version of the Express chassis, with the driver's cab alongside the four-cylinder petrol engine. Stratford Blue fleet numbers 11 and 12 were allocated, and their Stoke-on-Trent registrations (VT34 and VT580) gave a clue to their chequered histories. No.11 had been supplied in July 1927 to Thomas

Tilstone & Sons of Tunstall, while No.12 had begun life with J.E. Pritchard of Stoke in December of the same year. In 1933 both vehicles found their way to Kingfisher Services of Derby, who had new Willowbrook bodies fitted, and in March 1935 Kingfisher were taken over by Trent together with the two buses. They were not placed in service immediately and it is thought to have been October before No.11 was operational with Stratford Blue, with No.12 following in December.

More TSMs were bought in October, not from Trent as planned, but from another TBAT subsidiary, the North Western Road Car Co. of Stockport. Twelve were bought, allowing all the previous generation of vehicles to be replaced. The Thornycrofts went first, followed by the former Midland General Tillings, the Maudslays and finally the Guys. The new buses underwent a thorough preparation for service and it was well into 1937 before all were in service with Stratford Blue. They were numbered 1-10/14/15 (registrations DB5141/5152-5154/5184/5162/5157-5159/5140/5147/5130) and were from a huge batch of ninety similar vehicles delivered to North Western in 1928, thirty-five with bodywork by Brush and fifty-five with Tilling bodies. All were rear-entrance saloons. However, North Western routinely swapped bodies around on overhaul, and by the time the buses reached Stratford most, if not all, carried later bodies removed from 1930/1931 buses. These were also a mixture of Brush and Tilling products, and were rear-entrance 31-seaters. The price per bus was £50, without tyres.

In amongst this flood of second-hand vehicles, the company did buy one new vehicle – a Ford saloon car for use by Mr Agg, at the comparatively high cost of £135!

As 1936 drew to a close it became clear that another big expansion of Stratford Blue's activities was on the way. This was confirmed by an application to the Traffic Commissioners to take over the Road Service Licences held by Kineton Green Bus Services Ltd, with effect from 1 January 1937. The application was granted at a hearing in Coventry on 14 December, bringing Stratford Blue the following additional services (Kineton Green's licence application numbers are quoted as these were still used for administrative purposes):

| | |
|---|---|
| D1713 | Kineton – Fenny Compton – Banbury |
| D1714 | Kineton – Moreton Morrell – Leamington |
| D1715 | Kineton – Wellesbourne – Stratford |
| D1716 | Kineton – Avon Dassett – Banbury |
| D1717 | Kineton – Ettington – Stratford |
| D1718 | Kineton – Gaydon – Leamington |
| D1719 | Kineton – Radway |
| D2035 | Excursions and tours from Kineton |
| D6372 | Excursions and tours from Fenny Compton |

The origins of Kineton Green went back to about 1922 when Charles Hunt bought a 14-seat bus and began running bus services to Leamington and Stratford. At about this time the Hunts moved in quick succession from Bishops Itchington to Northend and then to Kineton. The services had started before the move to Kineton, where Charles continued with his transport interests. Initially, his daughter Ethel recalled, he had a large car which was used for a variety of purposes including carrying members of the village cricket team to away matches. Mr Hunt was a keen cricketer and for a time was Kineton's captain. After this he had a small charabanc which he kept at the corner of the Market Square, opposite the Methodist church, but in later years as business expanded he moved to Brookhampton Lane, near the railway station, where a purpose-built garage was erected.

By 1926 he was again running regular services to Leamington and Stratford, and then added a service to Banbury (Midland Red had already introduced their service 49c between Leamington and Banbury via Kineton). In September 1927 a brand new 14-seat Chevrolet (UE4971) was bought, very similar to those acquired at the same time by Stratford-on-Avon Motor Services, although probably with bodywork from a different supplier. It was registered in the name of Ethel Hunt, Charles's wife, who was also very active in the business, and was followed in March 1928 by another Chevrolet (UE6108). The next acquisition, in July, was a step up in size, being a 20-seater on an American Reo chassis (UE6792). March 1929 brought another Reo (UE7917) and a 14-seat Chevrolet LQ (UE8132), while a Reo 26-seater (UE9167) followed in October. The run of seven new purchases was completed in July 1930 by WD1057, a 20-seater BAT.

As well as the local services various excursions were run, including regular trips to Birmingham. It was on such a trip that a particularly tragic event occurred on 28 January 1930. The bus had left Birmingham at about 4.00 p.m. for the return journey to Kineton, but at Lapworth Hill, south of Hockley Heath, a van pulled out suddenly from a side road. The bus driver, Frederick Usher, swerved to avoid it but in doing so struck an oncoming lorry laden with pigs. According to the following Friday's report in the *Herald* 'the whole of the offside and part of the back of the bus were torn from the rest of the body, while the seats were smashed to matchwood'. Sadly, one of the passengers on the offside was the Hunts' younger daughter, Edna, aged 15, who was thrown onto the road and fatally injured. The following month, the van driver whose actions had caused the accident was fined £5.

It is not clear when the Hunts adopted the 'Kineton Green' trading name – it may have pre-dated the Stratford Blue name but it seems more likely to have been a deliberate attempt to project a similar image to their near neighbours in Stratford and even the Midland Red. Certainly by the time that Road Service Licences were applied for in 1931 the style 'Kineton Green Bus Service' was in use. Initially, seven licence applications were made, all of which were granted, and these licences passed to Stratford Blue. Midland Red had objected to the application for a Kineton – Wellesbourne – Stratford service and, although it was granted, Kineton Green's licence did not allow local passengers to be carried between Wellesbourne and Stratford.

Five buses were required to maintain the services contained in the July 1933 timetable although on some days the requirement was less; the only daily services were those to Leamington via Gaydon and to Banbury via Fenny Compton. At the other extreme the service to Stratford via Wellesbourne ran only on Fridays, leaving Kineton at 10.00 a.m. and 1.00 p.m. with a single journey back from Stratford at 6.00 p.m. Ethel Hunt was quoted as the proprietor on this timetable, which advised that 'bicycles, perambulators, live poultry etc., will not be carried'.

In 1934 the Hunts suffered a second devastating blow, when the entire bus fleet and the garage in Brookhampton Lane were destroyed by fire in the early hours of Monday 10 September. A railwayman on duty in the nearby signal box spotted the blaze at about 12.15 a.m., an hour after

Very few photographs of Kineton Green buses are known to exist, so this one has been included despite its poor quality. It shows a Daimler with conductress (Peggy Bruce-Moore) and driver at North Bar, Banbury, where the services of several small operators terminated. North Bar, where Mrs Cattern acted as the Hunts' parcels agent, was also described as the Buck & Bell in the company's timetable. Although not confirmed, the numbers '235' visible on the registration plate strongly suggest that this vehicle was GJ2356, a Charlesworth-bodied CF6 which was initially supplied to Arlington Motors, the well-known coach dealer, and would have been acquired by Kineton Green after the disastrous fire of September 1934. (*Author's collection*)

the last member of staff had left the garage. The police were immediately contacted, as was Charles Hunt, who arrived just before the fire brigade to see what he described as 'an inferno'. As he got there the asbestos roof fell in, and all efforts to control the fire failed. The garage and contents, including the Hunts' five buses, were totally destroyed. Three of the vehicles lost were Reos UE6792/7917/9167, while another was DF9216, said to have been a Guy, which had originated with Frank Martin in December 1929. It has not been possible to confirm the identity of the fifth vehicle.

The wooden frame of the building was still smouldering on the Tuesday morning when a reporter arrived from the *Herald*. Part of his report went as follows:

> *Little remained to indicate that vehicles had once stood there … in one instance only was a radiator left on a chassis. As it happened, this particular bus was the only one which had not been on service. The transmission was being repaired, and the vehicle still stood on the jack which held it, in spite of the intense heat. It seemed that the greater part of the bodywork of the buses had melted, for there was very little to be seen. All the glass had melted and lay about the floor in shapeless masses.*

To the great credit of Charles and Ethel Hunt services were running as normal by 8.15 a.m., barely eight hours after the blaze had started, using buses which had been hired in. Stratford Blue were amongst those who helped out in this way, initially at least, but in the longer term buses were sourced from further afield, including from the Red & White company in Chepstow, Monmouthshire. At least four Red & White vehicles were hired, and later five were offered for sale to Mr Hunt, but instead four Leylands were acquired from the Exeter-based Devon General Omnibus & Touring Co. and the last pair of Red & White buses was returned by the end of the year.

Two of the Devon General vehicles (UO7471/9690) were Lions dating from 1928/1929 while the other pair (UO7851/7852) were 1928 Lionesses. The Lions were of the more modern forward-control style, whereas the Lionesses had a long bonnet ahead of the driver. All four had bodies by Hall Lewis, the Lions having originally been 32-seaters and the Lionesses 26-seaters, both types having doorways at the front and rear of the saloon. The Lionesses offered greater comfort and had been bought by Devon General to establish a network of limited-stop services. Another vehicle to join the fleet after the fire was a forward-control Daimler coach, almost certainly GJ2356, a CF6 with bodywork by Charlesworth of Coventry. It is believed that there were also a couple of second-hand Guys.

In the meantime Kineton Green Bus Services Ltd was established as a limited company on 31 October 1934, with a registered office at Hallwood Road, Kettering, Northamptonshire. The directors were Charles Hunt and Harold Frost, and it was Frost who arranged the purchase of the Devon General Leylands. Frost had several business interests, and had only recently sold his own bus company, Frosts (Motors) Ltd of Kettering, to the Northampton-based United Counties Omnibus Co. He decided to stay in bus operation but his involvement in Kineton Green may have been purely financial, as Charles Hunt was still described as Traffic Manager in the June 1935 timetable. This was a very impressive publication, taking the form of a sixteen-page booklet entitled 'Official Time and Fare Tables of Omnibus

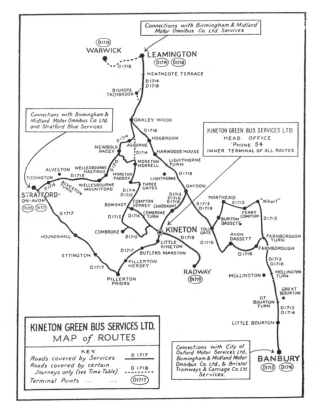

Kineton Green's timetable booklet of 1 June 1935 was a very professional production which would have put many larger companies' efforts to shame. It included this map showing all the services in detail, together with connections onto other operators' services. One quirk was that services were referred to throughout by the Traffic Commissioners' reference numbers, the Kineton – Moreton Morrell – Stratford service, for example, being given as 'Route D.1715'. No doubt this was a bit of a mystery to the passengers! Kineton Green did not use service numbers as far as is known.

Stratford Blue bought eighteen TSM Express buses from North Western in late 1936/early 1937. Together with the Trent pair they replaced the whole of the previous fleet and all the Kineton Green buses, which Mr Hunt disposed of himself. They had 1928 chassis and bodies dating from 1930 or 1931 but looked antiquated alongside the 1933-bodied vehicles acquired from Trent. Their career with Stratford Blue was short and few photographs exist; this rare view shows one of them at Kineton church with a cheerful-looking group, four of them uniformed busmen. It appears to be operating the former Kineton Green service to Stratford. Most of the batch were withdrawn by 1939, when some were scrapped and others were put to use on local Air Raid Precaution duties. (*Author's collection*)

Services'. It was dated 1 June and described as issue number one, and sold for 1*d*. By contrast the 1933 timetable had been a single sheet of paper, printed on one side only! The 1935 edition included a list of services, a map, details of times and fares, an index to the towns and villages covered and information on early closing and market days and parcel agents. The pattern of services shown in the book continued through 1936 until operation by Kineton Green ceased at the end of the year.

Examples of the fares charged were:

| | |
|---|---|
| Kineton to Gaydon | 3*d* |
| Kineton to Banbury | 1*s* 3*d* (2*s* 6*d* return or 7*s* 6*d* for a weekly ticket) |
| Kineton to Leamington | 1*s* 3*d* (2*s* return) |
| Stratford to Banbury | 4*s* return (changing at Kineton) |

The booklet also included advertisements for some of the company's other activities including regular summer excursions to Stratford from Farnborough, Fenny Compton and nearby villages at 1*s* 6*d* return, and private hires using 'saloon buses and sun saloon coaches'.

Following the takeover by Stratford Blue, Charles Hunt had a complete change of lifestyle to become licensee of the White Horse Hotel in Banbury, and on 19 January 1937 he was guest of honour at a celebration dinner at the Swan Hotel in Kineton which many former members of staff attended. Miss Peggy Bruce-Moore, a conductress who had worked for Kineton Green for eight years, referred to the good relationship which had existed between Mr Hunt and his staff and presented him with a barometer bearing the inscription 'Presented to the "Boss", Mr C. Hunt, by the employees of the Kineton Green Bus Service, Limited, on his retirement after 14 years as proprietor and managing director'.

Many of the staff transferred to Stratford Blue, including Miss Bruce-Moore and the other conductress, the Hunts' daughter Ethel – both of whom worked for just a week before handing in their notice! Speaking in 1989, they recalled that they were used to rather more freedom than they were allowed under the new régime. Ethel in particular took exception to being told that she was two minutes late for work on one occasion. Both had previously enjoyed their work on the buses, and particularly remembered the last runs back from Leamington on Saturday nights (there were two buses at 11.15 p.m., one via Gaydon and one via Moreton Morrell) when they used to call in at village halls on the pretence of looking for passengers, then have a couple of dances before returning to the bus. On foggy nights the job was much less enviable as they sometimes had to walk ahead of the bus with a white handkerchief tucked into the back of their belt to guide the driver through the worst stretches.

At the end of Kineton Green operations there were six buses, including the four Leylands bought after the fire. The new owners decided that there was no place for any of them in the Stratford Blue fleet, so the purchase price of £3,950 only included the garage and the goodwill attached to the services, and Mr Hunt was left to dispose of the Kineton Green fleet.

In anticipation of the takeover Mr Agg wrote to Mr Womar at North Western on 9 December 1936 stating that 'we may possibly be requiring three or four additional buses early in the New Year, and I should very much like to hear if you have any Tilling-Stevens for disposal now, similar to the type we recently purchased from you'. Mr Womar confirmed that he had, and another six buses from the same batch were taken, ensuring that there were more than enough buses available to cover all the Kineton services. They were given fleet numbers 16-21, following on from the earlier acquisitions and carried registrations DB5156/5177/5155/5163/5190/5166 respectively. Whilst the other were 31-seaters, Nos 20/21 were recorded as 35-seaters.

The last of the North Western buses took to the road in about May, and by then the fleet had been entirely transformed. Not one bus which had been in the fleet the previous July remained, having been swept away by the intake of twenty Tilling-Stevens Expresses (Nos 1-12 and 14-21; either the management were superstitious, or they felt that the public would refuse to travel in a bus which carried the number 13!). By June the fleet was covering around 13,500 miles a week – an impressive average of 675 miles per bus.

The takeover led to a dramatic expansion of Stratford Blue's area of operation and the Kineton Green garage, which had been rebuilt after the fire in 1934, was retained. Stratford Blue had previously come no closer to Kineton than Wellesbourne or Ettington, but now Kineton became a second focus of operations, with services radiating to Stratford, Leamington and Banbury, each via two different routes.

Following the takeover some further service alterations were to be expected and, at the Stratford Blue Christmas dinner at the Swan's Nest Hotel on 14 December 1936, Mr Power had gone so far as to say that he expected the company to double in size within twelve months. This turned out to be very wide of the mark, but it was not long before some changes were seen.

Kineton Green had not served Edgehill, but it was added to the Stratford Blue network from 10 May 1937 when Midland Red handed over two services which they had acquired in December 1935 with the business of Francis Bloxham of Tysoe. Both ran to Banbury, one via Ratley and Warmington and the other via Hornton and Horley. The Ratley service had originated with Chown's Primrose Bus Service (Mr Chown, of Twyford Road, Banbury, had obtained a Road Service Licence for an Edgehill – Banbury service in 1931). When the services were transferred to Stratford Blue, several journeys were extended beyond Edgehill to and from Kineton, incorporating the former Kineton Green service to Radway. The former Primrose service ran seven days a week, via Radway (on Wednesdays and Saturdays only), Edgehill, Ratley, Warmington and Shotteswell but the other ran only on Thursdays and Saturdays and followed the length of Edgehill to the top of Sunrising Hill and then ran via Upton House, Hornton and Horley. In discussing this transfer of services Mr Power was keen to point out that 'we are constantly going into the question of curtailing and marrying the various services in this district and wherever dead mileage can be saved by working services from Kineton or Stratford garages, we are doing so'.

From the outset Stratford Blue had used the 'Bell Punch' ticket system but in June 1937 this was replaced by 'Portable Automaticket' machines (often referred to as the 'Bellgraphic' system). The old system involved the use of a rack containing an array of pads of coloured tickets, each representing a different value or ticket type. On receipt of a fare, the conductor selected the appropriate ticket from the rack and punched a hole in it as he handed it to the passenger. For some fares more than one ticket was needed. The Bellgraphic system replaced the individually priced tickets with a continuous strip of carbonated tickets held inside the machine. To issue a ticket the conductor wrote the fare and category (single or return) on the ticket displayed on the top of the machine, and a copy was retained inside for accounting purposes. The conductor's task was greatly simplified by having only one serial number to record at the end of each run instead of probably twenty or more. Initially at least, twenty-four machines were hired from the Bell Punch Co. at 6s 3d each per quarter, less 15 per cent discount, and a supply of 480,000 tickets was obtained.

Towards the end of the summer the news broke that far-reaching changes were to take place in Leamington; from 30 September the 'Green' bus fleet of the Leamington & Warwick Transport Co., Stratford Blue's sister company, was to disappear. This was a drastic solution to the problem of an ageing bus fleet with a poor image, and resulted in the complete and permanent removal of the green and cream buses, to be replaced by standard Midland Red vehicles.

Although it had only been ten years since the Electrical Company (as it was then) had put its Reos onto the Myton route, the development of the company's bus services was complex, and the next chapter looks back at the 'Green' buses before developments at Stratford are taken up again in Chapter Seven.

# 6

# The Leamington & Warwick Green Buses

The history of the Leamington & Warwick tramway is outside the scope of this book, but a brief account is needed to set the scene for the Electrical Company's activities as a bus operator alongside Stratford Blue, which are described in this chapter.

The idea of a tramway between the two towns was first floated as early as 1872 but it was not until 1880 that the Leamington & Warwick Tramways & Omnibus Co. Ltd was established and started to translate the plans into reality. Construction began the following summer and public services started on 21 November 1881 with two horse-drawn double-deck cars. The line ran from Warwick High Street, near the Lord Leycester Hospital, to Avenue Station approach in Leamington, a distance of three miles. Within a year or so the fleet had grown to seven cars, allowing the frequency to be progressively increased.

Electrification of the Leamington & Warwick tramway was carried out during 1905 and this early view shows car No.4 descending the Parade, past Leamington Town Hall, on a journey from Warwick. Opponents of electrification felt that the overhead wiring poles would ruin the appearance of the Parade, but this photograph shows that an elegant design was chosen. Bicycles and a horse-drawn vehicle are the only other traffic in this view. (*Author's collection*)

The Leamington terminus of the tramway was outside the Manor House Hotel, close to the Avenue (LMS) Station. This car, No.1, was another of the original electric cars of 1905, but it is seen here in later days without its top-deck destination box and with a semi-enclosed platform, which gave the driver some protection from the elements. Note the clock and tram stop sign mounted on the pole to the left of the tram. (*National Tramway Museum*)

The cars were replaced during the 1890s (and the horses rather more often!) but the system was looking obsolete by the early years of the twentieth century. The British Electric Traction Co. had acquired the tramway in 1898, and in 1902 the local company was re-titled the Leamington & Warwick Electrical Co. Ltd, indicating BET's wider interests in electricity generation and supply. In the course of conversion to electric traction during the first half of 1905, most of the tramway was upgraded to double track. Public services resumed in July using double-deck electric cars, six of which were brand new and another six transferred from the BET system in Taunton, Somerset.

The Electrical Company branched into motorbus operation in 1908 when it hired three vehicles from BMMO in 1908, as described in Chapter One, but in 1912 the motorbus interests were transferred within the BET group to the British Automobile Traction Co. and it was not until 1928 that the Electrical Company operated buses again. At the end of 1912 BET sold the Electrical Company to Balfour Beatty & Co. Ltd, who controlled it through a subsidiary, the Tramways, Light & Power Co. Ltd.

Initially the electric tramway was a great success, but even before the outbreak of war in 1914 there were problems, and Leamington Town Council was expressing concern about the standard of service. By the end of the war matters were no doubt much worse, but for four years the state of the tramway had been the least of everyone's worries.

In 1916 the Electrical Company and the BMMO updated the 'non-competition' agreement which formed part of the terms of the 1912 sale. This had imposed on BAT a minimum fare of 5*d* within the boroughs of Leamington and Warwick, but BMMO were now allowed to charge fares below 5*d* provided they were at least double the tram fare. In

Six brand new cars and a similar number of 1901-built cars transferred from the BET-owned tramway at Taunton were used to start services in 1905. A former Taunton car is shown here at the depot at Emscote in the twilight years of the tramway system. Beside it is Reo No.7 (UE7087), delivered in 1928. Thornley's Gold Medal Ales were brewed at Radford Semele and the brewery survived until 1968, despite a merger with Kelsey's of Birmingham in the 1930s. (*National Tramway Museum*)

return the Electrical Company agreed not to run omnibuses in competition with the BMMO in Leamington or Warwick, and to pass on any bookings for the hire of omnibuses or chara-bancs in return for a 5 per cent commission.

With the return to peace, 1919 saw the start of a travel boom and during the year the tramway carried well over two million passengers, earning more than £18,000. These figures were about double the pre-war average, yet the annual car mileage had remained steady at about 180,000 (the fleet had been reduced to ten cars during the war after No.7 came off the rails in January 1916 and ploughed into the Castle Arms in Warwick and No.11 was withdrawn from passenger service). Although working expenses had also increased sharply, the company was able to pay a 5 per cent dividend, increasing to 6 per cent for 1920 and 1921.

A final new tramcar (No.14), a late replacement for No.7, arrived in 1921, and this was also the peak year for passenger and revenue figures, which then went into decline. Despite this, the trams soldiered on, running around 170,000 miles per year, until the greatest threat yet to their future – Stratford-on-Avon Motor Services – appeared in October 1927.

Two actions by the Electrical Company in February 1928 put the 1916 agreement with BMMO under severe pressure. First it decided to counter SoAMS by introducing four Tilling-Stevens buses transferred from Midland General (RA4002-4005) and then announced its intention to operate services to the new housing developments at the Cape and St Lawrence Avenue (off Stratford Road) in Warwick. Midland Red pointed out that these would contravene the agreement but in the event police objections to the use of 'heavy buses' on the routes forced the proposal to be shelved. Later in the month Midland Red accused the Electrical Company's manager, Percy Olver, of failing to make much progress against the competition from SoAMS and offered to drop their fares between Warwick and Leamington to assist. Naturally Mr Olver rejected the offer, which would have further weakened the Electrical Company's position, and pointed out that it would also breach the 1916 agreement.

More debate took place towards the end of the year, by which time the Electrical Company was operating its Reo 20-seaters (UE7085-7087) on the Myton route, which had started in September, and the Midland Red were running a service to Waverley Road (Rushmore Farm Estate) in Leamington. In the light of further accusations by the Electrical Company, Midland Red admitted that they may have 'technically' broken the 1916 agreement by charging 1*d* fares in Leamington, but claimed that this was done only 'to forestall the Stratford Blue Co.' and in any case had been agreed with Mr Olver.

The day-to-day arguments went on, but became overshadowed by the Electrical Company's parliamentary Bill seeking to abandon the tramway. In December 1928 Midland Red offered to pay £10,000 for the goodwill of the tramway, but the Electrical Company rejected the offer and instead offered to buy Midland Red's local routes, leaving Midland Red with the out-of-town services which would operate within the two boroughs at higher 'protective' fares. Eventually the squabbling stopped and an agreement was signed on 13 March 1929 under which Midland Red withdrew their objections to the parliamentary Bill.

A few days later the Electrical Company bought out Grail and Joiner's competing bus service over the tramway together with two Chevrolets (UE4664/4665) which were swiftly dispatched to the Mansfield District Traction Co., another Balfour Beatty company, probably without being used locally.

With these competition issues resolved, the Bill became the Leamington & Warwick Traction Act on 10 May, clearing the way for the abandonment of the tramway and giving the company exclusive rights to carry local passengers over the course of the tramway and on five other 'specified routes':

1  From High Street, Warwick, via Swan Street to the Market Place, returning via Old Square and Church Street back to High Street.
2  From Castle Hill, Warwick, via Banbury Road, Myton Road, Old Warwick Road and High Street, Leamington, to its junction with Bath Street.
3  Along the length of Castle Hill and St Nicholas Church Street, Warwick.
4  From Spencer Street, Leamington, via Bath Street, Clemens Street, Brunswick Street, St Helens Road, Tachbrook Road and Lower Avenue back to Spencer Street.
5  From Victoria Terrace, Leamington, via Priory Terrace, Church Street and High Street to its junction with Bath Street.

Fares were set at a maximum of 1*d* per mile or part thereof, and a day return fare of 6*d* had to be offered between Warwick Market Place and Avenue Station, Leamington. No variations were permitted without the approval of the Minister of Transport, although Section 10(1) of the Act made special provision for workmen:

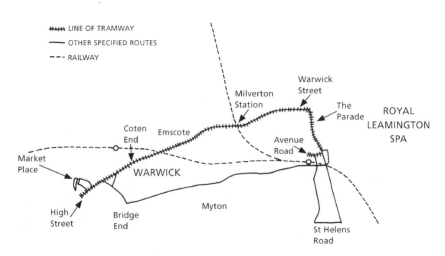

**LINE OF TRAMWAY**
**OTHER SPECIFIED ROUTES**
**RAILWAY**

The line of the Leamington & Warwick tramway and the 'specified routes' on which the company was given protection from competition by the Leamington & Warwick Traction Act of 1929.

> *The company after the opening of any omnibus route shall … run a proper and sufficient service of omnibuses thereon for artizans, mechanics and daily labourers each way every morning and evening (Sundays, Christmas Day and Good Friday always excepted) at such times not being later than eight in the morning or earlier than five in the evening respectively as may be most convenient for such workmen going to and returning from their work at fares not exceeding one halfpenny for every mile or fraction of that distance but the Company shall not be bound to take any fare less than one penny …*

Failure to comply would render the company liable to a penalty of up to £5 per day, as would failure to provide on the specified routes a service which 'may be reasonably required in the public interest', the Minister of Transport being the final judge of what was reasonable. The company's reward for accepting these conditions was absolute protection from competition; other operators would not be permitted to carry passengers between any two points on any of the company's routes.

The Act set a deadline of 31 December 1931 for the complete abandonment of the tramway. Fortunately, pressure had been eased by the removal of competition from SoAMS, and the ageing tramcars lived out their remaining months in relative peace. When the Act was passed the Electrical Company had seven single-deck motorbuses in operation, but it was clear that double-deck buses would be better for replacing the trams, which each seated around fifty passengers. However, headroom under Milverton Station bridge on Warwick New Road was restricted, and, although a double-deck Daimler was tried, single-deckers were chosen. The order went to Daimler, for twelve short-wheelbase 'CF6' chassis, a recently introduced model with a 5.76 litre six-cylinder sleeve valve engine noted for its quiet operation.

The first six were registered as UE9321-9326 on 28 September 1929 and were given the next available fleet numbers, following on from Reos 5-7 (the Tilling-Stevens were probably regarded as Nos 1-4, but on arrival of the Daimlers they were returned to Midland General).

*Above*: The service between Leamington and Warwick via Myton began in September 1928 using three newly delivered Reo 20-seaters which operated as one-man buses. This view shows No.5 (UE7085) in Warwick Market Place. The buildings in the background have long since been demolished and the site is now occupied by the Shire Hall extension. (*National Tramway Museum*)

*Right*: Many handbills of this style were issued by the Electrical Company to advertise its bus services. This November 1928 example announces timetable changes at the height of the competition with Stratford-on-Avon Motor Services along the tramway route. The Tilling-Stevens operated every twelve minutes on the 'track', while two Reos worked the Myton service.

---

**Leamington & Warwick Electrical Co., Ltd.**

# "GREEN" MOTOR OMNIBUS SERVICES

Commencing on MONDAY, 19th NOVEMBER, 1928, and until further notice, the following revised Time Tables will come into operation between

## WARWICK Market Place & LEAMINGTON Avenue Station
### via NEW WARWICK ROAD.

WEEK-DAYS.

WARWICK (Market Place), dep. 8-0 a.m., and every 20 minutes until 11-0 a.m., and then every 12 minutes until 8-36 p.m. (Saturdays, 10-36 p.m.)

LEAMINGTON (Avenue Station), dep. 8-20 a.m., and every 20 minutes until 11 a.m., then 11-18 a.m., and every 12 minutes until 8-54 p.m. (Saturdays, 10-54 p.m.

SUNDAYS.

WARWICK (Market Place), dep. 1-45 p.m., and every 20 minutes until 10-5 p.m.
LEAMINGTON (Avenue Station), dep. 2-5 p.m., and every 20 minutes until 10-25 p.m.

## WARWICK Market Place & LEAMINGTON Post Office
### via MYTON AND OLD WARWICK ROAD.

WEEK-DAYS.

WARWICK (Market Place), dep. 8-5, 8-25, 8-45, 9-10 a.m., and every 20 minutes until 8-30 p.m. (Saturdays, 10-30 p.m.)

LEAMINGTON (Post Office) dep. 8-20, 8-45, 9-0, 9-25 a.m., and every 20 minutes until 8-45 p.m. (Saturdays, 10-45 p.m.)

SUNDAYS.

WARWICK (Market Place), dep. 2-0 p.m., and every 40 minutes until 10-0 p.m.
LEAMINGTON (Post Office), dep. 2-15 p.m., and every 40 minutes until 10-15 p.m.

## Through Fare, 3d. each way.
## Return Fare, 5d. Available for the Return Journey on day of issue by either route or on any of the Company's Trams.

The Company will make every effort to maintain these Services, but reserve the right to alter, suspend, or withdraw any vehicle without notice, and will accept no liability for loss, damage, injury, or delay sustained by any passenger by reason of unpunctuality, or failure to maintain Service.

Any suggestion regarding the above Services will receive consideration.

**PERCY OLVER**, Manager.

Offices :—14, PARADE, LEAMINGTON SPA. 'Phone 601.
Garage:—TRAM DEPOT, EMSCOTE. 'Phone 602.

T. J. Kennard, Printer, Warwick St., Leamington Spa.—(11951a)

The buses that were always most closely associated with the Leamington & Warwick fleet were the twelve Daimler CF6s bought in 1929/1930 to replace the trams. The roof-mounted boards, designed to ensure that valuable advertising revenue was not lost when the trams were displaced, created a very distinctive appearance although here they are not in use. UE9323 was one of the first batch, registered in September 1929, and is seen here at the depot at Emscote. In 1934 it was transferred to Stratford Blue and fitted out as a coach with thirty comfortable seats and a number of other 'luxury' features. (*National Tramway Museum*)

Another of the first batch of Daimlers was No.11 (UE9326), shown here in Victoria Terrace, Leamington, opposite the General Post Office, on its way via the 'track' to Warwick. The legal ownership details clearly show Percy Olver as manager. In their early years the Daimlers carried destination boards on the side to supplement the small front blinds which looked rather lost amongst the advertisements. This photograph is believed to date from May 1930, when the morning peak workmen's trams were still operating. (*Author's collection*)

The second batch of Daimlers, dating from January 1930, included No.20 (UE9916), and their delivery allowed the phased withdrawal of the tramway service to start the following month. This view in Warwick Market Place illustrates the success of the roof boards, with space having been taken by Bovril, Gillette and Schweppes. The building to the right of the bus housed the Abbotsford Café. (*National Tramway Museum*)

As with Stratford Blue some years later, the number 13 was avoided, and UE9321-9326 are thought to have been numbered 10, 8, 9, 12, 14 and 11 respectively, although a pre-delivery photograph shows UE9321 as No.8 and UE9322 as No.10. The other six (UE9911-9916) were registered in January 1930 and numbered 19, 15, 16, 18, 17 and 20 respectively. All twelve had 32-seat forward-entrance saloon bodies, and Daimler records agree with those of the Electrical Company in quoting the first six plus UE9911/9916 as being bodied by Strachan & Brown, and UE9912-9915 by the Warwick-based New Avon Body Co. Strachan & Brown was a well-known coachbuilder of the day, but there is no other record of bus bodies having been built by New Avon, whose main business was specialist car bodywork. It may be that the New Avon bodies were built on frames supplied by another manufacturer.

The Cape and St Lawrence Avenue services had been able to start after further discussions had taken place with Midland Red and delivery of the smaller Reos had overcome the police objection. However from 23 December 1929 the lightly used St Lawrence Avenue run was withdrawn and instead the Myton service was extended to Tachbrook Road in Leamington. Percy Olver felt that the Tachbrook Road service was not likely to be a 'very fat trip' but would still perform better than the St Lawrence Avenue run in Warwick. Observations carried out by Midland Red's Resident Inspector Atkins confirmed the first part of his forecast; of the five journeys he looked at on the first day of operation, only one carried any passengers! Another Midland Red inspector had spoken informally to some of the Electrical Company's drivers and reported that they were 'very gloomy' about the new service, believing that it would perform much better as an extension of the main 'track' service via the Parade to Warwick rather than running via Myton. Contemporary reports from the local Midland Red staff give the impression that they had a better grasp of bus service operation than the management of the Electrical Company, and the same might even be said of some of the latter's drivers!

The arrival of the Daimlers allowed the final winding up of the tramway to begin. From 10 February 1930 all services after 9.00 a.m. ceased, but the morning workmen's cars continued for another six months. The final closure was on 16 August and work on lifting the track and making good the roadway began almost immediately afterwards.

During June Mr Olver brought to the attention of Midland Red the fact that they were charging 1*d* fares along the Parade on the Coventry services, in breach of the 1929 Act. Midland Red did not deny this but claimed that it had been forced upon them by the Red House Garage doing the same on their competing services, but they agreed to reinstate a 2*d* minimum (this would honour the 1916 agreement on competition, but still not comply with the Act). At the same time Mr Olver indicated that he had no objection to BMMO charging the 1*d* fare on their local services and the Bishops Tachbrook – Cubbington route, even though this was also contrary to the Act.

Towards the end of 1930, Sir Joseph Nall, the Electrical Company Chairman, wrote to Midland Red reiterating his wish to take over their local operations:

> *I think that the time has now arrived where we should ask you to discontinue your so called local services in Leamington so that the local services operating to Tachbrook Street, Waverley Road, Radford Road and Lillington can be operated by us, thereby enabling you to impose minimum fares on your services running into Leamington and give effect to the provisions of our Act and the agreement signed between the companies when our Bill was before Parliament.*

Not surprisingly, the response from Midland Red headquarters at Bearwood was less than enthusiastic; their revenue was already around £60 per week but with new housing developments at Lillington and Whitnash they felt this could double within two years.

Without any fresh agreement in place the early months of 1931 saw a frenzy of activity and a further worsening in relations. Midland Red again suggested buying out the Electrical Company, and this time Sir Joseph tentatively agreed, subject to the price being right. However, within days there was discord again as Sir Joseph refused to supply certain figures which he had promised 'because of the irregular competition which the BMMO is indulging in', suggesting that they should 'put themselves in order'. Midland Red then accused Sir Joseph of retracting from the deal, and offered to withdraw their Willes Road service if the Lillington – Rushmore Farm Estate service could operate without fares restrictions. Sir Joseph dismissed this proposal as ridiculous and Midland Red admitted internally that 'after considering our various services in Leamington ... we have laid ourselves open for prosecution for infringing the Leamington and Warwick Act of 1929', although undoubtedly this opinion was not broadcast!

A leaflet for Midland Red's 'Leamington Spa Town Services' dated February 1931 showed the following services:

| | |
|---|---|
| 548 | Cubbington – Warwick Street – Bishops Tachbrook |
| 549 | Warwick Street – Lillington |
| 563 | Warwick Street – Radford Semele (via Willes Road) |
| 564 | Cubbington – Warwick Street – Radford Semele (via Radford Road) |

## Leamington and Warwick Electrical Co., Ltd.

# GREEN MOTOR OMNIBUS TOWN SERVICES

Commencing on MONDAY, MARCH 23, 1931, and until further notice,
the following services will come into operation between

# Rushmore Estate and Lillington POST OFFICE

#### WEEK-DAYS.

**RUSHMORE ESTATE** depart 7-50 a.m., and every 20 minutes until 8-50 p.m. (Saturdays, 10-10 p.m.)

Buses will run from the junction of Scott Road and Waverley Road, via Brunswick Street, Bath Street, Parade, Warwick Street, Clarendon Street, Church Lane, Lime Avenue, to Lillington (Post Office), with the exception of Buses leaving at **8-50** a.m., and every hour until **7-50** p.m., which will run via Tachbrook Street, Tachbrook Road, High Street, Bath Street, Parade, Kenilworth Road, Cloister Crofts, Church Lane, Lime Avenue, to Lillington (Post Office).

#### SUNDAYS.

**RUSHMORE ESTATE** depart 11 a.m., and every 40 minutes until 10-20 p.m.

All Buses will run from the junction of Scott Road and Waverley Road, via Brunswick Street, Bath Street, Parade, Warwick Street, Clarendon Street, Church Lane, Lime Avenue, to Lillington (Post Office).

#### WEEK-DAYS.

**LILLINGTON** (Post Office) depart 8-10 a.m. and every 20 minutes until 9-10 p.m. (Saturdays, 10-30 p.m.)

Buses will run via Cubbington Road, Clarendon Street, Warwick Street, Parade, Bath Street, and Brunswick Street, with the exception of Buses leaving at **9-10** a.m. and every hour until **8-10** p.m. which will run via Church Lane, Cloister Crofts, Kenilworth Road, Parade, Bath Street, Tachbrook Road, Tachbrook Street, to Rushmore Farm Estate terminus, at junction of Scott Road and Waverley Road.

#### SUNDAYS.

**LILLINGTON** (Post Office) depart 11-20 a.m. and every 40 minutes until 10-40 p.m.

All Buses will run via Cubbington Road, Clarendon Street, Warwick Street, Parade, Bath Street, and Brunswick Street, to Rushmore Farm Estate terminus, at junction of Scott Road and Waverley Road.

The last Bus from Lillington (Post Office) will return to Depot via Warwick Street Corner.

# Warwick Street and Radford Oak.

#### WEEK-DAYS.

**WARWICK STREET** depart 7-45 a.m. and every 30 minutes until 8-45 p.m. (Saturdays, 10-15 p.m.)

Buses will run via Parade, Bath Street, High Street, and Radford Road, with the exception of Buses leaving at **10-15** a.m., **2-15** p.m., **4-15** p.m., and **7-15** p.m., which will run via Warwick Street and Willes Road.

#### SUNDAYS.

**WARWICK STREET** depart 2-15 p.m. and every hour until 10-15 p.m.

All Buses will run via Parade, Bath Street, High Street, and Radford Road.

#### WEEK-DAYS.

**RADFORD OAK** depart 7-52 a.m. and every 30 minutes until 8-52 p.m. Saturdays, 10-22 p.m.)

Buses will run via Radford Road, High Street, Bath Street, and Parade, with the exception of Buses leaving at **10-22** a.m., **2-22** p.m., **4-22** p.m., and **7-22** p.m., which will run via Willes Road and Warwick Street.

#### SUNDAYS.

**RADFORD OAK** depart 2-22 p.m. and every hour until 10-22 p.m.

All Buses will run via Radford Road, High Street, Bath Street, and Parade.

**LATE THEATRE BUSES WILL BE RUN AND SERVICES WILL BE SUPPLEMENTED AS AND WHEN REQUIRED.**

The Company will make every effort to maintain these Services, but reserve the right to alter, suspend, or withdraw any vehicle without notice, and will accept no liability for loss, damage, injury, or delay sustained by any Passenger by reason of unpunctuality or failure to maintain Service.

Any suggestion regarding the above Services will receive consideration.

**PERCY OLVER,** Manager.

Offices:—14, PARADE, ROYAL LEAMINGTON SPA. 'Phone 601.
Garage:—EMSCOTE, WARWICK. 'Phone 602.

February, 1931.

J. Kennard, Printer, Warwick St., Leamington Spa.

For a short period in early 1931 there was intensive competition on Leamington local services. This handbill dated 23 March announced new services to Rushmore Estate, Lillington and Radford Road, all in competition with the Midland Red. On 17 April they were withdrawn again on the instruction of the Traffic Commissioners, and the 'Green' buses never reached Lillington again. Bus operation was just one activity of the Electrical Company and the office in the Parade was shared with the associated Midland Electric Light & Power Co., 'contractors for electrical installations for residences, factories and farms', who also offered refrigerators, wireless receivers and cookers on hire or hire-purchase.

565     Cubbington – Warwick Street – Rushmore Estate
569     Cubbington – Warwick Street – Whitnash

It is thought that this pattern of services actually started on 2 March, the same day that the Electrical Company acted on the advice to reroute its Tachbrook Road service via the Parade and Emscote, instead of via Myton.

Intensive competition began on 23 March with two new 'Green' services directed against the Midland Red, from Rushmore Farm Estate to Lillington and from Warwick Street to Radford Road. The Rushmore – Lillington service ran every twenty minutes on weekdays and every forty minutes on Sundays, while the Radford Road service was half-hourly. Lillington and Rushmore Estate were completely new ground for the 'Green' buses, and were well away from any of their 'protected' routes. After only a week the pattern changed, and from 30 March the Lillington service was reduced to half-hourly and amended to run to Radford Road instead of Rushmore, while the Rushmore service continued every twenty minutes but only to and from Warwick Street.

As always, Midland Red's staff were watching every move of the Electrical Company, and there were many reports of irregular running in an attempt to gain a competitive advantage. An internal memo to Mr Power, Midland Red's Traffic Manager, reported that 'the latest alteration by the Leamington & Warwick Electric [*sic*] has evidently been made with the direct purpose of preceding our times at every possible opportunity, especially on the Lillington section. I understand they are even hanging back on our times.' These reports reveal that for the first week the Radford Road route was run by the Reos, but when it became linked to Lillington the larger Daimlers became the norm.

On 2 April Midland Red sent copies of recent Electrical Company handbills to the Traffic Commissioners to show that the services contravened the new Road Traffic Act (any service introduced after 9 February 1931 had to cease by 31 March). Either the Electrical Company were not aware of this, which seems unlikely, or they chose to ignore it, perhaps believing that 'their' Act gave them some sort of exemption. Under the Road Traffic Act they submitted eight applications for Road Service Licences, as follows:

D915    Warwick (Market Place) – Leamington (Avenue Station) via Emscote
D916    Warwick (Market Place) – Leamington (GPO) via Myton
D917    Warwick (Market Place) – The Cape
D918    Leamington (Warwick Street) – Radford Road (Oak Inn) via Bath Street
D919    Leamington (Warwick Street) – Radford Road (Oak Inn) via Willes Road
D920    Leamington (Warwick Street) – Rushmore Estate via Brunswick Street
D921    Leamington (Warwick Street) – Rushmore Estate via Tachbrook Road
D922    Leamington (Warwick Street) – Lillington (Post Office)

The applications were due to be heard at Birmingham Council House at the end of April, but before then circumstances changed again. On 9 April Sir Joseph and the Midland Red's Mr Howley negotiated an exchange of services and four days later the Traffic Commissioners instructed Mr Olver to withdraw the services introduced since February. Consequently the Electrical Company withdrew the Lillington, Rushmore and Radford Road services on

17 April, apparently without any warning to the public. Because of the new agreement with Midland Red the Lillington service ceased altogether, after little over three weeks of operation, while the Radford Road and Rushmore services were temporarily handed over to the Midland Red until the Electrical Company got its Road Service Licences.

Having given up its claim to Lillington the Electrical Company withdrew application D922, but the other applications were granted during August, albeit in modified form. Perhaps the most notable change was the use of the High Street as the Leamington terminus instead of the Avenue (LMS) Station. Knowing that this was likely to create a storm of protest from local councillors, Mr Olver was anxious to effect the changes as soon as possible – 'during August when lots of people are on holiday and things are quiet in general'. Midland Red wanted a little longer, but agreement was reached to introduce the new co-ordinated services from the last day of August.

At last a period of much greater stability began, with the 'Green Omnibus Services' established as:

- Warwick (Market Place) – Emscote – Leamington (High Street), continuing either to the Oak Inn (via Radford Road), Rushmore Estate, or Market Corner (either via Tachbrook Road or Brunswick Street and Tachbrook Street)
- The Cape – Warwick (Market Place) – Myton – Leamington (Spencer Street), with a few journeys extended via the Parade and Willes Road to the Oak Inn

Over the 'track', as it was still known to busmen for many years afterwards, the Daimlers generally ran every eight or nine minutes, increasing to every six during the late afternoon and early evening. On Sundays there was a ten-minute frequency. The Myton Road service was the preserve of the Reos and ran half-hourly during the week and hourly on Sundays.

The relationship between the companies improved somewhat, but the vexed question of Midland Red carrying passengers over the Electrical Company's 'specified routes' remained and in March 1932 Mr Olver requested that they stop carrying all local passengers over the relevant sections of route. This went unheeded and in July he reduced his demand to the removal of the 5d fare between Leamington and Warwick. Midland Red replied that they considered that there was a tacit agreement between the two companies. The dispute rumbled on, but matters took a turn for the worse in January 1933 when a Midland Red conductor was found to have charged a passenger 1d to travel from Warwick Street to Leamington Town Hall – the same fare as the Electrical Company. Displeased at having been caught out, Midland Red claimed that the whole episode had been 'set up' by a Leamington & Warwick inspector who knew that the conductor in question was from Digbeth Garage in Birmingham. In his report Midland Red's inspector stated that 'there is no doubt that this man ... had set himself to trap a man working in a strange district, and it is just the type of craft that he would get amusement from'.

Another source of friction was the Electrical Company's extension of the Tachbrook Road service to the Lockheed works, about 300yds beyond Market Corner. Midland Red felt that journeys should be operated there only to meet Lockheed's requirements, but by August 1932 the whole service was extended. This time, however, the Midland Red had to back down as the Electrical Company had quite properly applied for the extension.

As 1933 progressed, arguments arose over Leamington & Warwick running private hires using buses supposedly on hire to Stratford Blue, who issued the invoices. Many of the hires involved local football teams, and may not have been unconnected with the fact that Percy Olver was president of Leamington Town Football Club at the time. Speaking of one such hire Inspector Atkins said 'I doubt if the Blue Bus Co. knew the job had been on the books until they were asked to send through the accounts'. On the other hand, Mr Olver stated that he 'would not countenance Warwick Electrical men booking up private hire jobs when they knew full well they were not entitled to do so'.

A significant service change by August 1933 was the rerouting of the Electrical Company's Cape service to take in the Packmores Estate in Warwick. Alternate journeys ran via Cape Road and Millers Road, or via St Johns, Coventry Road and Lakin Road, with most continuing to or from Leamington via Myton.

Eventually the Traffic Commissioners became involved in the row over fares and urged the operators to come to an agreement. Midland Red were now trying a new tack, arguing that the Electrical Company were unable to meet demand and regularly leaving intending passengers behind. Further discussions ensued and various suggestions were put forward as to what Midland Red should charge and what percentage they should hand over to the Electrical Company, but still no agreement was reached.

The fleet of twelve Daimlers and three Reos had remained unchanged since 1930, apart from the long-term loan of Daimlers UE9323/9916 to Stratford Blue, but in 1934 a second-

The twelve Daimlers were the mainstay of the fleet until operations ceased at the end of September 1937. In later years a revised livery was carried with the town crests on the side instead of the inscription carried previously, as shown here by No.16 (UE9913). This bus was one of four with bodies built in Warwick by the New Avon Body Co., whose main output was car bodies. This view in Warwick Market Place shows the conductor in his summer uniform changing the unusual black on white destination blind. By now the 'wrapround' advertising boards have gone and a single offside advertisement for Flower's Ale is carried, together with several smaller adverts on the windows. (*The Omnibus Society*)

hand Guy Conquest (DG1311) was transferred from the Cheltenham District Traction Co. This became L&W No.9 (later renumbered to 4 when UE9323, the original No.9, returned from Stratford Blue) and was a 28-seater, identical to the four which Stratford Blue acquired a few months later. Also acquired in 1934 were two Stratford Blue Thornycrofts (UE6734/6494) which became L&W Nos 5/6 and replaced the Reos which previously carried these numbers (UE7085/7086). Like the Reos, which were sold to a Mr Hopkins from the Saltisford in Warwick, the Thornycrofts were 20-seaters dating from 1928.

The debate about fares and competition continued into 1935, but the situation was altered dramatically by an agreement dated 28 June between Midland Red and the Midland Counties Electric Supply Co., the Balfour Beatty subsidiary which now owned the Electrical Company. This resulted in the Electrical Company selling its electricity supply business and substituting the word 'Transport' for 'Electrical' in its title. Midland Red then acquired the Leamington & Warwick Transport Co. Ltd on 12 December, at the same time as they acquired Stratford Blue. It was announced that both companies would remain separate, with Leamington & Warwick continuing to provide overhaul and repair facilities for Stratford Blue as they had done for some years. Mr Olver did not transfer to the new régime so Midland Red appointed a new manager, Mr L.L. Christie.

On New Year's Day 1936 Mr Christie wrote a detailed report on the sixteen buses he had inherited. He concluded that 'taking everything into consideration and particularly the hard work which the vehicles have to do on the old tram track service, they are all in very fair

From 1929 to 1936 the Red House Garage ran bus services from its home city of Coventry to Leamington and Warwick, but on 1 March 1936 Midland Red acquired these together with five Maudslay buses. One of these was WK9708, a 1929 ML3B model, which originally carried Vickers bodywork but was rebodied by Willowbrook in 1932. Midland Red acquired the buses in order to pass them on, and WK9708 went first to Stratford Blue (No.23) and then in early 1937 to Leamington & Warwick (No.7). This view shows it in earlier days outside Annie Elkington's furniture shop in George Street, Leamington. (*National Tramway Museum*)

condition and with just a little more maintenance than they have been getting I think they ought to be good for another eighteen months or two years wear'. Despite this moderately optimistic overview, the Daimlers must have caused him some concern. No.8 for example was reported to have 'badly worn sleeves and pistons' using oil at 70mpg and petrol at 5½–6mpg. Several other Daimlers appeared to have serious body problems such as loose cab joints. The former Stratford Blue Thornycrofts, which ran as one-man buses on the Cape, Myton and Willes Road services, seemed reasonably sound, despite having the highest mileages (both had covered about 278,000 miles, whereas none of the Daimlers had exceeded 181,000). The surviving Reo and the Guy were also basically sound, but the Guy's engine was described as 'really inefficient for its size' and could only manage 5mpg.

Whilst Mr Christie may have been able to make do and mend for a while, it was clear that the fleet needed replacing soon and at the end of January he inspected the five Maudslays which Midland Red were due to acquire with the bus services of the Red House Garage and decided to take them for the Leamington & Warwick and Stratford Blue fleets. Consequently two 1929 ML3s with Buckingham 30/32-seat bodies (VC1619/2476) became L&W Nos 2 and 3.

Later in the year it was decided to replace the Thornycrofts, the Guy and the Reo by transferring the three Red House Maudslays from Stratford Blue and acquiring two others from the Trent company in Derby. The Thornycrofts were taken off the road at the end of August and sold for £20 apiece, but in the meantime Trent had found another buyer so the Guy and the Reo had to be retained until Stratford Blue could release their Maudslays.

Another Red House Maudslay was this normal-control version, almost certainly WK9631, shown here in Warwick Market Place. This vehicle had 26-seat bodywork by Midland Light Bodies, but in 1932 was drastically altered to forward-control and a new 'half-cab' Willowbrook body was fitted. During 1936/1937 it operated first for Stratford Blue before becoming Leamington & Warwick No.5, by then looking very similar to the bus in the previous photograph. (*National Tramway Museum*)

After service on 30 September 1937, the last day of operation by Leamington & Warwick, the whole fleet was driven to Stratford and parked up at Bridgetown ready for collection by Birds, the commercial vehicle dealer. This view shows three of the Daimlers after Darby's Advertising Agency had removed the roof-mounted advertising boards. Two of the Daimlers survived for a time with travelling fairs, although most were scrapped. (*Colin Martin collection*)

These finally came to Emscote in early 1937, having probably been required until then because of the Kineton Green takeover, and were numbered 5-7 (WK9631, VC7801, WK9708 respectively).

In November 1936 Mr Christie considered acquiring some of the fleet of Albions which Midland Red inherited that month with the business of Leicester & District. After inspecting seventeen of them, with a view to the possible replacement of the Daimlers as well, and finding them to be in very fair condition he recommended that six (RY6187-6190, 7961/7962) were bought for the Leamington & Warwick fleet. These would have replaced L&W's Maudslays, which were apparently not popular with passengers, together with the Guy and the Reo, but for some reason the idea was dropped. Instead the Maudslays were kept and with the transfer of the three from Stratford Blue all five Red House Maudslays were now reunited in one fleet.

Despite the fact that Midland Red now owned Leamington & Warwick, the issue of local passengers on the protected services remained. Colonel Redman, the Chairman of the West Midland Traffic Commissioners, had for some time wanted to see greater co-ordination and had threatened on occasions not to grant licence amendments until this was achieved. As well as wishing to standardise fares, Colonel Redman felt that the whole pattern of bus services in the two towns needed to be reviewed now that all were in common ownership and he particularly wanted to see a through service between Lillington and Warwick.

Early in 1936 Midland Red announced the introduction of local fares on several services, but the town clerks of Warwick and Leamington objected, alleging that the revised arrangements would breach the Leamington & Warwick Traction Act and that co-ordination of this kind could prejudice their opportunity to buy the Leamington & Warwick Transport Co. in

1959 (an option for the councils to purchase the undertaking on 31 December 1959 and every ten years thereafter was written into the Act). Mr Power assured Leo Rawlinson, the Leamington Town Clerk, that the fares were only being amended for the convenience of local residents, and suggested that in due course the councils would realise this. However, the councils won their case, and the Traffic Commissioners were obliged to accept that the Act stood, whether they liked it or not. Midland Red were now keen to point out that it was not they, but their predecessors, who had sought monopoly powers!

Another of Colonel Redman's hobbyhorses was that there were no 1*d* fares on Midland Red's Cubbington – Leamington – Bishops Tachbrook service, although it served what he called the dormitory areas of Leamington. One way to achieve this was to transfer the service to the Leamington & Warwick company and this was explored in some detail, but several difficulties were identified. Not least was the likelihood that L&W staff would demand BMMO rates of pay, so the idea was dropped. The difference in pay came very close to causing a strike during September, but this was averted at the last minute (L&W drivers received a flat rate of 1*s* 1½*d* per hour, and conductors 1*s* ½*d*, whereas after three years' service the equivalent Midland Red staff earned 1*s* 4*d* and 1*s* 2½*d*, respectively). Instead it was proposed that Midland Red should maintain the service but charge local fares and pass all the takings to the Leamington & Warwick company.

The eventual outcome went considerably further and by July 1937 the press was forecasting with relish the demise of the 'Green' buses. This followed the announcement of a public sitting in Birmingham on 29 July to hear an application by Midland Red to take over Leamington & Warwick's licences.

For some time the 'Green' buses had come in for a lot of criticism, and when Midland Red acquired the company at the end of 1935 some improvement was hoped for. This had not materialised and the *Warwickshire Advertiser* commented that 'the vehicles we have to use are of such a type that it is a punishment rather than a pleasure to ride in them. Many of the seats are old and rickety, and when a heavy person happens to drop with a bump immediately in front of you a nasty crack on the knees is not an infrequent occurrence'. The article went on to describe the situation which arose from the Act in the following terms:

> *People still wait at Emscote and suffer the mortification of seeing green buses go flying past fully loaded. To add insult to injury they see red buses and blue buses, all in that same combine, refusing to stop because that precious protective fare must be preserved for the greens, regardless of public convenience.*

Both councils opposed the licence applications, but on receiving assurances that the Leamington & Warwick Transport Co. would continue in existence, with all revenue credited to it even though the services would be worked solely by the Midland Red, they withdrew their objections. The licences were then granted for operation from 1 October, so that the last of day of operation by Leamington & Warwick was to be Thursday 30 September.

The *Advertiser* speculated that this may have resulted in the existing buses merely being repainted red, and obviously believed that some of them had already come from the Midland Red:

*...the groans and the squeaks which one may hear in the course of a penny ride from Warwick Market Place to St John's are sure symptoms of advanced senile decay, and it will be nothing but cruelty to motorbuses if the existing vehicles are made to practise further deception by reverting once more to red.*

Much of this criticism was justified and there is little doubt that most of the Daimlers were on their last legs. In his report of January 1936 Mr Christie had described the bodywork as poor on eight of them, and by March 1937 he was considering buying a second-hand chassis to help overcome a chronic shortage of spare parts. In July ten of the twelve were due for their annual PSV tests and several were found to have rotten timbers which required replacing. Fortunately a sympathetic Certifying Officer agreed that certain cosmetic work would be overlooked providing that safety standards were met, but only on condition that the vehicles involved were scrapped after the end of September.

The scepticism of the press proved to be unfounded and on completion of their duties on that final day, the entire fleet of Leamington & Warwick 'Green' buses was driven to Stratford and parked in the field adjoining Stratford Blue's Bridgetown Service Station to await collection by Mr Bird, who had bought them for £30 each, including tyres. As the residual value of the tyres, which belonged to the North British Rubber Co., was around £400, the net proceeds for Midland Red were little over £100 for the whole fleet.

In their place a number of BMMO's latest SOS 'SON' types was drafted into Emscote ready to take up service on Friday 1 October, when a new pattern of routes came into

From 1 October 1937 Midland Red replaced the Leamington & Warwick fleet with its own SOS 'SON' buses, such as No.2116 (DHA734). This post-war view shows it working the 'track' services in company with an underfloor-engined 'S8' of 1948 (No.3207; JHA807). The stencil-type service number L41 is just visible in the nearside front window of the 'SON', showing this to be a Rushmore Estate journey. Note the disappearance of Pearks' Stores from the backdrop of Warwick Market Place. (*A.B. Cross*)

89

operation. The new services, which were to remain broadly unchanged for the next forty years or so with Midland Red, were numbered into a new series with an 'L' (for Leamington) prefix, as follows:

L41   Warwick – Leamington – Rushmore Estate

L42   Warwick – Leamington – Lockheed Works

L43   Warwick – Leamington – Oak Inn (Radford Road)

L44   Warwick – Leamington

L45   The Packmores – The Cape – Warwick – Myton – Leamington (Rugby Road)

L46   Leamington – Whitnash – Heathcote Terrace

L47   Leamington – Old Rugby Tavern

L48   Leamington – Cubbington

L49   Leamington – Bishops Tachbrook

Initially, all buses engaged on these services displayed a 'Town Service' board with a green diamond symbol, so that they could be readily distinguished from buses on the other Midland Red services in the area. In due course however, they came to be regarded as 'normal' Midland Red routes, and whilst the Leamington & Warwick Transport Co. continued as a separate legal and financial entity, as an operating company it ceased altogether on the last day of September 1937.

# 7

# War and Peace
# 1937–1947

Following the disappearance of the Leamington & Warwick 'Green' buses from the beginning of October 1937, it again seemed only a question of time before the axe fell on Stratford Blue. The main reason for replacing the Leamington & Warwick buses was their age, but the Stratford Blue buses were older, the whole fleet dating from 1927/1928. Unlike Leamington & Warwick, Stratford Blue could easily have been wound up, but fortunately any fears that this might happen were to prove unfounded.

A minor alteration during the winter of 1937/1938 introduced Stratford Blue buses to Wormleighton, a mile or so from the Northamptonshire border on the road from Fenny Compton to Byfield. This gave villagers the chance of a Saturday evening in Banbury and entailed buses on the Kineton – Northend – Banbury service doing a 'double run' from Fenny Compton canal wharf up to Wormleighton and back. Several years later the evening service was replaced by afternoon journeys, but still only on Saturdays.

For the summer of 1938 Mr Agg arranged with City of Oxford Motor Services to operate a connecting service between Stratford and Oxford on Wednesdays, Saturdays and Sundays, giving the opportunity for a day trip from either end of the route. Through passengers had to change at Long Compton, six miles south of Shipston.

During July all twenty buses were busy, covering about 13,600 miles a week (the winter timetable operated in February had only required eighteen buses and the weekly mileage was around 13,000).

Generally the Tillings were reliable buses but problems with the 'Autovac' fuel system and the magnetos were fairly frequent. However, it was decided to replace the former North Western machines, which were now ten years old (the former Trent buses with their more modern bodies would be kept). This could have been the ideal opportunity to bring in the Midland Red's SOS buses, but again it was not to be. The replacements emerged as more Tillings – sixteen were bought from the West Yorkshire Road Car Co. of Harrogate in October 1938.

These vehicles were only marginally newer than those they replaced, coming from a batch of forty delivered in 1930. The original 32-seat bodies, built variously by Charles Roe, Tilling and United, were still carried, and had an entrance at the front of the saloon instead of at the rear as on the outgoing buses. At £32 10s 0d each (£520 for the lot!) plus tyres, they proved to be an exceptionally sound buy, forming the mainstay of the fleet throughout the war and most giving over ten years' service. The new buses became Nos 1-10/14-19 and

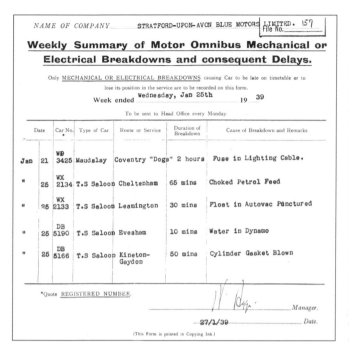

| NAME OF COMPANY | STRATFORD-UPON-AVON BLUE MOTORS LIMITED. | 157 |
| --- | --- | --- |

File No.

## Weekly Summary of Motor Omnibus Mechanical or Electrical Breakdowns and consequent Delays.

Only MECHANICAL OR ELECTRICAL BREAKDOWNS causing Car to be late on timetable or to lose its position in the service are to be recorded on this form.

Week ended **Wednesday, Jan 25th** 19 **39**

To be sent to Head Office every Monday.

| Date | | Car No. | Type of Car | Route or Service | Duration of Breakdown | Cause of Breakdown and Remarks |
| --- | --- | --- | --- | --- | --- | --- |
| Jan | 21 | WP 3425 | Maudslay | Coventry "Dogs" | 2 hours | Fuse in Lighting Cable. |
| " | 25 | WX 2134 | T.S Saloon | Cheltenham | 65 mins | Choked Petrol Feed |
| " | 25 | WX 2133 | T.S Saloon | Leamington | 30 mins | Float in Autovac Punctured |
| " | 25 | DB 5190 | T.S Saloon | Evesham | 10 mins | Water in Dynamo |
| " | 25 | DB 5166 | T.S Saloon | Kineton-Gaydon | 50 mins | Cylinder Gasket Blown |

*Quote REGISTERED NUMBER.

_____ Manager.

27/1/39 _____ Date.

(This Form is printed in Copying Ink.)

BET required its subsidiaries to provide reports on every aspect of their performance, including a weekly summary of breakdowns. Inevitably, with the age of the fleet, Mr Agg was rarely able to submit a 'nil' return. This one from January 1939 shows the fleet in transition with Tillings of both the 'DB' and 'WX' batches. The 25th was obviously 'one of those days', when four breakdowns occurred, the only ones all week to affect service buses. The other failure involved one of the recently acquired Maudslays on the Saturday night 'dogs' excursion. Note the use of the term 'car', a throwback to BET's early days as a tramcar operator.

had registrations WX2121/2131/2126/2134/2120/2152/2151/2148/2125/2130/2118/2133/2144/2141/2153/2150 respectively. Some took longer than others to prepare for service, but among the first to take to the road were Nos 1, 4 and 6, allowing the previous holders of these numbers to be sold by the end of 1938. The rest were in use by the spring of 1939 and progressively replaced the former North Western buses, the last into service being No.5 (WX2120) in May. Unlike others of its type the previous No.5 (DB5184) was retained, being renumbered to 22 and kept in service until early 1940 (it was the only survivor of the batch by July 1939, when it suffered a magneto failure while operating the Kineton – Stratford service).

Two other acquisitions in late 1938 reintroduced the Maudslay to the fleet after a brief absence. These were a pair of relatively modern ML3 coaches (WP3425/8277) from P. Owen & Sons Ltd of Abberley, Worcestershire, who had sold their bus operations to Midland Red in November. They dated from 1933 and 1935 and became Stratford Blue Nos 21/20, costing £550 for the pair (more than the sixteen Tillings!). They had 32-seat rear-entrance bodywork, by Beadle of Rochester (No.20) and W.D. Smith of West Bromwich (No.21). Initially at least they were used to replace Tillings on duties such as private hires and the regular Coventry Stadium 'dogs' excursions on Tuesday and Saturday evenings. They brought the fleet up to a total of twenty-one, all of which were in use over the busy 1939 Whitsun weekend.

The increasing fears about the political climate in Europe in the early months of 1939 were reflected in the gift of the previous No.21 (DB5166) to the Stratford Air Raid Precautions Committee and the sale of six other 'DB' Tillings to Warwickshire County Council, also for ARP use. The other seven taken off the road at this time suffered the same fate as the first three, going for scrap to Birds, the Stratford commercial vehicle dealer.

*Above*: At the end of 1938 two second-hand Maudslays were bought, the first luxury coaches since the AEC Regal of 1933, allowing a high-quality private hire service to be reintroduced. They came from Owen's of Abberley, whose bus services had just been acquired by Midland Red. No.20 (WP8277) was the newer of the pair, a three-year old ML3K with attractive Beadle coachwork, and this view shows it immediately after painting in Stratford Blue livery, in the garage yard at Stratford. (*The Omnibus Society*)

*Below*: The former Owen's Maudslays operated a range of excursions, which took them well away from Stratford, and No.20 is shown here at an unknown rural location, probably soon after acquisition. Both lasted through the war years, although laid up at times, and were sold for further use in 1946. (*The Omnibus Society*)

As matters deteriorated, preparations for a national emergency occupied much of the authorities' time, and in May Mr Agg was contacted by the local police superintendent who wanted two buses placed on standby for police use. Terms were agreed, although no guarantee was given that the vehicles would always be available. The company had also drawn up contingency plans and these were put rapidly into operation after the declaration of war on 3 September, with an announcement in the *Herald* of 15 September that services would be drastically reduced from Sunday 17th in response to a directive from the Ministry of Transport. The effect of this was to almost halve the scheduled annual mileage, from 639,561 to 321,765. Excursions and tours were cancelled immediately and contract mileage was also severely curtailed. Amongst the cancellations were several weekend tours to Blackpool for the illuminations, the first of which would have operated over the weekend of 16/17 September. On top of the 13s 6d fare (9s 0d for children), bed and breakfast was advertised 'from 4s 6d upwards'.

There were cutbacks on almost every service, the only exceptions being those to Claverdon and Loxley, which already only ran on Fridays, and the Alcester Grammar School run. The Stratford – Hampton Lucy and Kineton – Combrook – Stratford services were withdrawn altogether, whilst many others were discontinued on Sundays or reduced to run only on market days.

Even before this, on Saturday 2 September, buses had been taken off normal service to assist with the evacuation of civilians to Stratford from Birmingham, which was thought to be a likely target for air raids.

The journey to Oxford, about forty miles south-east of Stratford, was never a particularly easy one by train, requiring a change either at Honeybourne or at Leamington. Conscious of the potential summer traffic, Stratford Blue and City of Oxford Motor Services began a limited connecting bus service in June 1938, running three days a week. Following a successful season this was repeated in 1939, as shown here. The planned connections at Long Compton generally gave an end-to-end journey time of around two and a half hours.

The outbreak of war in September 1939 brought a sudden end to many of life's pleasures, including the Stratford Blue excursions and tours advertised here beneath a picture of Maudslay No.20. The Maudslays had helped to expand this activity. This is only an extract from the advertisement, and there was something to suit everyone, from afternoon tours to Bourton-on-the-Water through a night at the 'dogs' in Coventry to a weekend in Blackpool. Independent travellers could plan their own itinerary throughout the Midlands with the popular 5s 0d 'Day Anywhere' tickets (now valid on Midland Red and Stratford Blue services), but at this stage these were not available at weekends.

The enforced cuts led to eight vehicles (a Maudslay and seven Tillings) being delicensed from the end of September, leaving an active fleet of eight Tillings and a Maudslay coach at Stratford, and four Tillings at Kineton. Modifications made to comply with blackout regulations included restricted lighting inside and out and white painted markings at the front and back to improve visibility.

The company quickly experienced a shortage of staff as a result of all reservists being called up and others volunteering for military service. To fill the gap several conductresses were recruited, soon outnumbering men in this role. Everyone had to put in extremely long hours, sometimes as many as eighty to ninety per week in the case of conductors and conductresses. One of the latter, Rosemary McAteer, served for a time as the Transport & General Workers' Union branch secretary, and she recalled the difficulties of learning the routes at the start of the war when road signs had been removed to confuse the enemy in the event of an invasion. As well as the usual routes there were occasional stints on the Midland Red service to Birmingham, and from there to Coventry.

Approaches from the military authorities led to vehicles being put on standby for War Office use. One such arrangement involved up to ten buses for the Royal Artillery at Moreton Hall, Moreton Morrell, while another three were offered to the Adjutant of the 63rd Anti Tank Regiment at Walton Hall, near Wellesbourne.

A new timetable was issued in January 1940 and showed a few changes from the September 1939 pattern, including the introduction of Friday-only services from Stratford to Mickleton via Lower Quinton and to Alcester via Aston Cantlow and Great Alne, both of which probably replaced Midland Red services.

January 1940 saw some very harsh weather conditions around Stratford and in the middle of the month long stretches of the Avon were frozen over. The bitterly cold spell was followed by heavy snow which caused chaos to bus services, and then by a thaw which not only caused floods but forced large blocks of ice from the Stour onto the road between Alderminster and Newbold. Mr Agg praised the staff for keeping services running wherever possible in conditions which were made doubly difficult by the blackout.

During February the weather eased but there were many other problems to contend with. On Friday 16th a police constable stopped the 4.00 p.m. bus to Kineton as it left Stratford along Banbury Road, finding fifty-one passengers aboard the 32-seater bus. As a result the conductor, William Langford, and Inspector Reg Careless, who had been on duty in the bus station as the bus was loaded, appeared before the borough police court on 3 April. The company's defence described all the mitigating circumstances, including the shortage of staff, the halving of their petrol allocation and the wish to get children home from school before the blackout, but despite this Inspector Careless was fined 5s 0d. The case against the conductor was dismissed.

A notable addition to the fleet at about this time was the first double-decker, No.22 (JO2354), a 1931 AEC Regent bought from City of Oxford Motor Services for £70. It had Park Royal bodywork with seats for forty-eight passengers (twenty-four on each deck), well below the usual capacity of an early 1930s double-decker but still sixteen more than a Tilling. No.22 was put to work from Stratford garage, mainly on the Shipston service where the extra seats were most needed, but was to remain the solitary AEC and the only double-decker in a fleet made up almost entirely of Tilling-Stevens single-deckers. The Regent replaced the previous No.22 (DB5184) the surviving ex-North Western Tilling, which joined others of its batch on ARP work with Warwickshire County Council.

Concern was expressed by the Chairman, Mr Howley, that the reduction in mileage dictated by the war was not being mirrored by operating costs – between March 1939 and March 1940 these had leapt from 6.26d to 8.86d per mile, mainly because the same overheads still had to be covered despite the revenue-earning fleet being halved. The concentration of services on the busy days of Friday and Saturday had worsened the imbalance of work for the drivers and conductors, and to avoid laying them off they were engaged during slack periods on cleaning and other jobs inside the garage, but of course this brought in no income.

Fortunately, this situation did not last long and with the effects of the war not being felt too much at home, a slight relaxation was allowed. Some of the mothballed vehicles were put back on the road, and during the spring it was even possible to reintroduce a limited programme of local excursions.

As the summer approached, the reduced service network was increasingly stretched despite exhortations not to make unnecessary journeys. Stratford Blue helped Midland Red out by providing duplicate vehicles on the Stratford – Coventry service, particularly to help day-trippers get home to Coventry on Sunday evenings, although similar demands also arose on weekdays. As a result, on 13 July a pooling agreement came into force on the Stratford – Wellesbourne – Leamington service (518), which in pre-war years had been solely a Midland Red responsibility, and until the war was over Stratford Blue regularly operated certain journeys. By the August Bank Holiday the licensed fleet was back up to nineteen and revenue was comparable with the same period in 1939.

*Above*: The famous orchards of the Vale of Evesham have always been a springtime attraction, and as well as Stratford Blue the Warwickshire County Garage was also offering a tour on 28 April. Theirs was priced at 3s 6d, 6d more than Stratford Blue's blossom tour, and took an hour longer.

*Left*: The impact of the war was initially not too serious at home, and in Spring 1940 it was possible to offer local coach tours again, subject to the approval of the Regional Transport Commissioners. This advertisement from the *Herald* offers two local tours on 28 April and urges passengers to help the war effort by avoiding travel at weekends and not taking holidays in August.

Despite these slight relaxations, from July several BET companies, including Stratford Blue, had their registered offices temporarily moved from London to Midland Red's Bearwood headquarters.

Although bus driving became a 'reserved occupation', preventing a shortage of drivers, conducting did not have the same status and recruitment adverts were placed regularly. The first conductresses had been taken on at a rate of 8d per hour, plus a war bonus of 5s 3d per week. Negotiations with the Transport & General Workers' Union led to an increase in starting rates from January 1941, to 9d per hour for conductors and 1s 1d for drivers. A minimum of forty-eight hours per week was guaranteed, but much longer weeks were very often worked.

During 1941 it was possible to keep most of the fleet on the road, partly because of the constant demand for transport from munitions workers and military personnel, and in August all twenty-one buses were licensed. Even so, problems continued and both the Petroleum Board and the military authorities requisitioned petrol pumps and tanks, with the latter also taking over one of the lock-up garages at Bridgetown.

Another new timetable was published in September 1941. This showed very few service changes, but a notable point was that every service and variant was allocated a service number, as below:

| | |
|---|---|
| 1 | Cheltenham and Evesham via Teddington Hands (Bristol Blue service 66) |
| 1A | Cheltenham and Evesham via Kemerton (Bristol Blue service 66A) |
| 2 | Stratford and Evesham via Luddington, Welford and Bidford |
| 2A | Stratford and Evesham via Dodwell, Welford and Bidford |
| 2B | Stratford and Evesham via Luddington, Cranhill and Bidford |
| 2C | Stratford and Evesham via Luddington, Grafton and Bidford |
| 2D | Stratford and Evesham via Dodwell, Grafton and Bidford |
| 2E | Stratford and Evesham via Dodwell, Cranhill and Bidford |
| 3 | Stratford and Leamington via Snitterfield, Wolverton and Warwick |
| 3A | Stratford and Leamington via Blackhill, Sherbourne and Warwick |
| 4 | Stratford and Mickleton via Quinton (Midland Red service 524) |
| 5 | Stratford and Ilmington |
| 6 | Stratford, Langley and Claverdon |
| 7 | Stratford and Shipston-on-Stour (Midland Red service 519) |
| 8 | Stratford and Clifford Chambers (Midland Red service 524) |
| 9 | Stratford, Tiddington and Alveston (Midland Red service 518) |
| 10 | Stratford and Shottery |
| 12 | Stratford and Justins Avenue |
| 14 | Stratford and Banbury Road |
| 15 | Stratford and Alcester via Bidford and Broom |
| 15A | Stratford and Alcester via Billesley and Great Alne |
| 15B | Stratford and Alcester direct via Red Hill |
| 16 | Stratford and Hampton Lucy (Midland Red service 521) |
| 17 | Stratford and Loxley |
| 20 | Kineton and Stratford via Pillerton and Ettington |
| 21 | Kineton and Leamington via Gaydon |
| 23 | Kineton and Banbury via Fenny Compton and Northend |
| 24 | Kineton and Leamington via Moreton Morrell and Ashorne |
| 25 | Kineton and Banbury via Radway, Edgehill, Sunrising, Hornton, Horley and Hanwell |
| 26 | Kineton and Banbury via Radway, Edgehill, Avon Dassett and Warmington |
| 518 | Stratford and Leamington via Wellesbourne, Barford and Warwick |

Timetables for Midland Red services 150 (Stratford – Birmingham) and 529 (Stratford – Walton) were also included. The purpose of the numbers remains a mystery as they were not used for long and were almost certainly not displayed on the buses.

The problem of having just one double-decker in an otherwise single-deck fleet was illustrated by a mishap on Saturday 28 February 1942 when Mr Harold Jones took the Regent under a low roof at the Red Lion, bending the steel frame of the building and almost completely decapitating the bus. Fortunately he was travelling slowly, but four upstairs passengers needed treatment for cuts and abrasions. To avoid disruption to services while the bus was repaired Midland Red came to the rescue with another AEC Regent, one of many from London Transport's 'ST' class which they had on long-term loan. ST931, as it was known in London (registration GK1007), ran for Stratford Blue from early March until mid-April.

Throughout 1942 the company struggled on with its increasingly ageing and stretched fleet of Tillings, plus two Maudslays and the Regent. During the year Midland Red received a number of so-called 'unfrozen' double-deckers, assembled from parts manufactured earlier, followed by 'utility' vehicles of wartime pattern, but none came to Stratford Blue.

The staff shortage got worse and advertisements now had to be placed for drivers ('men used to PSV or Heavy Goods Vehicles'), as well as for conductresses 'age 17 to 18, or over 31' and garage hands 'over military age or not liable for service'. The adverts stressed that maintaining public transport services was vital to the war effort.

A minor drama occurred on the evening of 18 May when two RAF sergeants walked into Stratford garage and asked the cleaner if there were any more buses to Leamington. On being told 'no' and that they would be unlikely to find a taxi, they left, but a few minutes later a crash was heard as a bus which the cleaner had just parked collided with a gatepost at the Guild Street entrance. One of the men jumped from the cab and they fled but the police soon found them, hiding behind bushes in nearby Payton Street. Four days later they were fined for being drunk and disorderly.

As the shortages became serious, the Minister of War Transport directed that bus stops had to be at least a quarter of a mile apart. This would save fuel and tyre wear by cutting down on stopping and starting. This notice in the *Herald* gave details of the new stopping arrangements within Stratford from 9 November 1942.

## The Long and Short of it

Don't take a long-distance bus for a short journey —you may crowd out someone who wants to travel all the way. The number of long-distance buses is limited, and based on careful examination of the needs of the districts served; a missed long-distance bus may mean a long wait for the next one.

So use the local buses for local journeys and leave the long-distance buses for long distance passengers.

Many notices of this style were published during 1942/1943 in an effort to ensure that essential journeys could still be made. The 'British Buses' logo was used by the British Omnibus Companies' Public Relations Committee, who produced the adverts for local companies to adapt with their own titles. Earlier in the war various slogans were used, for example urging passengers to 'shop early and in daylight'.

Over the winter of 1942/1943 five of the Tillings which had been sold to the County Council for ARP use were repurchased, to be used for spares to keep other Tillings on the road. The hulks were then disposed of for scrap.

Early 1943 again saw the appearance of London Transport AEC Regents, with ST941 (GK1017) at Stratford from 8 March to 2 April and ST931 back from 10 April to 14 May. Another hired vehicle was DF7840, a 1929 Leyland Tiger 31–seat coach which came from Black & White Motorways of Cheltenham in July. It was probably not with Stratford Blue for long. As an alternative Mr Lapper, Black & White's General Manager, had offered a 1930 28-seater which he felt would be more suitable if the requirement was to transport servicemen rather than prisoners of war.

An innovation from 1 October 1943 was a 'Freedom from Accident Bonus', worth £6 0s 0d a year and paid quarterly to drivers with a clean record.

Unfortunately, Mr Power, who had been Midland Red's Traffic Manager since 1912 and was also one of Stratford Blue's most influential directors, died suddenly on 14 October. His replacement as a director was Mr D.M. Sinclair, Midland Red's Chief Engineer and from early 1944 their first General Manager.

Another three 'DB' Tillings returned later in 1943, two of them repurchased from Warwickshire County Council, and the former No.21 (DB5166) handed back after local ARP work in Stratford. Whilst the first two were used for spare parts, authority was given to spend up to £10 converting DB5166 into a tree-cutting vehicle. This went ahead and DB5166 was a familiar sight in this guise for several years, providing a vital service in clearing the lanes for the double-deckers which joined the fleet in the early post-war years.

At about this time the lease on the Red Lion bus park came up for renewal and representatives from Midland Red and Stratford Blue met the Hon. R.A. Erskine, Managing Director of Flowers' Brewery, to discuss the position. Mr Erskine stated that whilst he did not wish to terminate the agreement it had not boosted the trade of the Red Lion as had been expected, and the 'noise and disturbance' of the buses may even have had the opposite effect. He also felt that 'bus passengers were not the type of people to make use of such facilities'. Agreement was reached however, and the lease was renewed for another ten years.

Another new timetable came out in May 1944, featuring the 'British Buses' design on the cover. This showed surprisingly little change from the September 1941 edition, although the changes which had taken place were for the better, with some journeys reinstated. Also shown was a service operated temporarily on behalf of Midland Red, to Alcester Grammar School via several villages to the west of Alcester, including Inkberrow and Astwood Bank, which were very much in Midland Red territory.

Another bus was added to the hard-pressed fleet when No.23 (HA4942) was bought from Midland Red in 1944, at a cost of £25, plus £13 for painting into Stratford Blue colours. Although this finally introduced the Midland Red's excellent own-make SOS buses to the fleet, it did nothing to improve the average age, being a 1929 SOS 'M' (Madam) model, still carrying its original and by now antiquated-looking 34-seat Ransomes body. Nevertheless, in the circumstances of the time it was a very welcome arrival. Not all the fleet was blue however, as at least one Tilling (No.10; WX2130) was painted khaki in about 1944.

Three more vehicles were received during 1945, although unlike No.23 they were not actually bought. Nos 24/25 (JA6972/6973) were 1936 Leyland Tiger TS7s fitted with Harrington coachwork and belonging to Majestic Express Motors Ltd of Stockport, a company in which both Midland Red and North Western had an interest. Many surplus coaches had been requisitioned, but these two had spent much of the war working on hire to Midland Red. Sometime after arrival in Stratford, where they were used mainly as buses, they received blue livery. The luxurious bodies had forward-entrances and seats for either thirty or thirty-two, but it was their Leyland diesel engines – all previous Stratford Blue vehicles having been petrol-driven – which were to have the greatest impact on future vehicle policy. Amongst the coaches' features were canvas roofs which occasionally flew open during the course of a journey! The third vehicle was Midland Red's No.1675 (AHA619), a 1935 SOS 'OLR' which had started life as a 29-seat normal-control touring coach complete with sliding roof. For wartime service it had been converted along with the rest of its type to a forward-control service bus with seating for thirty-four, its Short Brothers body losing much of its original elegance in the process. It became Stratford Blue No.26, but remained in Midland Red livery. Three more TSMs were also acquired, again for spare parts, but this time the source is not known.

The January 1945 timetable showed another slight improvement in the level of service, although this was still well down on pre-war standards. Little further improvement had taken place by the time that another edition appeared in June, but by now the war in Europe was over and a slow return to peacetime conditions began. After joining in the initial celebrations, the company's management had to face the harsh realities of the post-war period, a very different era from the 1930s.

In October another new pay scale was agreed, with drivers starting at 1*s* 2½*d* per hour and 'junior' conductors (aged 18) at 9*d*. Forty-eight hours were still guaranteed, and eight days holiday per year were allowed after a year's service, rising to ten after three years.

After many difficult years 1946 saw some very welcome developments, and in July the board (now without Mr Howley, who had resigned after over ten years as Chairman) accepted a recommendation from Mr Sinclair to place an order which would completely transform the fleet. This called for eighteen brand-new Leyland buses, including eight double-deckers, at an estimated cost of £54,000. These would be the first completely new buses since Grail and Joiner's Thornycrofts of 1928 and would cost about £3,000 each; the majority of the buses to be replaced had cost little over £30 apiece! However, although some had benefited from the delivery of wartime 'utilities', operators everywhere were desperate for new buses and the manufacturers had very full order books. This meant long delays before some orders could be met, and as an interim measure Mr Agg found it necessary to buy second-hand again. After the mixed bag of arrivals during the war years it was now possible to be a little more selective but the choice was still not wide. The diesel-engined Leyland Tiger coaches from Majestic Express had performed excellently, leading to the large order for new Leylands, but similar vehicles were scarce on the second-hand market. Consequently Mr Agg opted for yet more of the tried and tested Tilling Stevens Express models, buying another eight in late 1946. They had belonged to the North Western Road Car Co., which had also been the source of those acquired in 1936/1937, but only four were bought direct (DB9362/9380/9389/9397, which became Stratford Blue Nos 28-31 respectively). The other four (DB9368/9375/9377/9395; Nos 27/20/21/26) came via a bus dealer, Frank Cowley of Salford, Lancashire. Their petrol-engined B10A2 chassis dated from 1930 but attractive new 31-seat Eastern Counties bodies

The first post-war acquisitions were eight further TSMs from North Western, reintroducing the rear-entrance layout for service buses. As Flowers were still usually the sole advertiser at this time, perhaps the 'Hovis' advert came with No.26 (DB9395) from North Western. In this picture in Stratford garage yard the bus is facing towards Guild Street. (*Shakespeare Birthplace Trust*)

No.5 (WX2120) was one of sixteen TSMs bought from the West Yorkshire Road Car Co. in October 1938, and had a 32-seat Tilling body. These buses dated back to 1930 but put in sterling service throughout the war and most continued to see intensive use until about 1948, No.5 lasting into 1949. It is shown here at the Red Lion before the fourteen-minute journey through Tiddington to Alveston on what became the L1 local service. There are already passengers on board, but no sign of the crew. The advertisement above the window proclaims Flower's Ale as 'the best beer brewed'. (*BaMMOT/R.T. Wilson*)

had been fitted in 1935, giving a much more modern appearance than the other TSMs in the fleet. They had rear entrances and comfortable seating, and although the chassis were dated they were to prove a sound buy at £195 each.

The new TSMs ousted the Maudslay coaches (Nos 20/21; WP8277/3425), one of which fetched £400, substantially more than had been paid for it eight years earlier, and presumably also the 'OLR' coach hired from Midland Red (No.26; AHA619), since this number was now taken by DB9395. The first of the former West Yorkshire TSMs (No.7; WX2151) was also sold, but with only four buses displaced the fleet expanded to twenty-nine vehicles – the largest it had yet been.

The effect of the return to peace and the start of the post-war passenger boom was to more than double the company's annual revenue, from £32,511 in 1945 to £78,598 in 1946.

The winter of 1946/1947 was one of the most severe ever recorded, and early March saw south Warwickshire in the grip of extreme conditions. On Wednesday 5th Mr Agg reported that his buses had covered only 906 miles out of the 2,857 scheduled. Snowdrifts of 9–12ft were commonplace and during the day five buses had to be dug out, but all were back at their garages by midnight. The next day conditions were even worse, with almost all roads blocked, and services were suspended completely. On the Friday barely a third of journeys were run, with only 1,035 out of 3,071 miles operated, and on the Saturday the figure was lower still, but the situation then eased so that by mid-day on Tuesday 11th Mr Agg could report that a full service had been restored.

Early in 1947 considerable attention was given to the Cheltenham – Evesham service, which was shared with the Bristol Tramways company. Although joint operation had started as far back as 1931, scope was identified to co-ordinate the two companies' activities more closely. For example, school bus passes were not interavailable, even though many children travelled by Bristol Tramways in the morning and Stratford Blue in the afternoon, or vice versa. This had become more of a problem with the closure of village schools along the route, leading to more children travelling to the large schools in Cheltenham and Evesham. The solution was a new pooling arrangement which is thought to have been operational by early summer, under which all tickets were fully interavailable on buses of either operator. Mileage and receipts were split on the basis of one-third Bristol Tramways, two-thirds Stratford Blue.

Although the war was over the transport of troops was still a very big part of the company's business but inevitably it brought a few hazards, especially with off-duty servicemen. In December there was an incident on a journey form Banbury when a group of soldiers from Marlborough Farm Camp jumped on to a bus while it was moving. Jan Drbal, a Kineton driver, stopped the bus to remonstrate with them but one of the men struck him in the face. This resulted in a court appearance and a hefty fine.

Fortunately as 1948 approached relief was finally in sight for the hard-worked fleet of twenty-nine vehicles, of which all but four were TSMs dating from 1927-1930, and the new Leyland diesel buses were awaited with eager anticipation.

# 8

# Recovery and Growth
# 1948–1958

The long wait for new vehicles ended on 24 March 1948 with the delivery of the Leyland Titan double-deckers, which became Nos 32–39 (GUE238-245), the fleet numbers following on from the last of the Tillings. They were Leyland products throughout, with chassis of the PD2/1 model, powerful 9.8 litre diesel engines and 56-seat open-platform bodywork built at the Farington body plant.

Their arrival was a huge boost to the company, which had not bought a single brand new vehicle for twenty years. They were put to work on a variety of services, most of which had never previously seen a double-decker, and were immediately popular with passengers, who for years had been accustomed to travelling in ageing and often crowded single-deckers. For those who ventured upstairs the Titans opened up new vistas of the South Warwickshire countryside over the tops of the hedgerows. Before they entered service a tree-cutting crew travelled the lanes with the specially modified Tilling (DB5166) to cut back any branches likely to damage the roofs.

The post-war fleet transformation began in March 1948 with the arrival of eight Leyland Titans (Nos 32-39; GUE238-245). Before receiving advertisements they were lined up for the official photographer, each with a different destination and service number display. No.32, on the left, is showing '64A Cheltenham via Beckford & Kemerton'. Previously there had only been one double-decker in the fleet, and many routes now saw double-deckers for the first time. (*P. Hudson collection*)

This view of No.39 (GUE245) in Stratford garage yard is one of many photographs taken on Sunday 30 April 1950, when a large group of bus enthusiasts were guests of the company. This was probably the first such visit as interest in buses was in its early days, encouraged by the appearance of the magazine *Buses Illustrated* in November 1949. The third issue, in March 1950, contained an illustrated article on Stratford Blue. (*The Omnibus Society*)

Among the buses directly displaced was the only previous double-decker, AEC Regent No.22 (JO2354), which had rarely strayed off the Shipston and Justins Avenue services. The others were Tillings 2 and 6 (WX2131/2152) and former Midland Red SOS No.23 (HA4942), but three more Tillings (Nos 1, 10 and 15; WX2121/2130/2133) were retired during the summer. None of these saw further use as buses, but some of the Tillings were bought by travelling showmen and the desperate shortage of vehicles in the early post-war years is reflected in the price – after ten years of intensive use they were sold for more than they had cost in 1938! Midland Red took the SOS back and converted it into a mobile workshop.

The summer of 1948 was busy and Mr Agg particularly noted the success of the connectional journeys to Oxford, which had been reintroduced after being suspended during the war. As a result he began talks with City of Oxford Motor Services with a view to introducing a jointly-operated through service which would operate all year and overcome the need to change buses at Long Compton. After lengthy discussions about how to share the mileage equally an agreement was reached and through operations began on 6 November 1949, using City of Oxford's service number (44). The journey of just over forty miles was scheduled to take two hours and twenty minutes. Each operator ran two full round trips on weekdays, but to achieve the mileage balance City of Oxford also operated a 4.30 p.m. journey from Stratford to Long Compton and back. On Sundays there were only three journeys each way, so on the morning run from each end passengers still had to change at Long Compton. Another difference on Sundays was that City of Oxford's 4.30 p.m. journey ran only as far as Shipston before returning to Stratford. Stratford Blue buses now became a regular sight in Chipping Norton, Woodstock and Oxford, which remained the southernmost point on the network.

Meanwhile the single-deck Tigers arrived between September 1948 and January 1949, with fleet and registration numbers (40-49; GUE246-255) following the Titans. The chassis were of Leyland's PS1 model with 7.4 litre diesel engine and the 34-seat forward-entrance bodies, to standard BET design, came from Northern Coach Builders Ltd of Newcastle-upon-Tyne, a small concern which won a few BET orders at about this time. They replaced another nine 'WX' Tillings, leaving No.5 (WX2120) as the last survivor. However, this was also sold during the first half of 1949, together with No.11 (VT34), one of the long-serving

The new buses had comprehensive destination displays and introduced another attempt at service numbering. This had more success than previous efforts, but the nine-minute run to Clifford Chambers was not known as service 24A for very long; a little later the blinds showed service number 524A, but this was also short-lived. No.36 (GUE242), shown here at the Red Lion, and sister vehicle No.37 were always distinguished by their chromium-plated radiators, the other six having more mundane blue-painted ones. (*Author's collection*)

No.34 (GUE240) is still looking as good as new in this view in the yard of Stratford garage before the new brick structure was erected. Already the original large destination blind has been replaced by a smaller single-line display – easier for the staff perhaps but less helpful for passengers. These buses had hand-painted number plates, No.34's having noticeably taller characters than some others. (*The Omnibus Society*)

Rear-view photographs are relatively scarce, but this picture of No.32 (GUE238) at the Red Lion nicely illustrates the blind display above the rear platform, which here reads '519 Shipston-on-Stour via Alderminster & Newbold'. Many operators had blinds fitted to the back of the bus but Mr Agg may have chosen the position above the platform to allow more space for advertising. Flowers have used the rear spaces on No.32 to advertise their Special Brew and the bottled Brown Ale. (*BaMMOT/R.T. Wilson*)

pair of Tillings bought in 1936. Typical of the sales of these vehicles was No.11, which was fitted with a set of scrap tyres in April 1949 and sold for £55 to a buyer in Leamington's Covent Garden Market, for use as a caravan.

Reverting to 1948, the Transport & General Workers' Union negotiated some much improved terms of employment for the platform staff. The standard working week was reduced to forty-four hours over six days and the starting rate for drivers was increased to just under 2s 2d per hour, with conductors getting about 1d an hour less ('junior' conductors under 21 were on a lower rate).

Following the receipt of the new buses several services, including the Stratford 'locals', had their frequencies increased, and by 1949 the Shottery service was running every twenty minutes (previously half-hourly), and the Alveston, Banbury Road and Justins Avenue services were all hourly instead of running at irregular, less frequent, intervals.

Twelve more Leylands arrived in 1950, starting with four Tiger PS2/3s with 35-seat Willowbrook 'dual-purpose' bodywork (Nos 50-53; JUE348-351) which arrived in March and April. They were followed in May by Nos 54/55 (JUE352/353), which were generally

No.40 (GUE246) was the first of ten Leyland Tiger PS1 saloons to arrive, in September 1948, and is shown here at the Red Lion Bus Station with its original full destination display. These buses, with 34-seat Northern Coach Builders bodywork, displaced Tillings dating back to 1930, and their registrations completed a series of eighteen consecutive registrations carried by Stratford Blue buses – a record which was never to be beaten. When photographed, No.40 carried a small plain fleet number on the cream band, rather than the usual gold-leaf style above the headlamp. In the background, Reg Careless, one of three inspectors employed by the company in 1948, can be seen chatting to a passenger. (*Author's collection*)

No.46 (GUE252) looks immaculate as it stands outside the Clifton cinema in Evesham, possibly during its first summer. Several passengers have already boarded, and it seems likely that all seats will be taken by the time the bus departs. The original large destination display shows another of the short-lived service numbers – '5B Stratford-upon-Avon via Bidford and Cranhill'. (*The Omnibus Society*)

similar but had more functional 34-seat saloon bodywork on PS2/1 chassis. The dual-purpose vehicles were distinguished by a cream flash on the side panels and carried a monogram instead of the usual fleetname. With coach-style seating and rear luggage boots, they were intended to be as much at home on excursions and other longer-distance work as they were on local stage carriage services. All six had the 9.8 litre engine as fitted to the double-deckers, giving them more power than the 'GUE' Tigers.

The transformation of the fleet was completed by the delivery of another six double-deckers (Nos 26-31; JUE354-359) in late July and early August. These were 56-seaters of almost identical specification to those delivered in 1948 and they allowed all remaining pre-war buses to be withdrawn.

The vehicles displaced were the two Majestic Express Tigers (Nos 24/25; JA6972/6973) and the final nine Tillings – No.12 (VT580), which had had a remarkable innings of almost fourteen years, and the former North Western machines acquired in 1946. This marked the end of the petrol-engined bus in the fleet, although No.29 (DB9380) survived for another five years as a tree-cutting vehicle after being converted to replace DB5166.

By August 1950 the fleet consisted of fourteen Titans (Nos 26-39) and sixteen Tigers (Nos 40-55), the oldest of which dated from March 1948. Stratford Blue almost certainly had the most modern bus fleet in the country and at last portrayed the image of a professionally run, high-quality operator, as befitted its status as a member of the BET group. Contrast this with little over two years earlier when most of the battle-scarred collection of second-hand vehicles was almost twenty years old!

Mr Agg and the staff were justifiably proud of the new fleet, and so were Leyland, who featured the company in an article entitled 'Show Fleet for a Showplace' which appeared in

The TSMs acquired in 1946 continued in service alongside the new Tigers for a couple of years, but were all withdrawn in the summer of 1950. No.27 (DB9368) had by now been repainted in the later livery style, with a blue roof like the Tigers. It is shown here in Stratford garage yard on 30 April 1950, still looking reasonably smart despite the battered front wing. Flower's Brown Ale (on the rear of the bus behind) was not among the range of brews later advertised on the side panels of the buses. (*Author's collection*)

Spring 1950 saw the arrival of four Leyland Tigers with Willowbrook semi-luxury bodies and No.53 (JUE351) was quickly taken to picturesque Welford-on-Avon and posed in Boat Lane. The result was this promotional postcard which claimed on the back 'our latest 1950 Leyland 33-35 seater coaches are specially designed for safety and comfort, and only experienced drivers employed'. The monogram, used in preference to the normal fleetname to give a further 'touch of class', is visible immediately behind the entrance. (*Author's collection*)

Illustrating the flexibility of the 'dual-purpose' Tigers are these contrasting early shots of No.50 (JUE348). Above it is seen at an unknown location helping out on a Midland Red express service, while below it sits in the familiar surroundings of the Red Lion ready to operate service 5A to Evesham via Temple Grafton. *(A.B. Cross)*

their house magazine in November 1951. This gave Mr Agg the opportunity to describe several facets of the company's operation. Because of the rural nature of almost the entire 350-mile route network, fuel economy was vital, and Leyland's six-cylinder diesel engines returned a very good average of 12.25mpg. The buses covered high mileages, often as much as 250 miles a day. Mr Agg considered himself fortunate not to have the peak-hour problem which many urban operators experienced, and whilst there was a morning and afternoon peak demand for school and work travel, it did not leave many buses surplus to requirements for the rest of the day (to illustrate the extent of this problem, a few years later Birmingham City Transport needed 1,473 buses during Monday to Friday peak hours, of which 928 sat idle in between!). Another feature of Stratford Blue's operations was the regular transfer of buses between the two garages to help with market-day requirements (Thursday, for example, was a particularly busy day for Kineton because of Banbury market, but it was early closing day in Stratford). To conclude the article Mr Agg could not resist a Shakespeare anecdote to highlight a unique aspect of the company's operations:

> *During the long season at our magnificent Memorial Theatre, final departures from Stratford at night are held up for theatre traffic, and our platform staff have become students of Shakespeare at least to the extent that they know they will have longer to wait if the play is* Richard III *than if it is* Othello *or* The Merchant of Venice.

Another 'JUE' registered vehicle was Mr Agg's new company car, an Austin saloon registered JUE165 which replaced his pre-war Ford (AWD507).

The two Tiger PS2/1s with ordinary saloon bodywork were licensed for service on 6 May 1950. Their Willowbrook bodies were of similar outline to the dual-purpose vehicles, but of more functional appearance, and carried the standard fleetname. Advertising for Flowers' brewery, not thought fitting for the dual-purpose vehicles, was carried in the usual position above the windows. No.54 (JUE352) stands in Evesham before a journey to Welford-on-Avon on service 5. (*S.J. Butler collection*)

Another six Leyland Titan double-deckers (Nos 26-31; JUE354-359) took to the road In August 1950. This view shows No.26 in original condition with large destination display, about to leave Bridge Street for Shottery on service L2. These buses differed from the 1948 Titans only in a few points of detail but could be identified by their unpainted aluminium radiators and by the horizontal sliding windows – on the earlier buses the windows were opened by lowering the top section. (*Author's collection*)

Another of the 1950 buses was No.30 (JUE358), shown here at the Red Lion before leaving for Alcester on service 353 – one of the services numbered in the Midland Red series. Flowers' brewery remained the sole advertiser on the buses, the adverts being painted using the fleet colours of royal blue and cream. This produced a useful supplementary income in a way which Mr Agg felt was 'distinctive without being discordant'. (*Dr M.A. Taylor*)

The 1950 Leylands completed the renewal programme started only two years earlier, and saw off all remaining pre-war vehicles, including No.12 (VT580). This long-serving machine was one of two TSM Expresses acquired from Trent in September 1936. They dated from 1927 and had originated with independent operators in the Potteries before being rebodied in 1933 while owned by Kingfisher of Derby. The slightly battered appearance and lack of fleetnames confirm that No.12 was withdrawn from service, awaiting a buyer, when this photograph was taken in Stratford garage yard on 30 April 1950. It fetched £14. (*National Tramway Museum*)

Stratford Blue had been a subsidiary of Midland Red since 1935 and had always appeared the 'poor relation' with its elderly second-hand fleet. The events of 1948-1950 changed all that, and, in this rare 1950 view at the Red Lion Bus Station, the traditional roles appear dramatically reversed. The Stratford Blue buses are No.31 (JUE359), on service 5 to Evesham, and No.35 (GUE241) on service 6 to Alcester. Beside them is Midland Red's No.2245 (FHA227), a pre-war 'FEDD' (forward-entrance double-decker) with Brush bodywork, on service 150 to Birmingham; at this time the 150 was still operated solely by Midland Red. (*A.B. Cross*)

The modernisation programme did not stop at the buses, and during 1950 trials were conducted with Setright 'Speed' ticket machines. These were found to have many advantages over the Bellgraphic system, which had been used since 1937, so forty-five machines were ordered. With a Bellgraphic the conductor had to write each ticket out by hand, whereas after appropriate setting of the dials a Setright printed the fare, the boarding fare stage, the date and the class of ticket. A sequential ticket number and the number of the ticket machine were also printed. Another major benefit was that the new machines recorded the total value of all tickets issued, which previously had to be laboriously added up by the ticket clerks and checked against the cash paid in by the conductor. The Setright machines were to prove extremely successful, and the system remained in use until the era of electronic ticket machines, which were introduced at Stratford garage in March 1989. A curious practice for many years was the use of green ticket rolls at Kineton garage and pink at Stratford; most companies managed perfectly well with one standard ticket roll and if Midland Red had taken the same approach they would have needed thirty different shades!

At about the same time consideration was given to establishing a car hire and taxi service. This would have been an unusual diversification for a bus company in the BET group, but the board approved the principle in July 1950 and in September gave authority to buy three Humber Pullman limousines at an estimated cost of £1,800 each. The taxi proposal was dropped but the 'private car hire service' started in early 1951 and the chauffeur-driven limousines soon became popular both for weddings and business use, although in the event only two were acquired (KUE178/179).

Unfortunately the very informative large destination blinds were soon replaced by this style of one-line display with 'Stratford Blue' applied to the top half of the glass. Apart from having this modification, No.33 (GUE239) was very much in original condition in this scene at the Mulberries, starting point for the L1 service to Tiddington and Alveston. Although working Stratford 'locals', No.33 was based at Kineton at the time. Note the car parking in the middle of Bridge Street. (*P. Hudson collection*)

Another view outside the Clifton cinema in Evesham, with No.39 (GUE245) awaiting passengers for Cheltenham on service 64 via Teddington Hands (most journeys ran as 64As via Kemerton). To the right is G.E. Buchanan's Guy Wolf, CPE222, on the service to its home village of Ashton-under-Hill. (*Author's collection*)

KUE179 was one of two six-seater Humber Pullman limousines acquired to launch Stratford Blue's chauffeur-driven limousine hire service in 1951. This was a useful sideline for a number of years but probably less profitable than Mr Agg had hoped. No further cars were added and the service ceased in 1962 after the original limousines had seen eleven years' service. (*The Omnibus Society*)

A fine view of Kineton-based No.32 (GUE238) at the Red Lion (or the 'Service Bus Station'), understood to date from April 1950. Although the blind is carefully set to show Kineton it also shows the service number 33, which was the service from Leamington to Kineton via Moreton Morrell; it should have been showing 30 for its journey to Kineton via Ettington, Pillerton Priors, Pillerton Hersey and Butlers Marston. The Red Lion never had a proper system of stands and buses awaited their passengers wherever there was a space available. Sometimes portable queue signs were used, as seen here to the left of the display boards, but even these did not always help – buses often loaded well away from the queue signs. On the left, on service X90 to Coventry, is Midland Red's No.3208 (JHA808), a 1948 'S8'. (*B. Knowlman*)

The new Stratford garage was a big improvement on the old premises and included modern office accommodation and an enquiry office (visible to the right, with Midland Red's wheel device above the window). The yard adjacent to Guild Street was also improved, and this early 1950s view shows it with a row of Titans alongside the garage, including No.31 (JUE359) and two of the 1948 buses, while on the left, showing '32A Kineton' on its blind, is dual-purpose Tiger No.51 (JUE349). All of them look immaculate. (*R. Knibbs*)

The Oxford terminus of service 44 was in Gloucester Green Bus Station, where No.29 (JUE357) is shown before its return journey to Stratford. Alongside, heading for Wallingford on service 33, is City of Oxford Motor Services' solitary wartime utility Bristol, a 1942 K5G with Duple lowbridge bodywork (No.L16, later L111; JWL418). *(P.M. Photography)*

During 1950 attention was also given to the garage and offices at Warwick Road, which by now had become thoroughly inadequate. Only fourteen of the twenty-two buses based at Stratford could be kept under cover so it was proposed to extend the garage by building over the bus washing area. A modern office was also needed for enquiries and bookings, preferably at the corner of the garage facing the bus station. To accommodate this and extra office space a two-storey building was proposed, with Mr Agg, the typists, the wages and statistics staff, the cashier and ticket clerks and the inspectors all having new offices on the first floor. There would also be a conductors' ticket room and a staff rest room. Stratford Blue's staff never benefited from a canteen, the traditional hotbed of busmen's gossip, although no doubt the grapevine functioned well enough without it! Board approval was given towards the end of the year and work was quickly put in hand.

The enormous investment in the new bus fleet and in the garage and ticket machines had been made possible by the huge upturn in passenger numbers during the post-war travel boom, but a pointer to the future lay in the company's first ever general fares increase, which took effect on 28 July 1951. Midland Red fares went up on the same day and the companies blamed the greatly increased costs of operation, especially the rise in fuel prices introduced by two successive budgets. Adult single fares below 1s went up by ½d and those from 1s to 1s 11½d by 1d, the minimum adult fare becoming 1½d.

Although rationing was still in force for some consumer items, the company's bus services were by now back to pre-war levels, and in most cases better. Demand was continuing to grow and private cars were still beyond the means of most people, although ownership was slowly rising. Another helpful factor was the growth in Stratford's population, from 11,600 in 1931 to around 15,000 in 1951, partly due to the number of wartime evacuees and refugees who chose to make the town their permanent home. In the surrounding area agricultural employment was declining, together with the population of some of the villages, but 24 per cent of jobs in the Stratford Employment Exchange area were still in agriculture in 1951, keeping demand for travel in the countryside buoyant.

Another service numbering scheme had been introduced in about 1948, with the numbers included on the destination blinds in the new buses. However, although they were now shown on the buses (probably for the first time) the service numbers did not at first appear in the timetables! Most of the numbers adopted at this time were to remain in use until the end although others, such as the No.7 for journeys to Snitterfield, quickly faded into obscurity. By the time the November 1951 timetable was published the list of services, together with their numbers and days of operation, was as follows (for joint services, only the days of operation by Stratford Blue are indicated):

| | | |
|---|---|---|
| L1 | Stratford – Tiddington – Alveston | Daily |
| L2 | Stratford – Shottery | Daily |
| L3 | Stratford – Justins Avenue | Daily |
| L4 | Stratford – Banbury Road | Monday – Saturday |
| 5/5A | Stratford – Bidford – Evesham | Daily |
| 6 | Stratford – Broom – Alcester | Monday – Saturday |
| 10 | Stratford – Hampton Lucy | Friday only |
| 11 | Stratford – Wellesbourne/Walton | Monday – Saturday |
| 30 | Kineton – Ettington – Stratford | Daily |
| 31 | Kineton – Moreton Morrell – Stratford | Friday only |
| 32/32A | Kineton – Gaydon – Leamington | Daily |
| 33 | Kineton – Moreton Morrell – Leamington/Warwick | Daily |
| 34 | Kineton – Fenny Compton – Banbury | Monday – Saturday |
| 35/35A/35B | Kineton – Warmington – Banbury | Monday – Saturday |
| 36 | Kineton – Hornton – Banbury | Monday – Saturday |
| 44 | Stratford – Chipping Norton – Oxford | Daily |
| 64/64A | Evesham – Beckford – Cheltenham | Daily |
| 90A | Stratford – Snitterfield – Leamington | Daily |
| 90C | Stratford – Snitterfield – Claverdon | Friday only |
| 339/353 | Stratford – Alcester | Monday – Saturday |
| 519 | Stratford – Shipston – Long Compton | Daily |

| | | |
|---|---|---|
| 524 | Stratford – Clifford Chambers – Chipping Campden | Monday – Saturday |
| 533 | Stratford – Ilmington – Stretton-on-Fosse | Tuesday, Friday and Saturday |
| Unnumbered | Stratford – Pebworth – Evesham | Friday only |

Numbers up to 36 formed the company's own numbering system, whilst the higher numbers were generally those used by joint operators (44 by City of Oxford, 64/64A by Bristol Tramways and the three-figure numbers by Midland Red). Nos 90A and 90C were the exceptions, apparently selected to infer that they were variants of Midland Red's X90 service (Stratford – Warwick – Coventry). Stratford local services had an 'L' prefix, while Kineton area services were in the range 30 to 36. Only the newly introduced Stratford – Pebworth – Evesham service had no number.

Despite the concerted efforts between 1948 and 1951 the haphazard approach to service numbering continued, and for the rest of their existence Stratford Blue buses were frequently to be seen showing their destination but no number. Midland Red's passengers almost always knew their bus by its service number, but Stratford Blue regulars simply talked about 'the Ilmington bus' or 'the Moreton Morrell bus'.

Scope for expansion was now more restricted as bus patronage reached its all-time high, but during 1951 a Friday-only service between Evesham and Stratford via Pebworth and Honeybourne had been introduced. This consisted of a single round trip for market day shopping in Stratford and brought Stratford Blue buses back to Pebworth after an absence of fifteen years.

In 1952 the fleet grew to thirty-three with the delivery of Titans 23-25 (MAC570-572). These were bought mainly for use on service 150 to Birmingham, on which Stratford Blue took a regular share of the operation from 31 May. The new buses were longer and wider than the earlier Titans, the regulations covering maximum dimensions having been relaxed. No.24 is seen here in original condition beside the Bridge Café after a journey from Shipston on the 519, a joint service with Midland Red. (*Author's collection*)

Friday is market day in Stratford, and on a summer afternoon in the mid-1950s No.39 (GUE245) makes the right turn from Rother Street into Wood Street, heading for the Red Lion on service 5. This shows the second style of advertisement carried by the double-deckers, still giving the message 'Flower's Ale Famous for its Flavour'. The clock on the American Fountain confirms that this is the 2.00 p.m. journey from Evesham, running exactly on time. Buses from Evesham continue to enter Stratford along Rother Street although they now have to pass the other side of the fountain, in front of the Old Thatch Tavern. (*P. Hudson collection*)

When new the 1952 Titans were also regular performers on the Oxford service. This commercial postcard view shows No.23 (MAC570) passing through Chipping Norton on the 8.40 a.m. journey from Stratford. (*Author's collection*)

The first major change since the start of the Oxford service in 1949 came on 31 May 1952 when Stratford Blue finally took a share in Midland Red's long-established 150 service between Stratford and Birmingham via Henley-in-Arden. This included a share of the revenue, which the two operators placed into a pool to be divided up according to a predetermined formula. At the same time the frequency was doubled to half-hourly and two Stratford Blue buses, each running four round trips a day, joined the three Midland Red vehicles on the service. Midland Red continued to operate all scheduled evening and Sunday journeys and also held the Road Service Licence, so Stratford Blue technically operated on hire. Previously Stratford Blue buses on regular service had ventured no further along Birmingham Road than the end of Justins Avenue.

Three new double-deckers were ordered for the 150 service, again Leyland-bodied Titans but of the updated PD2/12 model. Although broadly similar to earlier Titans, Nos 23-25

(MAC570-572) were easily distinguished by their extra width (8ft compared with 7ft 6in). They were also a foot longer, being built to the new maximum length for double-deckers of 27ft. This gave room for two additional seats upstairs (fifty-eight in total). The first of the trio was ready on time and was licensed on 30 May, but Nos 24 and 25 were not received until July. A distinguishing feature of No.23 was its predominantly green interior trim, giving rise to speculation that it was originally destined for another operator.

In the first half of 1952 thirteen lock-up garages were built at the Bridgetown Filling Station to add to the nine put up in 1939. Two were for the Humber limousines and the others for rental. Bridgetown was still a profitable offshoot of the main business and in 1951 it sold over 208,000 gallons of petrol, with a turnover in excess of £39,000 and four full-time staff.

The 90C service was amended in November 1952 to include Bearley village, which had not previously had a bus service, but for some reason this was not found to be successful and the service reverted to its old route, omitting Bearley, from February 1954. By 1955 Bearley had a separate service, consisting of one round trip to Stratford for the market on Fridays.

Another minor expansion was on the horizon at the end of 1952 when Samuel Bennett offered to sell his stage carriage operations to Stratford Blue. Mr Bennett's letterhead showed his address as Old Fox House, Ilmington, and used the dated term 'general carrier'. However he was also recognised as one of the finest traditional fiddle players and morris dancers in the country, and had travelled the world with dancing teams. His bus services ran from Ilmington to Stratford on Wednesdays and Fridays and to Shipston on Saturdays, using a 1939 Bedford 26-seater. The bus was of no interest to Stratford Blue but Mr Bennett was keen to retire and agreement was quickly reached for Stratford Blue to pay £175 for the goodwill, slightly over a year's takings.

'The Ilmington bus'. The PS1 Tigers were the mainstay of most of the rural services throughout the 1950s and No.41 (GUE247) is seen at the rear of the Red Lion on a dismal day in September 1955. Several passengers have already boarded for the journey to Ilmington, at the northern tip of the Cotswolds, and the interior is well steamed-up. For most of the '50s the Ilmington service ran on Tuesdays, Fridays and Saturdays, although Wednesday journeys were introduced in February 1953 to replace Sam Bennett's service. The latter only lasted until December 1956 when the 'Suez' crisis presented an opportunity to withdraw them, initially on a temporary basis. (*Roy Marshall*)

'The Moreton Morrell bus'. Service 33 ran from Leamington to Kineton via Moreton Morrell and No.47 (GUE253) is seen here at the Crown Hotel terminus in Leamington, about to embark on a short journey. The clock in the window of Miss Beasley's fruit stores suggests that this is the Saturday-only 3.45 p.m. journey to Moreton Paddox (Moreton Paddox is just beyond Moreton Morrell, but may not have been carried on the blind). Miss Beasley ran a Stratford Blue parcels agency, and had previously carried out the same function for Kineton Green. (*Author's collection*)

'The Claverdon bus' ran only on Fridays, when it fetched passengers to market from Claverdon and Langley (Claverdon also had regular trains to Stratford, but the station is nearly a mile from the village). Although it had previously been numbered 90C, buses on this service usually ran without showing a number. Here No.46 (GUE252) stands alongside the Red Lion with passengers already on board for the afternoon return journey. (*Author's collection*)

'The Edgehill bus' (No.43; GUE249) at North Bar, Banbury, with No.44 ('the Kineton bus') beside it. In this instance the lack of service numbers might cause a problem for unfamiliar passengers as the Kineton bus could be operating via Fenny Compton (service 34), Warmington (service 35) or Hornton (service 36)! No.43 has a later livery style with the waistband blue instead of cream. Both buses are already partly loaded, while the drivers, a conductor and a conductress are gathered in front of No.44. Midland Red's Banbury services terminated at the Town Hall but Stratford Blue, and Kineton Green before them, used North Bar, sometimes referred to in the company's timetables as the 'Buck and Bell', the Flowers' house whose sign is visible on the extreme right of the picture. (*R.H.G. Simpson*)

'The Combrook bus' left the Red Lion every Friday at 12.30 p.m. until the 'Suez' cuts of 1956, but this journey was then extended through to Kineton and the afternoon service was withdrawn altogether; Combrook was then no longer needed on the blinds. No.44 (GUE250) is seen in earlier days, for once displaying the service number (31). The tiny village of Combrook (spelled 'Combroke' for many years in the company's timetables) also had a bus to Leamington on Saturdays when one journey each way on service 33 made a detour from its normal route. (*Author's collection*)

MOTOR

COACH

TOURS

STARTING FROM

## WARWICKSHIRE COUNTY GARAGE

**WATERSIDE**      TEL. STRATFORD-UPON-AVON 3801–2

COACHES RUN DAILY THROUGHOUT THE
SEASON TO THE COTSWOLDS AND PLACES
OF HISTORICAL INTEREST

**Chauffeur-driven Limousines and Coaches are also
available for private hire and touring at very reasonable
rates.**

The Warwickshire County Garage was quick to buy the new Bedford SB model when it came on the market. The first was this 1951 example with Gurney Nutting coachwork (LNX488), alongside which Stratford Blue's Tigers looked positively utilitarian. Competition for the local tours market was stiff and these factors no doubt influenced Mr Agg's decision to buy the Royal Tiger coaches. Note that the County Garage also offered chauffeur-driven limousines, another area where the two concerns now competed.

The acquisition took effect from 18 February 1953 and led Stratford Blue to add Wednesday journeys on the Stratford – Ilmington service, which had previously only run on Tuesdays (when it continued to Stretton-on-Fosse), Fridays and Saturdays. The Saturday timetable was also revised to replace Bennett's service, with some journeys extended beyond Ilmington through Darlingscott to Shipston, a new stretch of route for Stratford Blue. The Wednesday journeys were not a success and were among the first to be withdrawn four years later when economies had to be made.

In May a new town service was introduced to the housing development at East Green Drive, off Alcester Road. This ran hourly and was treated as a variant of the L2 Shottery service, but buses initially showed the destination 'Redlands and Toll House'.

The latter half of 1953 was uneventful, but during the year an order was placed for two luxury coaches, an admission that Stratford Blue needed something considerably more stylish than the dual-purpose Tigers if it was to keep up with other local operators. This was partly due to a radical change in vehicle design in the early 1950s, which led to coaches with bonnets or 'half-cabs' rapidly starting to look obsolete. The County Garage wasted no time and in 1951/1952 bought a pair of Bedford SBs to the new 'full-front' style with 33-seat coachwork by Gurney Nutting (LNX488) and Duple (LWD567).

Stratford Blue's new coaches arrived on 9 April 1954, in time for the summer season, and were guaranteed to turn heads with their striking Burlingham 'Seagull' bodies. They were 37-seaters with a central entrance, and were numbered 56/57 (OUE11/12). The chassis were of Leyland's Royal Tiger model, which had been introduced in 1950, these particular ones being designated PSU1/16 by Leyland. Power came from a version of the O.600 engine which featured in the Titans and the PS2 Tigers, but on the Royal Tiger the engine was hidden away underneath the floor between the axles, allowing coachbuilders much more scope for imaginative styling. The Seagulls were the first new luxury coaches since the loaned AEC Regal in 1933, and replaced the dual-purpose Tigers on front-line excursion and tour duties. Nevertheless the Tigers continued to prove their worth for many years to come as back-up and duplicate vehicles during the busiest periods of the year.

In April 1954 the first ever brand new luxury coaches to be bought by Stratford Blue were delivered. Nos 56/57 (OUE11/12) were Leyland Royal Tigers with 'Seagull' coachwork by H.V. Burlingham of Blackpool, the first vehicles in the fleet with underfloor engines, and immediately took over the most prestigious duties from the dual-purpose Tigers. Notable features were the raised metal 'Stratford' fleetnames and the title 'Stratford Blue Motors' on the glass panel above the nearside windscreen. No.57 is shown outside Shakespeare's birthplace on Henley Street. (*P. Hudson collection*)

The Burlingham Seagull was one of the classic 1950s coach designs, and Stratford Blue's pair performed a wide range of work for ten seasons after delivery in 1954. No.56 (OUE11) is immaculately turned out for this private hire involving a party of businessmen. (*Author's collection*)

With their comfortable seating and larger engines than the earlier Tigers, the dual-purpose PS2s were well suited for the Oxford service when double-deckers were not needed. On this occasion, however, No.52 (JUE350) may not have been adequate, as another of the batch is visible behind showing 'Relief' on its blind, possibly having operated as a duplicate. City of Oxford Motor Services own the other buses in this view at Gloucester Green, Oxford, including on the right their No.724 (OJO724), a 1950 AEC Regal with a very similar Willowbrook body to No.52. (*R.H.G. Simpson*)

Kineton's operations expanded considerably during the 1950s to meet demand from Marlborough Farm CAD Camp and the RAF base at Gaydon, many journeys being subject to short-notice change in line with their requirements. These included late Sunday night journeys from the forecourt of Leamington Spa General Station for those returning from weekend leave. Most however left from 'The Crown', where No.32 (GUE238), one of Kineton's first pair of double-deckers, is awaiting passengers for the CAD Camp (the Central Ammunition Depot had opened in 1942). The departure stand was actually situated in Bath Place, just off High Street, across from the Crown Hotel. Although not shown, the service number would be 32 or 32A. (*Author's collection*)

On 1 February 1954, a new garage was opened at Kineton, adjacent to the old one in Brookhampton Lane. The latter had been built by Kineton Green after the disastrous blaze of 1934, but could only accommodate six single-deck buses (space for nine was required, including two double-deckers). Also replaced was the 'Nissen' hut alongside the old garage, which had been used as a ticket office and staff rest room. Mr Agg had first suggested a new garage late in 1951, although the land for it had been acquired in 1943. The design would be based on Midland Red's new Ludlow garage which had opened in January 1951, also accommodating nine buses. Initially the Regional Transport Commissioner refused a building licence due to the post-war steel shortage, but the problem was overcome and work began in March 1953. The old garage was kept for some time and offered to let, the Kineton Construction Co. being the tenant by July 1954.

Over the winter of 1954/55 the 1952 Titans had power-operated folding doors fitted to enclose their rear platforms. Stratford garage carried out the work and the first conversion was done by January 1955, at a cost of £280. The other two quickly followed, bringing Stratford Blue's contribution to the Birmingham service up to the standards offered by the Midland Red, who had specified platform doors on all new double-deckers since 1950. The 150 was almost invariably operated by double-deckers, and Midland Red frequently used some of the 100-strong 'LD8' class of 1952/1953 Leyland Titans which were very similar in many respects to Stratford Blue's 'MAC' Titans.

Seasonal variations in patronage had been a characteristic of Stratford Blue operations from the start, and holidaymakers and day-trippers greatly boosted the revenue. In February 1955 average weekly takings for the Birmingham service were £186, but in August this shot up to £533, helped only slightly by the company's second fares increase, which was approved in April. The Oxford service also doubled its takings, from £47 in February to £101 in August. Only the Stratford – Alcester service, which depended heavily on Alcester Grammar School, earned less in August than in February. Overall, revenue at Stratford garage was up by 60 per cent in August compared with February, whereas Kineton, being off the tourist track, had a much more modest 8 per cent increase.

Bus stations were the subject of much discussion during 1955, with redevelopment of the Royal Well Bus Station in Cheltenham being completed in April, the local council in Evesham proposing a bus station at Merstow Green to replace the stands on the High Street, and advance agreement being reached for use of the bus station to be built in Avenue Road, Leamington. The Evesham proposals came to nothing and today's bus station is at the same spot as the old High Street terminus, and it was to be several years before the plans in Leamington came to fruition.

Another event of note for 1955 was the departure from the fleet of the final Tilling-Stevens, five years after its bus career had ended. This was DB9380, the tree-cutting vehicle, which was replaced by DHA731, an SOS 'SON' acquired from Midland Red and specially modified for its new role.

Throughout the mid-1950s the route pattern remained constant, although co-operation between the operators led to Midland Red and Stratford Blue running occasional scheduled journeys on each other's behalf. An example was the 8.06 a.m. service 480 journey from Lower Brailes, which ran via Upper Brailes to Shipston and then continued to Stratford, effectively as a duplicate to service 519. Stratford Blue were running this by 1955 and the arrangement continued unchanged for many years. Later Midland Red's Digbeth garage regularly ran a morning journey on Stratford 'local' L3 to Justins Avenue, while by the late 1960s Stratford Blue could be seen operating Midland Red's Evesham town service E3 to Fairfield.

A fatal accident during a spell of severe weather in February 1956 started the year badly. In the course of an early morning journey from Shipston the driver had to stop the bus several times and leave the cab to scrape frozen snow off the windscreen. As he entered Stratford along Shipston Road, in appalling visibility, he had to swerve and brake to avoid a stationary car parked near the Railway Inn (now the Old Tramway). The bus skidded and struck the car, fatally injuring the owner who had been standing beside it.

March saw the delivery of another trio of Leyland Titan PD2/12 double-deckers (Nos 20-22; TNX454-456), but because Leyland had stopped bodywork production a new body-builder had to be found. The order went to Willowbrook, who had handled the 1950 Tigers, and 63-seat bodywork was fitted, complete with platform doors. The buses were put to use from Stratford garage, initially being favourites on the 150 to Birmingham, which, together with the 44 to Oxford, tended to be regarded as the company's 'flagship' service (since 1952 it had been possible with just one change of bus to travel all the way from Birmingham to Oxford by Stratford Blue double-decker, a distance of about sixty-two miles, mostly along the A34). The new buses brought the fleet to a total of thirty-eight (Nos 20-57), twenty of which were Titans.

Towards the end of the year a proposal was put forward to build ten lock-up garages at Kineton, between the old and new bus garages. Even if the company was losing passengers

The 'territorial' agreement with Midland Red excluded Stratford Blue from the main road route to Warwick via Black Hill, but there were a couple of exceptions, these being the little-known 90B service which followed Midland Red's X90 route to Warwick. No.36 (GUE242) is shown here at the Red Lion before setting off for Leamington, from where it would probably return as a school bus. (*D.A. Jones*)

A fine view of No.30 (JUE358) at the Red Lion on a bright summer's day, about to set off down the A34 to Shipston. Hemmed in to the right is one of Midland Red's dual-purpose 'S13's, on the infrequent 338 service to Bromsgrove via Alcester and Redditch. (*P.M. Photography*)

After less than three years the 1952 Titans had doors fitted to the rear platforms. This was to enhance their suitability for the longer services by reducing draughts and keeping in the heat on cold days. No.25 is shown passing through Henley-in-Arden, on its way back to Stratford on service 150. Flowers had by now taken to advertising individual brews rather than Flower's Ale in general, and advertisements for Bitter, Brewmaster, Dragon's Blood, Keg Bitter, Poacher Brown Ale and Sable Stout can all be seen in this chapter. They blended less successfully with the Stratford Blue livery, being painted in a variety of colours on the cream background. (*P.M. Photography*)

Three more Titans arrived in March 1956, this time with Willowbrook bodies, largely displacing the 1952 buses from the Birmingham and Oxford services. No.20 (TNX454) is shown at the old Bull Ring terminus in Birmingham, at the junction of Moor Street and High Street. This view dates from May 1956, before redevelopment work swept away everything in the picture apart from the façade of Moor Street Station (to the right of the Birmingham City Transport bus visible in the background). (*G.H.F. Atkins*)

to the private car, it was not going to give up the new generation of motorists as a potential source of income! For some reason the scheme did not proceed.

Tension had been rising during the year because of the 'Suez' crisis, and in December this led to fuel rationing. From 16 December a government edict forced the company to cut operational mileage by about 10 per cent, with the reductions spread across the whole network but concentrated on the least-used journeys. Mr Agg promised that essential journeys would be maintained but said that services on Sundays and the quieter weekdays would be hardest hit. There was also an increase in the price of diesel which he estimated would cost the company an extra £14,000 to £15,000 a year, hinting at another fares increase.

Despite the difficulties it was reported in January that fares revenue was actually up, due to the more stringent restrictions on private motoring (rationing was in force at the Bridgetown Filling Station from 17 December 1956 until 15 May 1957). Car sales around Stratford dropped, but demand for motorcycles and scooters was said to be at unprecedented levels. In fact 'Suez' may have been a blessing in disguise for Stratford Blue, allowing some of the most unprofitable journeys to be withdrawn as the number of passengers began a slow decline from its post-war peak. Although the situation eased during the spring, Mr Agg was able to satisfy Stratford Rural District Council that some journeys had carried an average of under two passengers, and that no complaints or requests for reinstatement of the suspended journeys had been received. The council therefore agreed not to oppose an application to the Traffic Commissioners to make some of the suspensions permanent. Amongst the casualties were the

Wednesday journeys to Ilmington which had replaced Sam Bennett's service in 1953, and the afternoon journeys on the Friday-only Stratford – Moreton Morrell – Kineton service which was reduced to one round trip a week, leaving Kineton at 9.30 a.m. and returning from Stratford at 12.30 p.m. Apart from these permanent changes, most services had probably reverted to normal by Easter.

Although many in the locality believed Stratford Blue to be a purely local concern, the truth was brought home by the events of July 1957, when the Transport & General Workers' Union called a national busmen's strike in pursuit of a pay claim. At the time the basic wage at Stratford Blue for a forty-four-hour week was £7 19s 11d, increasing to £8 4s 1d, while for an eighteen-year-old conductor or conductress it was £7 1s 6d. Any overtime and all Saturday afternoon and Sunday work was paid at time and a quarter. It was possible for a driver to earn £12 a week, but only by working seven days. The claim submitted nationally to the National Council for the Omnibus Industry was for an extra £1 a week, but Mr Agg felt that many Stratford Blue staff would have been happy with the 3s they had been offered and that the threat of strike action was a matter of loyalty to the Union. Mr O.J. Busek, the union branch secretary at Stratford, said, 'We do not want to strike, but it is necessary to bring to the notice of the public the conditions under which we are working.' He pointed out that the drivers' and conductors' rotas only included one 8.00 a.m. to 5.00 p.m. duty, most being 'splits', such as 7.45 a.m. to 9.00 a.m. then 2.40 a.m. to 11.20 p.m. When working these duties staff who lived some distance from their garage were often unable to go home in between, making for very long days. Although several staff were quoted as saying that it was

Another picture taken in Birmingham in May 1956 illustrates No.22 (TNX456) passing Midland Red's Digbeth Coach Station, with its journey from Stratford on service 150 almost complete. The hoarding behind the bus announces that new offices and passenger amenities were shortly to be erected on the site. (*G.H.F. Atkins*)

hard to live on their present wage, there was a reluctance to take the unprecedented step of a complete stoppage. Mr Busek confirmed this: 'there is no direct pay dispute between us and the Stratford Blue company ... we do not want to strike, but when we are told by the Union we have to support it 100%'.

All services were suspended from Saturday 20 to Sunday 28 July inclusive, the most serious disruption to bus travel that the area had ever seen. Perhaps most worrying was the lack of impact which the strike had, at least if contemporary press reports are to be believed. On 26 July it was headline news in the *Herald*, but the paper reported that 'far from having disrupted the life of the community, it has been accepted by the people of Stratford-on-Avon and district as "just one of those things" ... where villages are without railway facilities, young and old have by various means mostly managed to transport themselves to schools and places of employment'. It did concede however that schools were seriously affected, with an average of eighty boys a day absent from the Hugh Clopton Secondary School. Further examples of the 'wartime spirit' were quoted, with villagers fetching out 'an assortment of bicycles' and sharing cars or hitch-hiking. For those seeking an alternative, the classified columns offered a gents bicycle for £5, a 1952 James Commodore 98cc motor-cycle for £35, or for £265 a 1947 Hillman Minx car.

With their very different liveries and Midland Red's individual approach to design, there were few clues to the close relationship between Midland Red and Stratford Blue. On the right in this photograph is Stratford Blue No.24 (MAC571), after the addition of platform doors, and next to it Midland Red's No.4067 (SHA467), a 1953 'LD8' of almost identical specification. Both have Leyland 'Farington' bodies, but the concealed 'new-look' radiator on the Midland Red bus, together with the three-piece destination display and the unrelieved red livery make it look very different from No.24. Which looks better is a matter for individual taste, but at the time the Midland Red bus was probably considered to be of more modern appearance. Completing the picture is Midland Red No.4759 (759BHA), a 1957 'D7' about to return to Evesham via Broadway. Many years later, in Midland Red days, No.4759 ran from Stratford garage. (*P.M. Photography*)

In his 1958 interview for the *Leyland Journal* Mr Hirons singled out No.33 (GUE239) to illustrate the high mileages run up by the Leyland diesel buses delivered in 1948-1950. Having covered well over half a million miles in its first ten years, it was now due for an overhaul which would ensure that it lasted until 1963. This view shows it running past the Red Lion Bus Station towards Bridge Street, with the garage visible to the right. This stretch of road has carried only one-way traffic, in the opposite direction, since 1968. (*Author's collection*)

Eventually the Industrial Disputes Tribunal awarded an increase of 11*s* a week, and the industry journal *Bus and Coach* reported that this meant bus companies having to earn an extra 11*s* a week for each member of staff they employed in order to stand still. The inevitable result seemed to be more fare increases and more cutbacks on loss-making services.

After the strike services immediately reverted to normal, but the bank holiday at the beginning of August was the quietest Stratford had seen for many years. Mr Agg said that bus use was well down, concluding with resignation that 'it is only a week since we started running again, and people probably made other arrangements'. Although trade picked up again it must have become apparent to everyone that buses were no longer as indispensable as they had once been, and that this applied to Stratford Blue as much as to any other operator.

With its 100 per cent allegiance to Leyland, Stratford Blue was understandably popular with its main supplier and was the subject of another feature article in the *Leyland Journal* in May 1958. This was based largely on an interview with Frank Hirons, who was full of praise for the reliability of the thirty-eight Leylands he was responsible for. He quoted the case of No.33, one of the 1948 double-deckers, which was due for overhaul shortly after covering 544,000 miles on its original crankshaft. The high level of reliability allowed maintenance staff to be kept to a minimum; Stratford garage had a mechanical foreman with four semi-skilled assistants and an apprentice, a body foreman with two assistants, a general handyman whose duties included tyre maintenance, and a storekeeper who also looked after the ticket

This view of the inside of Stratford garage, looking towards Warwick Road, was used to illustrate the 1958 *Leyland Journal* article and was probably taken from the top deck of one of the Titans. Vehicles shown include PS1 Tiger No.40 (GUE246), Titan No.27 (JUE355) and Royal Tiger coaches Nos 56/57 (OUE11/12), No.57 over the inspection pit. (*Author's collection*)

machines, whereas Kineton, now home to eleven buses, had a semi-skilled foreman and three assistants. Kineton only handled running repairs as all major work was done at Stratford. This included repainting, each bus receiving a new coat of eggshell followed by a coat of varnish approximately every two years. In order to maintain a high standard of presentation buses were hand washed every night and cleaned internally both at night and when they returned to garage during the day. As in the previous article fuel consumption figures were quoted, the most economical buses being the PS1 single-deckers which averaged 13.5mpg during the summer and 13mpg in winter. The PD2/1 double-deckers were almost as good, achieving 12.8mpg and 12.3mpg, respectively.

According to the article the company intended to stick with Leyland for future purchases, with ten Tiger Cubs with Willowbrook bodywork being under consideration for 1959 delivery, although this is not quite what happened in practise.

During May Mr Agg drew up a list of twelve staff to receive long service awards, having completed at least twenty-five years with the company. Apart from Mr Agg himself, the recipients were J.T. Biddle, R.B. Careless, T.C. Davies, R.A. Dee, B. Dencer, G.A. Goode, P. Goode, R. Heritage, F. Hirons, T.J. Hughes and R.H. Jones.

Sadly this was to be among Mr Agg's last duties as he died on 15 July 1958 following a short illness, aged sixty-two. This signified the end of an era, as Mr Agg had been the company's manager for all but four of its thirty-one years, following his move from Cheltenham in 1931. The very fact that the company had maintained its separate existence for all this time, against all the odds, and now presented a thoroughly modern and professional image, was the ultimate testimony to the way Walter Agg ran Stratford Blue.

# 9

# The Last Years of BET Ownership 1958-1968

Following Mr Agg's death, Peter Scully was appointed as manager, taking up his position on 13 October 1958. Mr Scully was still in his twenties and, after following the BET graduate training programme, had spent three years as Assistant to the Traffic Manager at the Western Welsh Omnibus Co. in Cardiff. BET regularly used its smallest subsidiaries, like Stratford Blue, as a proving ground for potential senior managers, and those who made the grade could soon expect promotion to a larger company.

Mr Scully had a daunting task at Stratford as his predecessor had held the post for twenty-seven years and most of the staff knew only Mr Agg's style of management. The company was also having to face up to the relentless growth of private motoring, and during the previous year's strike Mr Agg had said that over half the services were uneconomic, some taking less than 1s a mile although 2s was needed to cover operating costs. There were similar problems throughout the country, but the road service licensing system ensured that the uneconomic rural services survived, in effect by protecting the profitable services from competition and allowing the proceeds to cross-subsidise the lightly used services.

Mr Scully inherited thirty-eight vehicles, with another five on order (not ten as had been proposed) to start replacement of the post-war fleet. These were Leyland Tiger Cubs with Willowbrook bodywork, and they entered service in February and March 1959. The Tiger Cub had an underfloor engine, like the Royal Tiger chassis of the 'Seagull' coaches, but was a lightweight model with a smaller engine. Nos 40-43 (2741-2744AC) had forty-one high-backed seats and a pleasing style of body with bright exterior trim and a cream waistband, while No.44 (2745AC) was a more austere-looking 45-seat service bus. Nos 40-43 replaced the dual-purpose Tigers as reserves for coach duties and often ventured well away from Stratford during their first few summers.

Following the new arrivals, the first five PS1 Tigers (the previous Nos 40-44) were sold to a used-bus dealer in Cheshire. Good quality post-war single-deckers were still scarce on the second-hand market so the Tigers quickly found buyers. Nos 40/43/44 went to South Wales, the first two to the associated Kenfig Motors and Porthcawl Omnibus Co., and No.44 to Eynon's of Trimsaran, while No.41 went to Purple Motors of Bethesda in North Wales and No.42 to Dunnets of Keiss, in the far north of Scotland.

Soon after his arrival Mr Scully ordered another three Willowbrook-bodied Titans, but to the maximum length of 30ft legalised in 1956 and using Leyland's PD3/4 chassis. They were delivered in February and March 1960 as Nos 17-19 (2767-2769NX). The extra length enabled the seating capacity to be increased to seventy-three (forty-one of which were upstairs), ten more than in the 1956 Titans. Another change was the forward entrance, a layout which became popular with many operators during the later 1950s and allowed the driver to oversee the operation of the doors. Only two buses were directly replaced, Tigers 48/49 (GUE254/255), which joined Nos 40/43 at Kenfig and Porthcawl and fetched £350 each.

In December 1959, pending the delivery of the new Titans, one of Midland Red's 'LD8' class Titans (No.4046; SHA446) was drafted in to assist at Stratford. It returned to Leamington garage in February 1960. Such loans were very rare, Stratford Blue being proud of its independence from the parent company, but no doubt it was a comfort to know that they were there in times of need.

At this time Midland Red were desperately short of staff and had to resort to hiring buses and drivers from other operators. With the increase in the fleet at the beginning of 1960, Stratford Blue were able to take up regular duties on Leamington garage's Stratford – Warwick – Leamington – Kenilworth – Coventry services, and for a time also provided conductors. The arrangement began in December 1959, and double-deckers were used, originally from the 'MAC' and 'TNX' batches which conformed to Midland Red practice with their enclosed rear platforms. Later they were fitted with blinds showing the Midland Red service numbers and destinations. Another operator to gain work was G&G Coaches of Leamington, set up by former Midland Red drivers Bernard Green and Tom Griffin in 1954. In October 1960 they bought a former Devon General AEC Regent double-decker which was regularly used on the same group of services, sometimes appearing in Stratford. These

The first underfloor-engined service buses arrived in early 1959 – five Leyland Tiger Cubs with Willowbrook bodies numbered 40-44 (2741-2745AC). They replaced the PS1 Tigers which previously carried these numbers, and the first two, Nos 41/42, were licensed for use from 1 February. A new backwards-sloping script fleetname was introduced, as illustrated by brand new No.43 at the start of a service 64A journey from Cheltenham to Evesham. Behind is No.31 (JUE359), the combination of Titan and Tiger Cub offering ninety-seven seats for this busy journey. Both vehicles have just left the Royal Well Bus Station and are waiting to turn from St George's Road into the Promenade. (*T.W. Moore collection*)

Another view of No.43 (2744AC), which was licensed from March. The dual-purpose role of Nos 40-43 meant regular forays on hire to Midland Red and Associated Motorways as express service duplicates. On this occasion soon after delivery No.43 was at Victoria Coach Station, London, probably after a journey from Birmingham. To the right is a Bristol MW coach owned by Crosville Motor Services of Chester, also new in 1959. These Tiger Cubs originally had a blue roof, and the dual-purpose vehicles lacked advertisements, which were not considered acceptable on vehicles which regularly deputised for coaches; even today coaches rarely carry commercial advertising. (*P.M. Photography*)

No.44 (2745AC) had a plainer external treatment than its dual-purpose cousins and was only suitable for local use. This interesting view shows it beside No.45 (GUE251), which was identical to the Tigers displaced by the new arrivals, and reveals how single-deck bus design had evolved in just a decade. Both are about to operate short-workings on the Evesham service, No.44 to Bidford-on-Avon and No.45 only as far as Luddington, probably as a duplicate. (*Photobus*)

While Stratford is known the world over, Kineton, home to Stratford Blue's other garage, is well off the tourist trail and little known outside the immediate locality. The garage was a little way from the centre of the village, tucked away down Brookhampton Lane, off Warwick Road. It was not a place that was likely to be stumbled on by accident, and this view of Tiger No.54 (JUE352) on the garage forecourt was taken on an organised visit in April 1959. This garage was built alongside the previous one, and opened in 1954. (*Mike Sutcliffe*)

During 1959 Midland Red's long-established terminal stands at Birmingham's Bull Ring were dispersed to nearby streets to allow the Bull Ring Shopping Centre to be developed (this 1960s complex, which included one of the most unpleasant bus stations ever built, has already been demolished to make way for a twenty-first-century version). Service 150 moved to Jamaica Row, now long since vanished, where No.21 (TNX455) is awaiting passengers in this August 1959 view. In the background a sign shows where to queue for the Stratford bus. Although Stratford Blue now had regular workings on the 150, Midland Red held the Road Service Licence so the destination blind showed 'On hire to Mid. Red' as well as the service number and destination. (*G.H.F. Atkins*)

arrangements were to continue until about 1967, by which time Midland Red's staff situation had improved sufficiently to allow them to cover all work with their own staff.

A very different Leyland was operated on 6 and 7 February 1960, on loan from Leyland Motors. This was 398JTB, a rear-engined Atlantean double-decker with seventy-eight seats, then regarded as the highest capacity achievable. It was evaluated on services 44 and 519, but later orders suggest that Stratford Blue was not yet ready for such an advanced vehicle.

In the early months of 1960 consideration was given to selling the Bridgetown Filling Station, which could have been affected by proposals for the A34 trunk road. However in both 1958 and 1959 the filling station had produced a profit of over £4,000 so it was decided to wait and see whether an alternative site was offered; it was hoped that this might lead to a better offer from one of the petrol companies.

Mr Scully was keen to introduce one-man-operation in an effort to contain costs (Midland Red had started this on rural routes in 1956, but Stratford Blue had never tried this method of operation, even in the early days) and the next new buses were ordered specifically with this in mind. Staff costs were a very significant proportion of the overall costs of operation, and one-man-operation was seen as the only way to make substantial savings without reducing services. The Traffic Commissioners' authority was needed to run full-size buses without a conductor, whose role was not just to collect fares but 'to ensure the safety and reasonable convenience of passengers'. Mr Scully was confident that he would get approval, but a greater obstacle was the company's Transport & General Workers' Union branch, which understandably feared for its members' jobs. The buses arrived in November; four Leyland Tiger Cubs with 45-seat Park Royal bodywork numbered 45-48 (3945-3948UE). Because negotiations with the union had not been concluded, they were initially put to use with conductors.

The 1960 double-deckers were 30ft long, and broke with tradition by having forward entrances on their 73-seat Willowbrook bodies. No.19 (2769NX) was still quite new when photographed in about September 1960, possibly on a works contract. The location is unknown but there must be a story to the bicycle, with shopping bag over the handlebars, propped against the doorway! (*Author's collection*)

Only three of the PS1 Tigers (Nos 45-47) survived the arrival of the 1960 double-deckers, but they looked smart right to the end. On 18 September 1960, with only a few weeks' service left in front of it, No.45 (one of two with chrome radiators) is seen parked at the rear of the Red Lion, with only the roof showing much sign of wear. By now Flowers were advertising their Keg Bitter on the bus. (*G. Mead*)

In December 1959 Stratford Blue took over a regular duty 'on hire' to Midland Red's Leamington garage, which was suffering a serious staff shortage. This mainly involved operations on services 517, 518 and 590 between Stratford, Leamington and Coventry, and Stratford Blue double-deckers became regular visitors to Pool Meadow Bus Station, Coventry, where No.24 (MAC571) is shown on 25 April 1960. To accommodate this work the Stratford Blue fleet was increased to thirty-nine in March 1960. The 517 was Midland Red's trunk service from Leamington to Coventry for over fifty years, at times running as frequently as every ten minutes. Behind No.24 is a Midland Red 'S14' on service 538, which followed a less direct route to Kenilworth and terminated at Elmdene Estate. (*Alan Broughall*)

Another four 45-seat Tiger Cubs took to the road in November 1960, their numbers following on from the previous batch. Nos 45-48 (3945-3948UE) had Park Royal bodies, the only ones supplied to Stratford Blue by this manufacturer, which built many of London's buses. They were bought with a view to pay-as-you-enter operation, but it took some time to reach the necessary agreement with the trade union. The first conversion involved the Kineton to Banbury services, and No.45 is shown at North Bar, Banbury, on 22 June 1962, with the request to 'pay as you enter' to the right of the destination blind, where many intending passengers might not notice it. For this type of operation the driver's cab was modified to provide a fixed mounting for the Setright ticket machine. (*Martin Shaw*)

No.58 (3958UE) seemed a surprising purchase, a lightweight Ford Thames and the first non-Leyland in the fleet for over a decade. It was delivered for the 1961 season and had a Duple 'Yeoman' body of a style popular with countless smaller independent operators. This view, probably in London, shows it working on hire to Midland Red, if the awkwardly placed 'destination' blind is to be believed (in practice the blind may not have included any destinations, but could certainly show 'Private' and 'Tour'). This vehicle and the 1961 Tiger Cubs were the first to take advantage of Warwickshire County Council's willingness to issue 'matching' registrations to tally with the company's fleet numbers, but only limited use was subsequently made of this facility. (*Photobus/G. Turner*)

Another view of No.58, this time at Pool Meadow, Coventry, on 24 July 1965, with the later fleetname style in which the lettering slanted forwards. The company name also appeared on the front using individual polished alloy letters, each about 3in high, while the roof quarterlights along the side and the glass panel at the front gave the coach a particularly airy feel internally. No.58 fulfilled a useful role for five years, but this was to be its last summer with Stratford Blue. The blind shows that it was again on hire to Midland Red. In the background are a Midland Red 'LD8' and a Coventry Corporation Daimler. (*Peter Relf*)

At this time the fleet had only two coaches – the 1954 Burlingham Seagulls – and these were in their seventh season and staring to look shabby internally. With only two coaches it had been difficult to meet demand during the summer of 1960 and the coach-seated Tiger Cubs acted as back-ups, but there was no escaping the fact that they were essentially dressed-up service buses. Mr Scully felt that they presented the wrong image and that another proper coach was desperately needed. Instead of a Leyland, which would have to work for many years to offset the high initial cost, he proposed to buy a cheaper lightweight model which could be replaced before it began to look too dated. Many of the small local operators had a similar policy, sensible given the speed with which coach designs and fashions changed. In August, after getting the approval of the directors, he ordered a Ford Thames Trader chassis with 5.4 litre diesel engine from Arden Garages and a 41-seater 'Yeoman' body from Duple Motor Bodies. This of course broke the company's 100 per cent Leyland monopoly, but at under £1,200 the Thames chassis was about half the price of Leyland's more sophisticated products. No.58 (3958UE) arrived in February 1961 and raised the fleet total to forty for the first time.

The new Tiger Cubs displaced an equivalent number of Tigers – Nos 45-47 (GUE251-253), the last three PS1s, and No.55 (JUE353), the first PS2 to go. As before, the PS1s soon found buyers, another two going to Welsh independent operators and the third becoming a works' bus in Liverpool (the only one of the ten to stay in England). The PS2 was retained by Stratford Blue and reappeared in August 1961 as a double-decker!

The PS1 Tigers were the first post-war buses to be sold, after short but useful lives of ten or eleven years. All were quickly snapped up by smaller companies for further use, something which had happened to very few former Stratford Blue buses since the 1930s. Amongst the first to go, in February 1959, and certainly the furthest travelled, was No.42 (GUE248). This found its way to Dunnets Motors of Keiss, Caithness, where it regularly operated their Wick to John O' Groats service, as shown here. (*R.F. Mack*)

Welsh operators obviously recognised a good second-hand buy, taking eight of the PS1s. No.44 (GUE250) was also displaced by the 1959 Tiger Cubs, and went to Eynon's of Trimsaran, Carmarthenshire. Here it shows the slightly anglicised spelling of Llanelli on its destination blind, something which would not be considered acceptable today. (*R.F. Mack*)

*Above*: Less than six months after the photograph on page 142 was taken, No.45 (GUE251) was with Phillips of Rhostyllen, Denbighshire. Neatly painted by its new owner, it is seen here in Wrexham Bus Station on the service to Rhosllanerchrugog, perhaps sensibly abbreviated to 'Rhos'. After its days of public service were over it ran for a contractor in Wrexham. (*Author's collection*)

*Left*: The 'new' double-decker which arrived in August 1961 was not quite what it seemed. The clue lay in the registration ... hiding under No.16's Roe body was the refurbished chassis of Tiger No.55 (JUE353), which had become surplus to requirements but was considered too good to sell. The new body had a particularly upright frontal appearance and initially only a very small blind aperture. This view shows it at Gloucester Green, Oxford, on 7 September 1961, only weeks after entering service as a double-decker. To the right is City of Oxford's No.184 (WJO184), a 1956 AEC Regent. (*Martin Shaw*)

The problem of what to do with the 1950 PS2s had been thought about for some time. They were solid and powerful machines and had covered only about 250,000 miles each, so there was plenty of life left in them. However, their appearance was now dated and with only 34/35 seats they were of limited use. Other companies had faced this dilemma, amongst them Yorkshire Traction, the BET subsidiary based at Barnsley in the West Riding of Yorkshire. Their solution since the mid-1950s had been to remove the bodies from PS1s, and later PS2s, overhaul the chassis and fit new double-deck bodywork. This seemed an ideal answer and as Mr Scully needed another double-decker he arranged for Yorkshire Traction to convert No.55. It was therefore despatched northwards where its single-deck body was removed and it later became a changing room on a Barnsley playing field. After a thorough overhaul and some minor modification, the chassis went to Charles Roe's Cross Gates factory in Leeds to receive a new 63-seat forward entrance body.

On delivery to Stratford in August few would have known that No.16, as it became, was not a completely new bus, although the 1950 registration (JUE353) rather gave the game away (the authorities in Barnsley were more generous and Yorkshire Traction's conversions were registered as if they were brand new). Initially No.16 was intended to replace one of the 1948 double-deckers, but because of the possibility of extra work from Midland Red these were all retained.

The other five PS2s continued in service, although orders were placed during 1961 for a similar number of Tiger Cubs to replace them. The body order went to a relatively unknown concern, Marshalls of Cambridge, from whom BET had received a favourable tender to supply a large batch of bodies. Mr Scully was wary, but reluctantly accepted the recommendation of BET's Engineering Department.

In later years the dual-purpose Tigers were relegated to bus work with the cream flash on the side panels painted over and advertisements applied, but still with the monogram rather than the usual fleetname. Even then their superior seating led to occasional use on tours, as shown here in August 1960 by No.53 (JUE351). The board leaning against the nearside wing offers an afternoon tour to Bourton-on-the-Water for 6s 3d (4s 2d child), or an evening tour starting at 6.15 p.m. for 4s 0d (2s 8d child). (*Photobus*)

In the meantime a serious accident occurred, forcing changes to the replacement programme. On the afternoon of 3 January 1962 two buses on the Evesham service collided head-on on a narrow ice-covered stretch of road at Barton, between Bidford and Welford. Nineteen passengers and crew were hurt. Both buses were seriously damaged, and the road was blocked for two hours until they were towed away. Although the single-decker, a Tiger Cub, looked worse, it was the double-decker, No.35 (GUE241), which was beyond economic repair, requiring expenditure of about £400. As it was due for replacement within a year this could not be justified, so it was stripped for spares and the hulk sold to a local scrap merchant, Frank Wyatt Motors, for £20. An extra 6s was added to the proceeds when the salvaged staircase mirror was sold separately!

Relief was soon at hand as the first of the Marshall Tiger Cubs arrived in February. This was No.49 (5449WD), the only one to service bus specification, with only eleven seats fewer than the scrapped double-decker. Nos 50-52/55 (5450-5452/5455WD) followed in April and May and were 41-seaters of the dual-purpose style, intended to replace the 1959 Tiger Cubs as reserves for the coach fleet. No.55 was finished to a particularly high standard, with extensive brightwork on the exterior and a cream roof instead of the usual blue, and had a two-speed rear axle to improve its performance on long-distance work.

It had been intended to convert all the remaining PS2s to double-deck but because of the loss of No.35 only four could be released and No.54 was retained. The others were taken out of service and sent to Barnsley for Yorkshire Traction to deal with along with another nine for their own use, but this time with bodies from Northern Counties of Wigan.

The PS2 service buses, Nos 54/55, led a quieter life than their more luxurious counterparts, but were regular performers on Stratford services such as the 'locals', the 5/5A to Evesham and the 90A to Leamington, when double-deckers were not needed. No.54 (JUE352) outlived its twin, which re-emerged as a double-decker in 1961, but was withdrawn early in 1963 and sold to Hills of Tredegar. This view shows it setting down in the Red Lion Bus Station on 18 September 1960. (*G. Mead*)

A view of the front of Stratford garage on 9 December 1961, with a pair of Titans catching the winter sun (No.31 of 1950 and No.33 of 1948). Also visible is Tiger No.52 (JUE350), while partly obscured on either side by the folding doors are the Burlingham Seagull coaches, laid up for the winter. (*Alan Broughall*)

Towards the end of its fourteen-year life, No.35 (GUE241) is seen in Leamington beside a Midland Red 'C3' class coach of 1954 (No.4203; UHA203). Unfortunately No.35 came to grief on an icy road at Barton on the third day of 1962 and had to be scrapped, the first post-war double-decker to go. By contrast the Midland Red coach had its original Willowbrook bodywork removed and a new Plaxton body fitted, lasting in this form until 1971. (*P.M. Photography*)

A busy scene at the Red Lion in about 1960, with schoolchildren, shoppers and workers all returning home on the 4.30 p.m. buses on service 90A to Leamington via Snitterfield (the enclosed-platform Titan on the extreme left), service 30 to Kineton (No.33; GUE239) and service 44 to Long Compton (City of Oxford No.946; WJO946). Just visible on the right is a Midland Red 'LD8' which will be the 4.35 p.m. service 518 to Leamington via Wellesbourne, and behind the double-deckers a PS1 Tiger and a Tiger Cub can be seen. (*P.M. Photography*)

The third and final batch of Tiger Cubs arrived in 1962, bringing the total of this model to fourteen. This time the bodywork was by Marshall of Cambridge, and within the batch there were three distinct styles, No.49 (5449WD) being unique as a service bus with the traditional fleetname. It arrived in February and is seen here in Pittville Street, Cheltenham, after operating service 64A from Evesham. In 1962 the Bristol Omnibus Co. ran a third of the weekday journeys and half the Sunday journeys on the joint 64/64A services. (*P.M. Photography*)

Tiger Cubs 50-52 had this style of body with cream waistband and the backward-sloping fleetname. Forty-one high-backed seats were fitted, more suitable for long-distance work but hardly necessary for the nine-minute run to Justins Avenue on service L3! The skyline in this Birmingham Road scene is dominated by Flowers' brewery, which was closed by Whitbread in February 1969 and demolished in 1973. Production of what had been Stratford's local brew for over 130 years switched to Cheltenham, or Luton in the case of the keg version.
(*P.M. Photography*)

Although it had the same body shell as the rest of the batch, No.55 (5455WD) was fitted out to a superior specification with coach seats and a cream roof. This official photograph was taken at Mary Arden's house at Wilmcote. Although barely four miles from Stratford, Wilmcote had no bus service until the 1950s, when one journey each way on the Alcester service was diverted through the village on Fridays. Before that all public transport needs had been met by the railway, with trains to Birmingham, Leamington and Stratford.
(*Author's collection*)

Following the delivery of the 1962 dual-purpose Tiger Cubs, the similar 1959 vehicles were relegated to bus work. In this 1962 view inside Stratford garage, No.43 (2744AC) has just been repainted into standard bus livery, with a blue waistband and a cream panel above the windows for the familiar Flowers' Keg Bitter advertisement. Note the reversion to the traditional style of fleetname. (*H.W. Peers*)

On 1 April 1962 the coach operations of the Warwickshire County Garage were acquired, together with their newest coach. 8222NX became Stratford Blue No.59, and was a 1960 Bedford SB3 with Duple 'Super Vega' coachwork. Its petrol engine made it completely non-standard and it was sold after less than twelve months, to Walls of Kingsey, Buckinghamshire. This view shows it in London on hire to Midland Red on express service duty. (*R.F. Mack*)

In March 1962 it emerged that Mr Scully and Mr Hayward of the Warwickshire County Garage had concluded an agreement for Stratford Blue to acquire the latter's coach operations. The County Garage had been running charabancs and coaches since about 1919, starting with a lorry which doubled up at weekends as transport for a cricket team. A successful excursion business was built up and during the 1930s two coaches were operated, although the main activity was car sales. In 1939 the owners offered to sell the coach side of the business to Stratford Blue, but no deal was reached. By 1951 the fleet had expanded to four, but ten years later the partners decided to concentrate on their BMC agency and made another approach to Stratford Blue. As well as an Excursion and Tour Licence for eighty-eight destinations, the County Garage had a healthy private hire business and Mr Scully was keen to acquire this. There were four coaches in the fleet at the time: HUE400, a 1949 Bedford OB/Duple 29-seater; LNX488, a 1951 Bedford SB/Gurney Nutting 33-seater;

LWD567, a similar 1952 SB but with Duple bodywork, and 8222NX, a 1960 SB3/Duple 41-seater. They were all petrol engined and would have been thoroughly out of place in the all-diesel Stratford Blue fleet, but nevertheless the purchase price of £5,000 included the 1960 coach.

The Traffic Commissioners granted the necessary Road Service Licence on 13 March, and 1 April was set as the date for the takeover. The acquired coach was handed over to Stratford Blue the following day and quickly received a partial repaint with blue side panels. It was given fleet number 59 for a busy summer's operation alongside the other coaches, Royal Tigers 56 and 57, now refurbished internally, and Thames Trader No.58. Although there were many differences in styling No.59's Duple 'Super Vega' bodywork was similar in general outline to No.58's 'Yeoman' body, but without the roof quarter-lights on each side.

None of the County Garage's drivers passed to Stratford Blue and one of them, Bill Spicer, who had been with the company since April 1923 was not sorry, stating that 'the roads are so congested now, and traffic so dense that all the pleasure has gone out of the job'. He also recalled the days when he could park his chara in the middle of the street in the centre of Oxford without any difficulty. What would he have made of the level of traffic at the start of the twenty-first century?

After protracted negotiations with the trade union, one-man-operation finally became a reality at Kineton garage, starting with the Banbury services. These traversed many steep and narrow lanes, especially on the slopes of Edgehill and at Warmington, and had always been the preserve of single-deckers, Kineton's Titans sticking to the busier services towards Leamington and Stratford and rarely, if ever, venturing into Oxfordshire. Exactly when one-man-operation

A much earlier Warwickshire County Garage coach was this 1937 Bedford WTB with a 25-seat Duple body. It carried the wording 'Tours in Shakespeare's Country' on the waistband, and was seen on the Waterside on 14 June 1951. This location, opposite the garage, served as the departure point for the company's tours. BNX882 lasted in service until 1952 when a new Bedford SB replaced it. (*R.H.G. Simpson*)

From 1948 Kineton regularly had a small number of double-deckers, mainly for the Leamington and Stratford services, the Banbury services being maintained by single-deckers. No.32 (GUE238) was a Kineton bus for many years, and this summer view shows it heading along Warwick Road from the garage to take up service at the church. The Red Lion, then owned by Hunt Edmunds' Banbury brewery, is now a private house, but the Midland Bank is still in business at the same location, albeit as an HSBC branch. (*P.M. Photography*)

No.34 (GUE240) was another of the long-serving 1948 Titans, and is seen here at Leamington Bus Station, which replaced the Crown Hotel as the terminus for the Kineton services. This location was never a great success, and within five years of its opening the adjacent Avenue Station, visible in the background, was closed. This view again highlights the inadequacy of the destination blinds, failing to show whether No.34 is to run via Gaydon (services 32/32A) or the completely different route via Moreton Morrell (service 33). (*P. Trevaskis*)

With the exception of No.35, wrecked in a crash a year earlier, the 1948 Titans survived until January 1963. This view shows No.39 (GUE245) at the Mulberries in its later years, with the driver and conductress chatting through the cab window before a run to Banbury Road. The L4 was Stratford Blue's shortest service, about a mile in length and taking five minutes each way. 39 was the highest number carried by a double-decker until 1970; between 1950 and 1970 double-deckers were numbered in the range 1-39 and single-deckers and coaches from 40 up to 62. (*R.H.G. Simpson*)

was introduced is not clear. The necessary clearance was given by the Traffic Commissioners early in 1961, but it was certainly some months after that – the date may have been 25 September 1961 – when timetables for the Banbury services were very slightly revised. The first vehicles used were Nos 45-48, which from now on were always associated with Kineton garage.

During August 1962 the board approved the replacement of the original Setright ticket machines, which had been in use since 1951, and forty-three new ones to the same basic design were ordered. Some existing machines were retained to give a total stock of fifty-two.

At the year end Mr Scully left the company, after a little over four years, to become Assistant Traffic Manager at Southdown Motor Services, the very large Brighton-based BET subsidiary. His replacement at Stratford, Mr D.D.N. Graham, took office on 1 February 1963. Another notable change in personnel was the retirement of Frank Hirons, the company engineer, at the end of February 1963. Mr Hirons, who was sixty-six, had been there from the start, having been the driver of Stratford-on-Avon Motor Services' first bus to Alveston and Shottery in April 1927. His mechanical expertise was recognised early on, and he was responsible for maintenance of the fleet for most of his thirty-six years with the company. His replacement was Mr J.T. Biddle, another of the original staff from 1927.

January 1963 saw the return of the Tigers which had been away for rebodying, together with the arrival of another four Leyland Titan PD3/4s. The Tigers kept their original registrations, JUE348-351, becoming Nos 32-35, while the Titans were Nos 36-39 (536-539EUE). Their forward-entrance bodies by Northern Counties were of generally similar appearance, but the Tigers were shorter and narrower and had sixty-three seats compared to the Titans' seventy-three. Notable features included fluorescent interior lighting and illuminated offside advertising panels.

These buses replaced the remaining 1948 Titans (Nos 32-34/36-39; GUE238-240/242-245) and the final single-deck Tiger (No.54; JUE352). By now, thoughts of rebodying the Tiger had been abandoned and it was sold together with the Titans, which had knocked up very considerable mileages during their fifteen-year careers. Five Titans were sold locally, to Priory Coaches of Leamington, where they lasted for up to three years, mostly carrying schoolchildren, and it was reported that one of them was then exported to India. The Tiger and Titan No.37 both went to Hills of Tredegar in South Wales (the Titan only as a source of spare parts), while the other Titan, No.39, became a van with Chipperfields Circus.

With his usual watchful eye on the local coach market, Mr Scully had noted that Black & White Garages of Harvington (not to be confused with the much larger Black & White Motorways of Cheltenham, a BET subsidiary) had bought a 51-seater AEC Reliance to the new maximum length of 36ft. Not wanting to be outdone, he swiftly ordered a 36ft Leyland Leopard with Duple's latest 'Alpine Continental' bodywork, to replace the former Warwickshire County Garage Bedford. Delivery was due in April but in the event the new No.59 (436GAC) was not delivered until 11 June. It was a 49-seater and looked very striking in a livery of cream to the top of the wheel arches and blue above. Operationally this may have been impractical as the areas of cream and blue were reversed when it was repainted. In the meantime the Bedford was sold in February.

*Above*: The new Nos 32-35 retained their 1950 registrations. No.32 (JUE348) is shown here during the severe winter of 1963/1964 on one of the regular 'on hire' duties operated for Midland Red's Leamington garage, cautiously approaching Coventry from Kenilworth on service 517. (*T.W. Moore*)

*Opposite*: In January 1963 eight new double-deckers with Northern Counties bodywork (Nos 32-39; JUE348-351 and 536-539EUE) replaced the surviving 1948 double-deckers, the original carriers of these numbers, and the last half-cab single-decker. The new Nos 32-35 were based on the refurbished chassis of the dual-purpose Tigers, while Nos 36-39 were brand new Titans. This view of Nos 37 (537EUE) and 34 (JUE350) soon after delivery clearly shows the width difference, the Titan having the now normal 8ft-wide bodywork, while the Tiger has a 7ft 6in body on its 1950 chassis. The Titans were also longer, giving room for ten more seats. No.37 is about to operate service 519 to Shipston, while No.34 is on hire to Midland Red, on service 518 to Leamington via Wellesbourne. (*Mike Sutcliffe*)

Another rebodied Tiger (No.35; JUE351) is seen here in April 1964 near the Central Ordnance Depot at Ashchurch, working service 64A from Evesham to Cheltenham, with the slopes of Bredon Hill visible to the right. This was about as far west as Stratford Blue bus services went. Philip Wallis, who took the photograph, was one of a group of Thornycroft employees who had just delivered a batch of tank transporters to the base and had to wait for No.35 to start their return journey to Basingstoke. The illuminated off-side panels were not a great success and were not repeated; they carried a new style of advertisement for Flowers, but as it turned out these were the last new buses to promote Flowers' ales, bringing a long tradition to an end. (*P.R. Wallis*)

Like the similar 1960 buses, Nos 36-39 were Leyland Titan PD3/4s with seventy-three seats. No.37 (537EUE) is shown in Leamington Bus Station before returning to Stratford via Snitterfield on service 90A. 'Matching' registration numbers were again obtained (536-539EUE), although this practice was then dropped until another No.36 (XNX136H) arrived in 1970. Nos 36-39 were renumbered to 24-27 in 1965, undoing any advantage gained by the matching numbers! Remarkably No.37 was still in use in 2003, earning its keep in the Netherlands. It was converted to open-top in 1979 while on the Isle of Man and then saw sporadic use with at least two UK mainland operators before moving to the Republic of Ireland in 1995, where it gained its fifth registration, ZV1466, and operated tours of Galway city until 2001. (*Colin*

Of the original post-war fleet, only the six 'JUE' Titans of 1950 survived beyond January 1963, and the following summer was to be their last. This June 1961 view shows No.29 (JUE357) about to work service 525 to the Royal Engineers' base at Long Marston, the destination shown being 'Long Marston No.1 E. S. D.'. Special fares applied to journeys operated to meet the requirements of military personnel, and in 1959 the fare from the camp to Long Marston Railway Station was 4*d*, and to Stratford Station 1*s* 1*d*. (*Alan Broughall*)

The 1950 Titans were busy on all-day service right until their withdrawal at the end of 1963, and still looked very presentable. This view shows no No.30 (JUE358) heading towards Sparkhill on its way to Birmingham on service 150, with some of Birmingham City Transport's distinctive circular bus stop signs visible on the shelters to the right. (*P.M. Photography*)

Also in its later days is No.31 (JUE359), passing a rural filling station on its way to Evesham on service 5. During 1963 there were eleven JUE-registered double-deckers in service; only in that year did the careers of all the rebodied Tigers and the 1950 Titans coincide. (*P.M. Photography*)

Photographs at the Red Lion in the snow seem to be scarce and this view on a cold winter's day shows a rather unsuitable open-platform Titan (No.27; JUE355) on the Birmingham service; the later Titans with platform doors were the usual choice for the 150 and certainly better in this kind of weather. Alongside is Tiger Cub No.41 (2742AC) bound for Evesham, and on the left Titan No.20 (TNX454) on the 90A to Leamington. (*Author's collection*)

1. High-quality colour photography only came into its own in the last few years of the original Stratford Blue company. Amongst the best 1960s photographs found in the course of preparation of this book is this one of Titan No.17 (2767NX) passing through Luddington on its way to Evesham on 25 May 1964. (*Martin Llewellyn*)

2. Also seen on 25 May 1964 is 1956 Titan No.20 (TNX454), in Bridge Street on service L1 to Alveston. It had recently been repainted with a script fleetname and the simplified style of fleetnumber. The flags are flying to celebrate the 400th anniversary of the birth of William Shakespeare in the previous month. (*Martin Llewellyn*)

3. Parked between trips at the Red Lion is Tiger Cub No.51 (5451WD), clearly showing its 'Please Pay on Entry' sign. A ticket machine is visible on the cab door, confirming that its next run, to West Green Drive on service L5, will be without a conductor. (*Photobus*)

4. 1956 Titan No.20 seems to have been Stratford Blue's most photographed bus, perhaps helped by its long spell in service; it was the only rear-entrance double-decker to last beyond 1967. This earlier picture shows it at the Royal Well Bus Station in Cheltenham, about to return to Evesham on service 64A. (*Author's collection*)

5. The final pair of Titans entered service in 1966. No.8 (GUE2D) is seen here at Gloucester Green Bus Station, Oxford, the south-easterly extremity of the network. The advertisement for the *Sporting Life* was unusual. Alongside is a City of Oxford AEC Regent tow-lorry, which until 1965 had been a double-deck bus. (*Photobus*)

6. The first one-man-operated double-decker was No.9 (NAC415F), shown in the snow at Cheltenham Coach Station, where it had been taken after suffering a defect on the run from Evesham. The Atlanteans did not match the Titans' excellent reliability standards, and were not always the best-presented buses, but No.9 looks smart here. (*Colin Martin*)

7. The first significant Stratford Blue revival came with the minibuses of 1986. Their white 'MINI-BUS' logos were perhaps intended to discourage more derogatory terms for them! They made quite an impact and helped to revive patronage on the flagging town services, but here No.469 (D469CKV) is operating to Shipston. The similar vehicle behind, in an advertising livery, looks even more van-like. (*Photobus*)

8. Shown outside Shottery Memorial Hall on 30 September 1990, during the very successful reunion organised by former employees Alan Giles and Joan Lockett, is Plaxton-bodied Leyland Leopard No.4 (230HUE). It was originally Midland Red's No.786 (BVP786V) but later received the traditional Warwickshire 'UE' registration which somehow made it look more appropriate in Stratford Blue colours. (*Author*)

9. Mercedes No.410 (J410PRW), now named *Sovereign*, is shown in Rother Street on 7 June 1995 on service 218 to Evesham, beside the magnificent 1950 Daimler CVD6 which Guide Friday used for a time on the Cotswold tour. This was new to J. Bullock & Sons of Featherstone, Yorkshire, and carried the same style of Willowbrook body as Stratford Blue's 1950 Tigers. (*Author*)

10. A green and yellow Stratford Blue bus! No.940 (PEU511R) was acquired by Western Travel from Badgerline, and gained Stratford Blue fleetnames on its previous owner's livery. It is seen in Guild Street, returning to the Avenue Farm garage after working the X20 from Birmingham on 29 June 1994. (*Author*)

11. Leyland Tiger coach No.91 (CDG213Y) carried an uninspired all-over blue livery and a unique 'Stratford Blue Coaches' fleetname. Despite its unsuitability it regularly operated rural services, as shown here after reaching Wood Street from Lower Quinton on service 215. Overtaking is 'Avon Shuttle' Transit No.378 (C709FKE), on its way to Justins Avenue. Both have 'Stagecoach Stratford Blue' windscreen logos. (*Author*)

12. Newmark's Stratford Blue fleet included several one-time National Bus Company Leyland Nationals, in a bold blue and white livery. Former East Yorkshire Motor Services' NAT198V is shown in Ettington on 19 February 2000, operating service 270 from Banbury to Stratford via Tysoe. Although the original company ran from Kineton to both Stratford and Banbury, there was never a through service. (*Author*)

13. The Status Group applied a white/blue/yellow Stratford Blue livery to a few vehicles, including Leyland Tiger GSU554, shown on service 22 to Moreton-in-Marsh on 26 January 2001, just weeks before the company ceased trading. Behind it is a Johnson's DAF on service 278 from Edgehill – this was also run by Stratford Blue until the County Council took away the contract. (*Author*)

14. In June 2002 Ensignbus bought Guide Friday and the current revival of Stratford Blue began, using the striking mid-blue and silver livery which Ensign had introduced during the 1980s. First to appear was former Guide Friday bus No.613 (H613NJB), seen in Bridge Street on its way to Justins Avenue on 6 September 2002. (*Author*)

15. Another Optare Metrorider is No.653 (K853RBB), which was new to Northumbria Motor Services in 1992. It is seen in East Green Drive, heading for West Green Drive (destination of the original Stratford Blue L5) on 6 September 2002, technically operating on hire to Guide Friday. (*Author*)

16. One of the preserved survivors from the original Stratford Blue is No.62 (HAC628D), shown carrying passengers in Kidderminster in conjunction with an event at the Severn Valley Railway on 10 October 1999. Unfortunately its original elaborate front grille has gone. (*Author*)

Soon after acquiring the County Garage's excursions and tours business, Mr Scully ordered a new coach to replace the inherited Bedford. The new No.59 (436GAC) was fitted with Duple 'Alpine Continental' coachwork on a Leyland Leopard chassis and arrived in June 1963. It was the first Stratford Blue vehicle to the new permitted length of 36ft and the last to enter service with the backward-sloping style of fleetname. This view shows it in the corner of the Red Lion Bus Station, probably during its first summer. (*H.W. Peers*)

The first buses ordered under Mr Graham's leadership were six more Leyland Titan PD3s, which arrived in December 1963. Perhaps to denote the start of a new régime they were numbered 1-6, the first buses to carry these numbers since the 1938 intake of Tillings. Registrations were 668-673HNX, and bodywork to the now usual 73-seat layout was by Willowbrook. A number of other firsts were the use of a forward-sloping script-style fleetname, destination blinds with lower-case lettering for intermediate points, and a fibre-glass bonnet assembly which concealed the radiator to give a much more modern frontal appearance than previous Titans. There were no illuminated advertisement panels as Flowers had not considered these a success and the company was still unwilling to accept advertising from anyone else.

Nos 1-6 replaced the last of Mr Agg's initial post-war fleet, 1950 Titans 26-31 (JUE354-359), which were also the last open-platform buses. Four were sold to operators in Leamington, Nos 26/30/31 going to Priory Coaches and No.27 to G&G Coaches, while the other pair went to Kenfig Motors in South Wales. No.27 immediately appeared in G&G's blue livery on regular hire to Midland Red.

The fleet now stood at forty-two; six rear-entrance double-deckers (Nos 20-25), eighteen forward-entrance double-deckers (Nos 1-6, 16-19, 32-39), fourteen Tiger Cub single-deckers (Nos 40-52/55) and four coaches (Nos 56-59).

The Titans delivered in late 1963 (Nos 1-6; 668-673HNX), looked very different from earlier Titans, having the so-called 'St Helens' glass-fibre front. No.3 is shown leaving Stratford garage soon after entering service, with No.19 (2769NX) alongside illustrating the earlier exposed-radiator style. This photograph was used on the cover of the April 1964 edition of the magazine *Buses Illustrated*. (*T.W. Moore*)

This view in North Street, Cheltenham, illustrates the style of destination blind which these buses introduced, helpfully showing that No.2 (669HNX) is running via Kemerton and Beckford on its way to Evesham. Another Stratford Blue bus is visible behind, suggesting that this is probably the 4.30 p.m. departure, which required two buses. Both ran as 64As, but beyond Beckford one went via Ashton-under-Hill and the other via Dumbleton; the Ashton-under-Hill variant was sometimes referred to as the 64X to distinguish it from the Dumbleton bus. (*Colin Routh*)

The new Titans were also capable of showing less informative destinations, such as 'Stratford', so in this view on Birmingham Road No.5 (672HNX) may be coming from Justins Avenue on service L3, or from Birmingham. Flowers' brewery is on the left of the picture while behind No.5 a couple of double-deckers can be seen at the premises of Birds, the second-hand bus dealer which scrapped many pre-war Stratford Blue vehicles. (*BaMMOT collection*)

On retirement from Stratford Blue service No.27 (JUE355) was sold to G&G of Leamington, who, like Stratford Blue, were regularly hiring buses to Midland Red to ease them through their protracted staff shortages. As a result it was often to be seen back at the Red Lion Bus Station, on this occasion working service X90 to Coventry via Warwick. The 'on hire' notice appears beside the platform, while the service number is shown in the nearside front window. No.27 ran with G&G from 1964 until it was scrapped in 1967. (*P.M. Photography*)

One-man-operation was extended on 3 October 1963 with the conversion of most journeys on service 33 (Kineton – Leamington via Moreton Morrell). In this view at Leamington Bus Station, No.44 (2745AC) is about to operate a short working to Moreton Paddox. No.44 was the odd-man-out amongst the 1959 Tiger Cubs, with its rather spartan appearance and forty-five service bus seats. (*P.M. Photography*)

Negotiations in early 1964 to buy the coach operations of Black & White of Harvington were unsuccessful but had the outcome been different Stratford Blue's sphere of operation would have expanded greatly. At the core of Black & White's operations were the services to the Maudslay works near Alcester, and only a short time earlier these required the use of double-deckers including these smartly turned-out former London Transport 'RT' class AEC Regent IIIs, which dated from 1949 and were snapped up by Black & White in 1956. The leading bus (JXC174, formerly London Transport RT1411) stayed with Black & White until 1960 when it was sold to Priory Coaches of Leamington. Priory kept it until 1962, replacing it with a 'GUE' Titan bought from Stratford Blue. It was then sold for scrap, yet many very similar RTs lasted in service with London Transport until as late as 1979! (*Author's collection*)

The following year, 1964, was expected to be a record year for tourism in Stratford, being the 400th anniversary of the birth of its most famous citizen. To capitalise on this Mr Graham argued successfully for the early retirement of the 1954 'Seagull' coaches and the acquisition of another two Leopards, of the shorter L2 variety with 41-seat coachwork by Plaxtons of Scarborough. An order was placed, and the Seagulls became surplus at the end of the 1963 season. Priory Coaches, who were negotiating to buy the Titans, learned of this and made an offer which Mr Graham accepted after confirming that if necessary he could hire coaches in from Black & White Motorways until the Leopards arrived. The Seagulls were released to Priory Coaches in January 1964, bringing the number of former Stratford Blue vehicles bought by Priory since December 1962 to ten.

At about this time serious consideration was given to buying a minibus for use on small private hire jobs, but the idea was not pursued.

At the start of 1964 there were discussions which could have led to a massive expansion of the company's coach operations. Black & White Garages (Harvington) Ltd had been put up for sale by the Marsh family and they already had an offer for the filling station and car sales operation, leaving the coach side of the business. There were twenty-one coaches (eight AECs and thirteen Bedfords) and almost half the income came from lucrative contracts to serve the Maudslay works at Great Alne, from points as far apart as Birmingham, Pershore, Redditch and Stratford. Most of the rest came from private hire and school contracts. A potential problem for Stratford Blue was that if they acquired the business, higher 'union' rates of pay would have to apply, but an offer was still made. Unfortunately this fell well short of the Marshs' expectations and as no compromise could be reached negotiations closed in

The 1954 'Seagull' coaches were replaced in 1964 by two Leyland Leopards with attractive Plaxton 'Panorama' bodies, Stratford Blue's only bodies from this leading manufacturer. These were built in Scarborough, whereas the Seagulls and the previous year's Alpine Continental coach came from rival resort Blackpool. They were collected from Scarborough by Stratford Blue drivers, Alan Giles being one of them. No.56 (AAC21B) is seen here in Stratford garage yard with the company Land Rover (230EUE) just visible to the right. In the background, across Guild Street, is the rear entrance to the Red Horse Hotel, on the site now occupied by Marks & Spencer. (*Author's collection*)

The 1964 Leopards (Nos 56/57; AAC21/22B) and the 1954 Royal Tigers (also Nos 56/57; OUE11/12) were the only two identical pairs of Stratford Blue coaches, every other coach being unique in the fleet. The second of the 1964 pair is shown here on a wet day in London, working on hire to Midland Red, a common duty for Stratford Blue coaches (Stratford Blue never ran any long-distance express services in their own right). Passing it is one of London Transport's 'RF' class Green Line 'coaches' – actually an elderly bus – on the long cross-London service 701/702 from Gravesend to Ascot and Sunningdale. (*Author's collection*)

March. In the absence of any other buyer the Black & White coaches continued their independent existence for several more years.

The new Plaxton coaches were ready on time at the beginning of May, becoming Nos 56/57 like their predecessors. They were given registrations AAC21/22B, amongst the first of the 'year-letter' style issued by Warwickshire County Council, who adopted the new system from 1 May 1964 without using the 1963 'A' suffix. The 32ft-long bodies were to Plaxton's 'Panorama' design, with long side windows giving excellent visibility, and the entrance was at the front (centre entrances, as on the Seagulls, had gone from fashion during the 1950s).

The new timetable dated 9 May featured the usual portrait of William Shakespeare which had adorned the cover since the 1930s, but flanked with the dates 1564 and 1964 and the cover design had a theatrical theme. Between the covers it differed little from previous editions, although in another twist to the service numbering saga, the rural services which had for some years been unnumbered were listed as follows:

| | |
|---|---|
| 6 | Stratford – Evesham via Pebworth |
| 7 | Stratford – Walton/Wellesbourne |
| 8 | Stratford – Shipston/Stretton-on-Fosse via Ilmington |
| 9 | Stratford – Bearley and Stratford – Claverdon |
| 11 | Stratford – Hampton Lucy |

An interesting view of No.20 (TNX454) at the Red Lion, accompanied by Midland Red and Black & White Motorways coaches. The destination display and the supplementary board on the bulkhead suggest that this must be a Friday, when the 12.45 p.m. 5A journey ran to Exhall via Temple Grafton and Ardens Grafton, instead of to Broom as on other days of the week. This was the only bus of the week to Exhall. By 1964 the Red Lion was handling about 44,000 bus departures per year, of which Stratford Blue operated almost 26,000 and Midland Red about 18,000. (*P.M. Photography*)

Service 44 was improved during 1964 with through fares and a faster journey time. This Chipping Norton view shows Stratford Blue No.16 (JUE353), the first double-deck conversion, and City of Oxford No.984 (984HFC), a 1960 AEC Regent (Stratford Blue's first double-decker was a former City of Oxford Regent, but a very different bus, dating from 1931). Both are working service 44 and the time is probably about 5.40 p.m., with No.16 on the 4.35 p.m. departure from Oxford and the Regent on the 4.30 p.m. from Stratford. The 'bus waiting room' for passengers is visible below the canopy of No.16. (*Roy Marshall*)

As usual there seemed to be little logic to this, especially in the case of service 9 which in fact had been two entirely separate services, to Bearley via Birmingham Road and to Claverdon via Snitterfield, since the short-lived circular service was withdrawn in 1954. Apart from the Red Lion Bus Station, there was not a single common point! To avoid confusion the Bearley service was later numbered 12, although it seems fairly unlikely that either number was ever actually displayed on the buses.

The company was still not short of ideas and the timetable advertised the extensive programme of half-day tours to stately homes and other places of historical interest, a free pushchair loan service for mothers arriving in Stratford by bus, and the filling station, described as a 'free house' offering a wide choice of leading brands of petrol.

During the year Mr Graham and his opposite numbers at City of Oxford Motor Services got together to make some improvements to the Oxford service, resulting in the end-to-end journey time being reduced by eighteen minutes to just over two hours and through fares becoming available to eliminate the need to 're-book' at Long Compton. This probably happened with the reintroduction of the winter timetable.

As predicted 1964 turned out to be a busy year, and the year-end figures showed a healthy increase in all areas of the business, as the figures below illustrate:

| SOURCE OF INCOME | 1963 (£) | 1964 (£) |
|---|---|---|
| Stage carriage services | 176,846 | 183,088 |
| Private hire | 12,146 | 13,598 |
| Hire to other operators | 6,529 | 6,650 |
| Excursions and tours | 2,776 | 3,148 |
| Parcels | 1,311 | 1,440 |
| | 199,608 | 207,924 |
| Less hire from other operators | 691 | 841 |
| TOTAL TRAFFIC RECEIPTS | 198,917 | 207,083 |

The investment in new coaches appears to have paid off, with revenue from excursions and tours up 13.4 per cent and private hire up 12 per cent, while the increase for stage carriage services was 3.5 per cent. It is notable that the carriage of parcels brought in nearly half as much as the excursions and tours, and for a fraction of the investment. The parcels business is often overlooked, but had long been a supplementary source of income and provided a valuable service to many local traders. Parcels were carried on any service bus, and could be picked up at or delivered to any point along the route. There were several local parcel agencies, and in 1964 these included Mrs Viggers at the café in North Bar, Banbury, the Falcon Stores at Bidford, the Central Stores at Ettington, and the Bird in Hand at Newbold. Charges were determined by the weight of the parcel and the nature of the contents, but not, it seems, by distance. Special rates applied for newspapers and periodicals, and bundles of local papers were a common sight on the buses. Items which were not conveyed included bicycles, perambulators, accumulators, wet fish and loaded firearms (it is not clear whether conductors were trained to check to see if firearms were loaded!).

Another Leyland Leopard single-decker arrived in January 1965, four months behind schedule because of a strike at the bodybuilders. No.60 (CWD33C) was a 36ft model with a

Weymann bus body to the attractive standard BET design and was intended primarily for use on service 44, but also to provide back-up for No.59, the 36ft-long coach. To suit it for these roles it was fitted with forty-nine luxury coach seats supplied by Plaxtons. It was a particularly astute purchase as the Oxford service always required double-deckers on Saturdays and summer Sundays, freeing up No.60 exactly when it was most needed to act as a coach.

After only two years Mr Graham left the company at the end of January, to take up a post with Ribble Motor Services in Preston. For a month Mr Levell took charge, as he had done after Mr Scully's departure, but a successor, Mr D.G. Codling, was appointed to start on 1 March.

Another 36ft Leopard, No.61 (DAC753C), came in June. This was a 49-seat coach with Duple 'Commander' body, very similar to the forty-nine 'LC7' class coaches delivered to Midland Red in 1965. Although it may be thought that the parent company ordered a batch of fifty and allocated one to Stratford Blue, this was not the case; No.61 was a separate Stratford Blue order and differed from the 'LC7's in having a manual gearbox, as usual for coaches at Stratford, rather than the semi-automatic option preferred by Midland Red. Mr Graham had been particularly interested in expanding the coach business and had identified scope for more private-hire work at Kineton, particularly from the nearby military bases where the married quarters were to be extended. No.61 was intended to provide another full-size coach for Stratford, allowing the Ford (No.58) to move to Kineton, which had never before had a coach on a regular basis.

The new style of destination blind introduced with Titans 1-6 was soon fitted to some of the other double-deckers, unfortunately not always with due attention to detail. This was the case with No.18 (2768NX) and as a result intending passengers for this journey to Evesham via Luddington on service 5 cannot read the whole display. The advertising for Mackeson stout is to the order of Whitbread, who by now owned Flowers' brewery in Stratford. (*Author's collection*)

On the same busy spring day as the previous photograph, No.36 (536EUE) pulls away from the Red Lion with a much neater destination display than No.18, visible to the left. Operation of service 525 (Stratford – Chipping Campden) was shared with Midland Red, who also ran through to Broadway via Chipping Campden on service 524. The Northern Counties double-deckers were the last to have the traditional style of fleetname and number, but the metal blanking plate across the radiator slightly mars the otherwise very impressive appearance of No.36. (*Author's collection*)

In January 1965 a second full-length Leopard was put into service. No.60 (CWD33C) had forty-nine coach seats in a Weymann bus body and initially took over weekday duties from a double-decker on service 44 to Oxford, where it is seen at Gloucester Green. Taking a leaf out of Midland Red's book, separate destination and 'via' blinds were fitted, together with individual number blinds, allowing the very comprehensive display shown here. (*R.H.G. Simpson*)

Another view of No.60 in original condition, this time near the inspectors' office in Leamington Bus Station. The blinds are neatly set for the return journey to Stratford. Notice the absence of opening windows, made possible by the use of forced air ventilation and the provision of skylights but totally inadequate for hot summer days when engaged on stop-start local service work. (*M. Collignon*)

By 1965 Midland Red had owned Stratford Blue for thirty years, but throughout this time an entirely different buying policy had applied. Then came No.61 (DAC753C), which had a Duple 'Commander' body and looked almost identical to Midland Red's 'LC7' class coaches placed in service the same year. The main difference – but not a visible one – was No.61's manual gearbox. This view shows it outside the office in the Red Lion Bus Station, ready to operate a half-day tour. (*R.H.G. Simpson*)

Soon after Mr Codling's arrival four double-deckers had their fleet numbers changed, No.16 (JUE353) becoming No.31, and Nos 17-19 (2767-2769NX) becoming 28-30. This seemed a fairly futile exercise but it did group together the twelve exposed-radiator forward-entrance double-deckers as Nos 28-39.

With the arrival of Nos 60/61 the fleet increased to forty-four, a new maximum. No.60 should have replaced a double-decker, but it was decided to hang on to this until the future of the stopping trains between Stratford and Evesham via Honeybourne was resolved (this was the 'Beeching era' when many local rail services were under threat). The British Railways Board had proposed that the stopping trains should be withdrawn and replaced by a bus service. This would have been operated jointly by Midland Red and Stratford Blue but as it would need an extra bus from Stratford Blue it was decided to put 1952 Titan No.23 into storage at Kineton garage rather than sell it, pending the outcome of an inquiry. By October there was still no decision but Mr Codling had a potential buyer, having been asked by the Green Bus Co. at Rugeley if he had a double-decker available. As a result he advised British Railways that he could not start a replacement service before January 1966, when two new buses were due. Mr Whieldon's offer of £399 including tyres was then accepted, and in early October No.23 left for Rugeley, where it was to run for another five years.

No.16 (JUE353) was renumbered to 31 during 1965, as shown here inside Stratford garage. By now the aperture for the destination blind had been enlarged, permitting a two-line display. Snitterfield was rarely seen as a destination as very few journeys finished there – the last journey for No.31 on this occasion may well have been the 10.40 p.m. journey on a Saturday night. Unfortunately No.31 was written off after overturning on an afternoon run from Alcester Grammar School on 23 September 1968. (*R.F. Mack*)

The rebodied Tigers appeared on a wide variety of routes, almost always from Stratford garage. No.34 (JUE350) is seen in Leamington on 1 March 1966, travelling down the Parade past the Cadena Café on service 90A. The author well remembers childhood milkshakes in the Cadena, and was ten years old when this picture was taken. (*T.W. Moore*)

During Mr Graham's period as manager in the mid-1960s, the image of the fleet was subtly modernised, the new style of fleetname and simplified number transfers being introduced with Titans 1-6. Both are clearly visible in this view of No.5 (672HNX) at the Red Lion while engaged on school contract work on 26 May 1967. (*Peter Relf*)

From the mid-1960s further Tiger Cubs were converted for one-man-operation (usually referred to then as 'pay as you enter'), mostly for use on rural services. Amongst them was No.55 (5455WD), here with the sign on the front covered over as there is a conductor on this journey on the Friday-only service to Hampton Lucy. Hampton Lucy was only needed on the destination blind on Fridays, and in inimitable Stratford Blue fashion the service was shown in timetables without a service number in the late 1950s and early 1960s, yet before that it had been the 10 and later it became the 11! To the right is Midland Red 'S14' No.4284 (UHA284) which had worked service 525 from Lower Quinton and shows a more prominent 'Pay as you enter' sign. This is another photograph taken on 26 May 1967. (*Peter Relf*)

Although still having a blue roof, No.47 (3947UE) has been repainted with the later style of fleetname and number in this view at North Bar, Banbury. It is working a 'pay as you enter' journey to Ratley, possibly on service 35 via Warmington but perhaps more likely on the 36 via Hornton and Edgehill. Stratford Blue passengers were expected to have a strong sense of intuition!  To the left is a 1965 six-wheel Bedford VAL coach belonging to Supreme Travel (E. Bonas & Son Ltd) of Coventry. (*R.H.G. Simpson*)

Another two 73-seat Leyland Titans entered service in January 1966, bringing the total of this type to fifteen. Nos 7 and 8 (GUE1/2D) were very similar to Nos 1-6, but had large Midland Red-style blind displays. This view shows No.7 heading out of Birmingham on its way back to Stratford on the 150. The other bus is Birmingham City Transport's No.2460 (JOJ460), a remarkably modern-looking 1950 Crossley with the 'new look' front pioneered by this operator, on a '17J' short working to Sheldon Heath Road (the main 17 service ran to the Meadway terminus on Garretts Green Lane). (*M. Collignon*)

A busy scene at the Red Lion as No.8 (GUE2D) picks up a good load for Birmingham. Unfortunately the lower blind is showing 'via Hatton Rock', perhaps because the conductor had searched in vain for 'via Henley-in-Arden'. The 1966 buses were to be the last of thirty-five Titans bought by Stratford Blue and by coincidence, like the first, they had 'GUE' registrations. Whereas Stratford Blue took two 1965 C-registered vehicles and three 1966 'D's, parent company Midland Red had no less than 180 'C's and 164 'D's. (*Author's collection*)

The new buses were 73-seat Willowbrook-bodied Leyland Titans of the PD3A/1 model, very similar to Nos 1-6. They were delivered at the end of 1965 and licensed from 1 January 1966 as Nos 7/8 (GUE1/2D). A distinguishing feature was the Midland Red-style destination display at the front, using separate blinds for the destination, 'via' points and service numbers. This layout, introduced on Leopard No.60, had not been used before on double-deckers, but was obviously considered a success as all but No.2 of the 1-6 batch were later altered to the same style. Although it meant more work for the conductor, the new layout was undoubtedly better for the travelling public – at least when proper use was made of it, which was not always the case. Another change was that the roofs were cream instead of the distinctive silver used previously on double-deckers, this becoming standard for subsequent repaints.

After further discussion, 3 January 1966 was fixed for the withdrawal of the stopping train service and the closure of Milcote, Long Marston, Pebworth, and Littleton & Badsey stations (the line continued to be used by through trains for a few more years). The replacement bus service, numbered 396, was run by Stratford Blue except for two round trips from Evesham to Stratford operated by Midland Red. Stratford Blue ran a round trip from Stratford to Evesham and several short journeys as far as Pebworth or Honeybourne. The route closely followed the railway in order to serve the communities around the closed stations, but journeys requiring double-deckers had to follow a different route because of the low bridge next to Pebworth Halt. In order to connect with trains, buses ran to the station forecourts in Evesham

Since the 1930s Midland Red and Stratford Blue between them had operated virtually all bus services around Stratford. The exceptions were a handful of infrequent village buses which were a lifeline to the communities they served, but were little known outside. Generally operation was confined to market days and perhaps one or two other days, and two Friday visitors to Stratford were Matthews of Brailes and Ellis & Bull of Moreton-in-Marsh. Each ran a service from their respective home bases and for many years parked up on the Warwick side of the Red Lion, away from the busy Midland Red and Stratford Blue departures, as seen here. Bedford coaches characterised these small operators; Matthews' HNX687 is a 29-seat OB of 1948, while Ellis & Bull's DDG393 was a 1939 WTB and served the company for an amazing thirty years until 1969. Both had Duple bodywork. (*Author's collection*)

and Stratford but also served the main bus terminals on the way. The service was subsidised by the British Railways Board, and was additional to service 6 which provided a market-day bus on Fridays from Evesham to Stratford and back via a very similar route.

The May 1966 timetable included timetables for four small private operators whose services would previously have been unknown to most people outside the villages they served. Three of them had services into Stratford, terminating at the municipal car park near the Unicorn; Barry's of Moreton-in-Marsh ran a Blockley – Paxford – Hidcote Boyce – Stratford service on Fridays (also on Tuesdays during the summer), Matthews of Brailes ran from Lower and Upper Brailes via Shipston on Fridays, and Mr Rouse of Oxhill ran from Tysoe and his home village on Tuesdays, Fridays and Saturdays. The other service included was Sumner's from Hornton and Horley to Banbury, which followed the same route as the Stratford Blue 36.

There had also been changes to the local services in Stratford, with some journeys to West Green Drive now numbered L6 and running via Masons Road.

In the meantime an order had been placed for a short Leyland Leopard with Marshall dual-purpose bodywork, and this was delivered in May 1966 as No.62 (HAC628D). It was licensed from 1 June and replaced the Ford coach (No.58), which was quickly sold to Evans (Pentre Motors) of Llanrhaiadr, Denbighshire. No.62 had a BET-style body finished to a very high standard and fitted with forty-one high-backed seats. Although the Ford had made occasional

Reg Rouse's 1947 Bedford OB with SMT body (HTF586) was a regular visitor to Stratford for many years. Mr Rouse, who lived at Oxhill Post Office, bought the coach second-hand in 1950 and used it to maintain his stage carriage services until he retired in December 1972. By this time he was sixty-nine, and it was reported that he had been running his bus services for forty-seven years. Latterly at least the services ran four days a week: from Oxhill and Tysoe to Stratford on Tuesdays, Fridays and Saturdays, to Banbury on Thursdays, and to Shipston on Saturdays. On his retirement the services were taken over by David Grasby, also of Oxhill. HTF586 was new to Warburtons of Bury, Lancashire, and survives to this day in the Museum of Transport in Manchester, restored in Warburtons' mainly black livery. This view shows it parked in Stratford, with the Red Lion in the background, already half full of passengers for the journey home. *(Author's collection)*

After a short time No.60 (CWD33C) lost its blue roof and gained blue window surrounds, subtly changing its appearance. It was then taken to Alveston church and posed for this photograph with a carefully set destination display for service L1, including a mention of the Youth Hostel. The resulting picture was used on the cover of the May 1966 timetable book. (*Author's collection*)

forays onto stage carriage work during its days at Kineton it was not well suited to the task, whereas No.62 was ideal for both service work and private hires.

The sale of No.23 left five rear-entrance double-deckers and it was intended to replace these in 1967. However, Mr Codling was conscious that the subsidy for the rail replacement service might not last and was reluctant to order new buses for a service with an uncertain future so he decided to keep two 1956 buses and order only three replacements. These had to be double-deckers but there was a lively debate about which model to go for. Mr Biddle, from his engineer's viewpoint, felt that more of the tried and tested Titans would be the cheaper and more reliable option, although this time with semi-automatic gearboxes. Mr Codling was less conservative and preferred the rear-engined Atlantean with its higher seating capacity and, in his view, greater level of comfort. Another factor was that the new buses would have to last until about 1980, by which time Mr Codling thought that one-man-operation of double-deckers would be possible, and only the Atlantean would be suitable for this. The matter was referred to the directors, who opted for the Atlantean. As a result an order was placed with Leyland Motors for three chassis, to be bodied by Northern Counties for delivery in August 1967.

Mr Biddle visited Northern Counties at Wigan on 27 June to inspect progress but it was clear that the buses would not be ready for August. Even so No.25 (MAC572), which had been delicensed for some months, was sold in August to Smiths of Tysoe. Contrary to the earlier plan, two of the 1956 buses were also sold, Nos 21/22 (TNX454/455) joining No.23 (MAC570) with Green Bus of Rugeley. Green Bus were told that they would probably not be able to take delivery until late September.

In 1966, after an interval of five years, the fleet reverted to 100 per cent Leyland when the Ford coach was replaced by No.62 (HAC628D). This was another Leopard, but a short version with attractively finished Marshall bodywork. It was used for private hires as well as service work and Mr Codling reported that it quickly attracted favourable comment from hirers. A retouched version of this posed photograph appeared in several company advertisements. (*P. Hudson collection*)

In December 1967 three Leyland Atlanteans (Nos 9-11; NAC415-417F) were delivered, four months late. Although the Atlantean had been available for almost ten years, and a demonstrator had been tried in 1960, Stratford Blue had previously stuck with the familiar Titan. The new buses, with their distinctive (some might say ugly!) Northern Counties bodies, introduced a new look to the fleet. The rear engine position allowed an entrance beside the driver, a particularly important feature as Mr Codling looked forward to the day when one-man operation of double-deckers would be possible. No.11 is shown here in Shottery village on the L2 local service, still looking brand new. (*T.W. Moore collection*)

In the event the Atlanteans were delayed further, and in order to release the Titans to Rugeley, two BMMO 'D7' double-deckers (Nos 4146/4767; THA146, 767BHA) had to be hired from Midland Red's Digbeth garage and were used at Stratford. By now Midland Red had sold virtually all their Leyland double-deckers, hence the loan of two of the less familiar 'home-built' buses.

The Atlanteans finally arrived in December, the first pair being delivered on the 7th. They were numbered 9-11 (NAC415-417F) and had 75-seat bodies of very distinctive appearance, making the previous year's Titans look conservative and dated. Their arrival allowed the return of the Midland Red 'D7's and the release of No.24 (MAC571), whose sale to the Porthcawl Omnibus Co. had been negotiated in November – yet another former Stratford Blue bus to lead an active retirement in South Wales. No.24 had the distinction of being the longest-serving Stratford Blue bus, its spell of duty from July 1952 to December 1967 never being equalled.

The fleet was now back to forty-four, after a brief high of forty-five, and after the Atlanteans had been placed in service the allocation to garages was as follows:

|  |  |  | Stratford | Kineton |
|---|---|---|---|---|
| Double-deck | Leyland Tiger rebuilds | (5) | 31-35 | — |
|  | Leyland Titan PD2 | (1) | 20 | — |
|  | Leyland Titan PD3 | (15) | 2-8, 29, 36-39 | 1, 28, 30 |
|  | Leyland Atlantean | (3) | 9-11 | — |
| Single-deck | Leyland Tiger Cub | (14) | 41, 42, 49-52, 55 | 40, 43-48 |
|  | Leyland Leopard | (2) | 60 | 62 |
| Coaches★ | Leyland Leopard | (2) | 59, 61 | = |
| TOTAL |  | (42) | 31 | 11 |

★Leyland Leopard coaches 56/57 are excluded as they were delicensed for the winter.

Consideration was given to replacing the last rear-entrance bus (No.20; TNX454) and the first of the Tiger Cubs during 1968, but the idea was shelved so for the first year since 1958 no new buses entered the fleet. It was also intended that no buses should leave the fleet, but that suddenly changed on Monday 23 September when No.31, the original Tiger double-deck conversion, ran out of control on Bordon Hill on the afternoon journey from Alcester Grammar School to Stratford via Welford. The bus veered across the road to the right, struck the kerb, and then span round and overturned. Six passengers were hurt but only one was detained in hospital. No other vehicle was involved and the cause of the accident remained a mystery. The driver reported that the skid had been caused by a wheel locking, but the Ministry of Transport inspectors could find no mechanical fault (only two months earlier No.31 had been recertified for a full five years). Unfortunately the impact twisted the body frame and it was quickly realised that the bus was a write-off. It was then dismantled, with usable parts including the seats being retained for the engineering stores, and the shell was sold for scrap before the end of the year. Mr Codling decided to keep going through the winter without a direct replacement by using a coach as an occasional duplicate on service work.

Mr Codling was keen to introduce modern one-man-operated single-deckers onto the Stratford town services, but the board was cautious and insisted that he gauge passenger reaction first, so a demonstrator for Leyland's rear-engined Panther model was tried during September. JTJ667F was a typical late 1960s city bus, a 48-seater with two doorways (the centre door serving as an exit) and capacity for a large number of standing passengers. After the trial Mr Codling reported that the bus had been well received by staff and passengers and that no-one had complained about having to stand; in fact he claimed it was easier for a housewife with a child and shopping to stand than to negotiate the steps of a double-decker. His arguments convinced the board, and the orders were placed in December, for five chassis from Leyland Motors (other suppliers were apparently not even considered) and bodies from Marshall of Cambridge. Delivery was to be in late 1969 and the intention was to replace No.20 and three double-deck conversions.

For some time it had been apparent that Harold Wilson's Labour government was proposing some far-reaching legislative changes for the bus industry, and the BET group had campaigned publicly against the proposals. Nevertheless it had sensed which way things were going and from 1 March 1968 it sold its UK bus interests (which included Midland Red and Stratford Blue) to the state-owned Transport Holding Co. Towards the end of 1968 a new Transport Act received royal assent, bringing about many changes such as empowering local authorities to subsidise loss-making services, the withdrawal of direct

As usual with new double-deckers, the Atlanteans were quickly put to use on the busy services along the A34 to Birmingham or Oxford, where their 75-seat capacity was particularly useful. No.9 (NAC415F) was barely a week old when photographed at the Robin Hood roundabout in Hall Green, Birmingham, on a fine winter's day, 16 December 1967. By this time Stratford Blue had been involved in the operation of the 150 for over fifteen years, yet buses were still required to show 'on hire to Midland Red' instead of something more useful to passengers such as 'via Henley-in-Arden'. So far no advertisements are carried, and No.9 looks much better without them. (*Malcolm Keeley*)

Harold Wilson's Labour government of the late 1960s brought about a radical overhaul of public transport and in 1967 the Minister of Transport, Barbara Castle, proposed in a White Paper that each major conurbation would have its own Passenger Transport Authority. The BET group, which owned Stratford Blue, fiercely opposed this and No.7 (GUE1D) is shown carrying a political statement rather than the usual commercial advertising ('Passenger Transport Authorities would charge their losses to the rates. PTA's will get you nowhere!'). In a similar vein No.39 (539EUE) had one reading 'Passenger Transport Authorities would mean coach passengers would have to go by train'. The campaign was unsuccessful and instead BET voluntarily sold its bus interests to the state. The West Midlands PTA was set up in 1969 together with a Passenger Transport Executive which took over the bus fleets of Birmingham, Walsall, West Bromwich and Wolverhampton Corporations, and later acquired a significant slice of Midland Red's operations. (*Author's collection*)

subsidy for rail replacement services like the 396, and the introduction of capital grants for new buses conforming to certain specifications (the Panthers would be eligible). One of the biggest changes was the establishment of the National Bus Company, which from 1 January 1969 acquired the THC's bus interests in England and Wales. Under THC control state ownership had made little difference to Stratford Blue, but the status quo was not to remain for long under the National Bus Company.

# 10

# The National Bus Company
# 1969–1970

When the National Bus Company began life on 1 January 1969 it had almost 21,000 vehicles operated by over fifty subsidiary companies throughout England and Wales. Stratford Blue, with a fleet of just forty-three, was amongst the smallest.

At first the new ownership made little difference locally. Mr Codling continued as manager, but now under the direction of Mr F.K. Pointon, Chairman of NBC's West Midland region which also comprised Midland Red and Potteries Motor Traction (generally known by its initials, PMT).

Mr Codling's biggest worry was a shortage of staff, a situation which had plagued Midland Red through most of the 1960s, and an advert was placed in the *Herald* on 3 January seeking conductors/conductresses for Stratford and a driver for Kineton. However until more staff could be recruited Mr Codling had to rely on voluntary overtime to cover some duties.

One early change, although probably not an NBC edict, was the adoption of white instead of cream in the livery. Tiger Cubs 50/51 were the first to be treated and other buses soon followed, creating a brighter and more refreshing appearance. Another change affected Leopard No.60 (CWD33C) which although only four years old was demoted to service bus status, with its coach seats replaced by fifty-three bus seats recovered from the wreckage of double-deck Tiger No.31 after its disastrous descent of Bordon Hill. In its new form No.60 was renumbered 54 and was the highest-capacity single-decker in the fleet, becoming a familiar sight on local services.

Eight other vehicles were renumbered in 1969 and early 1970, Titans 36-39 (536-539EUE) becoming Nos 24-27, Tiger Cub 55 (5455WD) becoming No.53 and Leopards 59, 61/62 (436GAC, DAC753C and HAC628D) taking new numbers 55/58/59 respectively. As with the 1965 renumbering there seemed to be very little point in the exercise.

March 1969 saw the company withdraw from Stretton-on-Fosse when the Tuesday journeys on service 8 were taken off; Warwickshire County Council had decided not to exercise its newly acquired powers to provide a subsidy to keep them going.

By now Saturday 3 May had been confirmed as the last day of operation of the Stratford – Henley-in-Arden – Birmingham passenger train service, with the closure of all stations between Wilmcote and Tyseley. Its replacement was to be a new bus service (the 103), similar to the long established 150 Stratford – Birmingham service except that between Hockley Heath and Shirley it would run via Wood End, Earlswood, Tidbury Green and Whitlocks End (also Tanworth-in-Arden on some journeys) to cover areas served by some of the stations. The

103 was to be operated jointly by Stratford Blue, who would run all through journeys, and Midland Red, who would only run between Birmingham and Henley. In Birmingham the terminus was to be the gloomy Bull Ring Bus Station, which had opened in November 1963 and was conveniently close to New Street Station, while in Stratford all journeys would serve the Red Lion Bus Station with most continuing to or from the railway station.

Closure of the rail line had attracted fierce opposition and was contested to the very last minute. On the Monday before closure five local councils (Warwickshire, Solihull County Borough, Bromsgrove Rural District and Stratford Urban and Rural Districts) sought a High Court injunction to prevent it from going ahead. Despite having their case dismissed and being ordered to pay costs, the authorities challenged the decision, and on Friday 2 May, a day before the last train was due to run, the Court of Appeal overturned it. Thanks to this historic reprieve service 103 was never introduced, and although the future of the North Warwickshire line was insecure for a time, more than thirty years later closure would be unthinkable.

This news was obviously too late for that day's *Herald*, which reported that the final train from Birmingham via Henley would reach Stratford at 11.41 p.m. on Saturday 3 May, with all trains running via Hatton from the Monday. Less controversial was the withdrawal of the remaining passenger trains between Stratford and Evesham, which went ahead with the last train from Stratford to Evesham leaving at 10.00 p.m. on the Saturday night.

Leopard No.60 (CWD33C) saw several transformations during its relatively short career. After an early livery change it was converted for one-man-operation. Then, during the winter of 1968/1969 it was downgraded to a 53-seat service bus using the narrow seats retrieved from Tiger No.31 after its mishap on Bordon Hill. It emerged in the brighter blue and white livery introduced in 1969, with a plain front panel which did little for its appearance, carrying fleet number 54. The photograph was taken on 27 June 1970, and shows No.54 pulling away from the Red Lion with a combination of destination displays – West Green Drive was served by the L5 town service, not the 90A. (*Peter Relf*)

Another view of No.54 at the Red Lion Bus Station, but in very different weather. Its previous trip on this bleak winter's day had been from Alcester on service 339. (*Author's collection*)

After ten years of service the Willowbrook-bodied Tiger Cubs of 1959 had become expensive to maintain, but thoughts of replacing them prematurely came to nothing. In this view beside the Red Lion No.41 (2742AC) appears to be having problems, with an engine panel lifted, instead of operating the 519 to Shipston. It has recently been repainted, and carries an advertisement for the Chinalight Chinese Restaurant in Henley Street. (*Author's collection*)

During the 1960s staff shortages were a constant problem for bus operators and in 1969 City of Oxford were so short of mechanics that they ran out of serviceable buses. Along with several other companies Stratford Blue came to the rescue, first sending Titan No.29 (2768NX) for a couple of days in July, and then No.38 (538EUE), which stayed into August. No.38 (also showing temporary fleet number S2) is seen here in a residential area, on the city service to Cowley and Minchery Farm. (*Author's collection*)

The 103 timetable had an intensive morning peak-hour service and Stratford Blue's share of the operation needed four buses. No extra buses were acquired, or ordered, and it must be assumed that the necessary vehicles were to be borrowed from Midland Red, at least in the short term.

In the meantime Mr Codling was looking at acquiring second-hand buses to replace the oldest Tiger Cubs, but he was not optimistic that anything suitable was available. The light-weight Tiger Cubs were less sturdy than the rest of the fleet and Mr Codling reported that 'they do not seem as likely to last their full term as the vehicles with larger engines, and in fact are even at this stage proving relatively costly to maintain'.

During May another Leyland Leopard coach was ordered, with coachwork by Alexanders of Falkirk – a new supplier for Stratford Blue. Delivery was scheduled for June 1970 and the intention was to displace the 'Alpine Continental' coach (No.59, soon to become No.55) from front-line duties.

Over the summer of 1969 City of Oxford Motor Services, also now a National Bus Company subsidiary, suffered a chronic shortage of maintenance staff and began to run out of serviceable buses. Replacements were drafted in from a variety of sources to assist and in late July Stratford Blue sent two PD3s (Nos 29 and 38), which were used on the important cross-city services 1 and 2 with temporary Oxford fleet numbers S1/S2.

The law had now been amended to allow one-man-operation of double-deckers, so Atlantean No.9 (NAC415F) was converted and tried out at Stratford garage. The trial was a success and the other two Atlanteans were similarly converted in 1970.

The intended conversion of the town services to one-man-operation was dependent on the delivery of the Panthers; they were due in September 1969 but by the end of the year there was still no sign of them.

At the end of the first year of NBC ownership thirty-one drivers were presented with safe driving awards. The Mayor, Cllr Malcolm Ray, made the presentations and mentioned in his speech that Stratford Blue was the first company he had been aware of as a child. Among those receiving awards were four drivers with over twenty years of accident-free driving behind them: Roland Dee (thirty-one years), Thomas Hughes (twenty-four years), Victor Kinnin (twenty-three years) and Stanley Freeman (twenty-one years). Mr Codling also spoke, and pointed out that on average Stratford Blue drivers covered 31,511 miles a year, equivalent to 630,000 miles over twenty years, so Roland Dee had probably driven almost a million miles without incident. The conductors were similarly recognised, and nineteen of them received awards for a total of 129 years' service.

Statistics show that in the year to 31 March 1970 the total mileage operated was 1,470,941, of which 421,401 (29 per cent) was by one-man-operated single-deckers. One-man double-deck operation, which started part way through the year, accounted for only 1,513 miles.

Double-deck one-man-operation was legalised in 1966, and although a few operators made rather awkward conversions of front-engined buses (including City of Oxford, who used them on the 44), only the rear-engined models were really suitable. Stratford Blue's first conversion was Atlantean No.9 (NAC415F) and in this view the 'Please pay as you enter' sign is clearly visible although not illuminated. The one-way system at Bridgefoot was opened in April 1968, leading to considerable extra mileage for the company, and here No.9 is heading past the Red Lion to return to Bridge Street for a journey to Shottery on service L2. (*P.M. Photography*)

A sight which would never have been tolerated in earlier years was a Stratford Blue bus in service with accident damage. Here however, Atlantean No.10 (NAC416F) has suffered noticeable frontal damage and there is also evidence of a 'botched' repair with an ill-fitting side panel. In this view it has yet to be converted for one-man-operation and a conductor is carried for the journey to Evesham on service 5. The advertisement for Watney's Special Bitter – a much-reviled product of the late 1960s and early 1970s – would have been equally unthinkable during the 'Flowers era'. (*R.H.G. Simpson*)

By 1969 one-man single-deckers covered almost a third of all mileage, as in this view of Tiger Cub No.48 (3948UE) at Banbury Bus Station with the request to 'Pay as you enter' displayed on a blue background on the nearside blind. No.48 had recently been repainted, with the fleetname now in a position above the wheel arch to allow room for adverts below the windows. The driver's hand can be seen on his Setright machine as he sets the dials to issue a ticket before setting out for Radway. Banbury Bus Station opened in 1968 and replaced North Bar as the terminus for all Stratford Blue services into the town. (*Author's collection*)

The staff shortage continued into early 1970, and from 1 March matters were compounded by new regulations which reduced the maximum daily driving time from eleven hours to ten and the maximum shift length from fourteen to twelve and a half hours. The legislation was intended to improve working conditions and safety standards, but many bus companies were already desperately short of staff and the reduced potential for staff to work overtime exacerbated the position. It was not only Stratford Blue who were short of drivers and in January Coventry Corporation Transport were advertising for staff in the Stratford area. Shorter shifts and loss of overtime inevitably had a serious effect on pay, and by the end of May three more drivers and another conductor had left. Mr Codling was in a very difficult position and the trade union representing the platform staff was angry.

In May the Panthers were finally ready for delivery from Marshalls at Cambridge, eight months late, but there was an unresolved problem with the outward-opening centre-exit doors, and until this was rectified the Ministry of Transport's Certifying Officer would only allow the front doors to be used. Without the centre doors in use, the 41-seat buses would only be allowed to carry twelve standing passengers, instead of the intended thirty, restricting their ability to replace double-deckers. That was not the only problem; the trade union had not agreed a rate for driving the so-called 'standee' buses, and decided to black them until the matter was resolved.

Mr Codling's radical choice of 'standee' buses to operate the Stratford town services proved to be something of a disaster and never actually came to fruition. Originally scheduled for delivery in Autumn 1969, the Leyland Panthers were not ready for collection until May 1970. Even then there were problems with the centre-exit doors, leading to a dispute with Marshalls, the bodybuilders. Technical problems aside, they were attractive buses and the 'Camair' bodies had up-to-the-minute styling. This view shows what should have been No.35 (XNX135H) in original condition at Marshalls. It was never to run for Stratford Blue, and after several months in storage all five were repainted in Midland Red colours, but Midland Red did not really want them either and nor did any other National Bus subsidiary. In November 1971 they were sold, still unused, to Preston Corporation Transport, where No.35 entered service with registration AUE313J. Roy Marshall, who took the photograph, was the municipal transport manager at Burton-on-Trent and was instrumental in the sale, having mentioned to his colleague at Preston that the Panthers may be available. (*Roy Marshall*)

While this was happening Mr Codling was away on a management course and Mr Levell, his assistant, felt that he lacked the necessary authority to resolve the situation. On his return Mr Codling took a firm stance and refused to accept the Panthers until they were properly fit for use as intended. This at least removed the urgency from the need to negotiate a 'standee' rate with the trade union.

On a brighter note, May also saw the delivery of the Leopard coach, No.36 (XNX136H). It had a 49-seat body to Alexander's 'Y-type' design, which had been in production for almost ten years but still looked modern, and wore a new livery of white with a single blue band below the windows. The Y-type body lent itself to demotion to a service bus in due course. The same could certainly not be said for the Duple Alpine Continental body on No.55 (436GAC), which No.36 replaced, but even so that was to be its fate. The ungainly transformation into a one-man-operated bus involved fitting a roof-mounted blind display and replacing the manual one-piece door by power-operated folding doors, in similar fashion to the conversions carried out by Midland Red on their 'C5' class coaches.

The fleet and registration numbers for No.36 followed on from the Panthers, which for some reason were allocated Nos 31-35 (XNX131-135H). As this clashed with the surviving double-deck Leyland Tigers (Nos 32-35) these became Nos 132-135 in April, the only Stratford Blue buses ever to carry three-figure fleet numbers (No.62 was otherwise the highest).

In the 1969/1970 period Stratford Blue's fleet numbering policy seemed particularly erratic. Quite unnecessarily the Panthers were allocated fleet numbers 31-35, four of which were already in use, so the double deck Tigers became Nos 132-135 – the only buses ever to carry numbers above 100 (62 had previously been the highest, on the 1966 Leopard). The futility of the exercise was only compounded by the fact that the Panthers never entered service! Carrying its new fleet number but no service number, No.132 (JUE348) is operating a journey on services 5/5A to Broom, on the day after the overtime ban was lifted, 27 June 1970. (*Peter Relf*)

In contrast to the Panthers, Leopard No.36 (XNX136H) was delivered a month ahead of schedule and entered service immediately, in May 1970. As it turned out it was to be Stratford Blue's last new vehicle and the only one to enter service in the final livery using white rather than cream. It displaced the first Leopard in the fleet (No.55; 436GAC) from coach work. Although Alexander bodies were a popular choice in many BET fleets during the 1960s, this was the only one bought by Stratford Blue. After a chequered career during which it carried many different liveries, No.36 was acquired for preservation and restored to much of its former glory. This posed shot when brand new was taken for possible publicity use. (*Author's collection*)

After seven seasons of front-line coach work from 1963, the Alpine Continental coach was ousted from its main duties by No.36. After renumbering from 59 to 55 in 1969, it was rebuilt to make it suitable for one-man-operation in 1970, the conversion having little consideration for its appearance. The idea probably came from Midland Red, who had similarly downgraded several of their own coaches. In its new form it is seen at the Red Lion on 27 June 1970, sandwiched between No.132 and a City of Oxford double-decker on service 44. 436GAC was the third No.55, the others being JUE353 and 5455WD, although numbers 37-54 had only been used twice. (*Peter Relf*)

More problems came with the announcement that another fare increase was to be sought, to take effect in July. This was said to be necessary in order to increase wages to assist recruitment and to compensate for the enforced loss of overtime. Stratford town council objected, amid much criticism of the company's performance both from members and the general public. At least someone had some sympathy for the company's dilemma – an anonymous pensioner wrote to the *Herald* blaming the difficulties on Barbara Castle and the Labour Government for imposing the restrictions on working hours.

In June the trade union imposed an overtime ban at Stratford garage where the thirty-five drivers and twenty conductors wanted the same basic wage as their counterparts at Midland Red, as well as the extra 4½d per hour bonus for one-man-operation which applied at Kineton garage but not at Stratford. This action brought the company to its knees, and on one day alone over 120 scheduled journeys were missed, causing chaos for passengers. Talks were rapidly convened and on 26 June, a week into the overtime ban, the management conceded the union's two main demands and the dispute ended.

In the meantime, and probably with a sigh of relief, Mr Codling left Stratford Blue for another post within NBC, becoming Traffic Manager with Yorkshire Traction. In a significant change of policy it was decided not to replace him and to place the company under the

Buses of the City of Oxford Motor Services were first seen at the Red Lion in 1949 when joint service 44 between Stratford and Oxford began, and for the next twenty years COMS also ran a short journey on Sunday afternoons from Stratford to Shipston and back. In 1969 the Sunday timetable for the through service was reduced and a second round trip to Shipston was squeezed in, and this view shows the 3.35 p.m. departure (although the Stratford Blue timetable showed the service number as 519, COMS regarded these journeys as 44s – another source of confusion for passengers). No.607 (417DHO) was a 1962 AEC Reliance acquired from Aldershot & District in 1970, and behind it is a Midland Red Daimler Fleetline ready to work the 3.40 p.m. service 524 to Broadway and Evesham. (*Author's collection*)

Kineton garage, with its higher proportion of rural mileage, led the way with one-man-operation, the drivers benefiting from a bonus payment which did not apply at Stratford. No.62 (HAC628D) was always closely associated with Kineton garage, and is seen here in Leamington Bus Station after a journey via Moreton Morrell on service 33. Under the 1969/1970 renumbering No.62 became No.59, previously allocated to the Alpine Continental coach and before that the former Warwickshire County Garage Bedford. In this photograph it still carries its original fleet number but has been modified for one-man-operation. (*Author's collection*)

wing of Midland Red's South Division for day-to-day management purposes. This was the most obvious threat to Stratford Blue's autonomy in thirty-five years of Midland Red ownership.

Behind the scenes there were negotiations over the Bridgetown Filling Station, which Shell-Mex and BP Ltd had offered to buy in late 1969. The offer was rejected but an increased bid of £111,000 was accepted in early 1970, and a formal handover date of 28 September was agreed.

Although services returned to normal after the disruption earlier in the year the company's reputation seemed tarnished, and the morale and goodwill of the staff, even after the pay increase, was not the same under Midland Red management. Inevitably Midland Red began to question the wisdom of keeping Stratford Blue as a separate company; it certainly made little sense from a financial point of view now that the staff enjoyed Midland Red pay rates.

Rumours of the impending demise of the company were rife, although no official statement was made. However, the clearest possible indication of the future was given in early December when Titan No.6 (673HNX) emerged from the paintshop – in full Midland Red livery including fleetnames! The only reference to Stratford Blue was in the legal ownership details. Still there was no formal announcement but confirmation soon emerged that Thursday 31 December was to be Stratford Blue's last day of separate existence, with Midland Red taking over fully from 1 January 1971.

From 1968 most of the 1963/1964 Titans were fitted with larger destination screens requiring two separate blinds as well as three-track number blinds, almost in Midland Red style. Another sign of Midland Red influence was the adoption of their style of fleet number transfer on later repaints, as shown here on No.3 (670HNX). Similar No.1 was to be the last vehicle repainted in Stratford Blue colours. Beside No.3 in Stratford garage yard is coach No.56 and, just visible to the rear, the ex-military Austin tow-truck, RWD567G. (*Alan Broughall*)

The news was received with some sadness but it was clear that the enormous regard which Stratford's citizens once had for their local bus company had mostly vanished, and the general attitude seemed to be one of indifference.

One man who treated the news with a great deal of interest was Dr Keith Lloyd, a member of the Omnibus Society, who on five days during December travelled on as many Stratford Blue routes as he could. Given that he lived in Southampton this was quite an achievement! He later wrote up his experiences in the OS journal, the *Omnibus Magazine*, in an article entitled 'Farewell to Stratford Blue'. The following paragraphs are based on this, and give a useful insight into the final days of Stratford Blue operations.

Dr Lloyd's first trip was on Saturday 12 December. After reaching Oxford by train he travelled to Shipston-on-Stour on the 9.15 a.m. service 44 journey. This was operated by a City of Oxford AEC Renown double-decker, which although not ideally suited for the purpose was one-man-operated as far as Chipping Norton. Here the driver left the bus to return to Oxford at the wheel of the Stratford Blue bus on the 9.10 a.m. Stratford – Oxford journey, and the Stratford Blue driver and conductor returned northwards with City of Oxford's AEC, taking it on a detour via Cherington, which was only served on Saturdays. Progress here was impeded by a herd of cattle being driven along the road, both on the way into the village, where the bus reversed, and on the way out. After a break in Shipston Dr Lloyd's Stratford Blue travels really began, starting with the 12.10 p.m. service 8 to Stratford via Ilmington, operated by Tiger Cub No.50. Connecting with this journey was Reg Rouse's service from Stretton-on-Fosse, worked by the Bedford OB (HTF586) which he had owned for about twenty years. Apart from a convoluted route in Ilmington involving another reverse, there was little to note on the journey to Stratford, where Dr Lloyd took a ride to Justins Avenue and back on local service L3 and then rejoined Tiger Cub No.50 for the short run to Clifford Chambers and back on service 525. Next he travelled to Evesham on the 2.05 p.m. service 5. Intending passengers for this journey had to be careful about their choice of bus as on Saturdays there was a more direct 5A at the same time, which reached Evesham in forty-nine minutes instead of the hour taken by service 5. The 5 was operated by Tiger Cub No.49, which next took Dr Lloyd on his last Stratford Blue journey of the day, as far as Aston Cross on the Cheltenham service (although this was now numbered 540 No.49 showed service number 64A, which had not been correct since 1967!).

Four days later Dr Lloyd caught the same AEC Renown from Oxford but this time travelled all the way to Stratford, where he sampled the Banbury Road (L4) and West Green Drive (L5/L6) services. After that it was a journey on the 12.45 p.m. service 5A to Broom and back via Temple Grafton and Ardens Grafton. This was operated by Tiger Cub No.52, showing only 'Broom' on its blind, without a service number. After a quick run to Shottery and back on the L2, he took the 90A to Leamington via Snitterfield, worked by Titan No.8, and from there the schoolday-only 90B to Henley via Claverdon. This was also worked by No.52, which had preceded him by running the 2.05 p.m. 90A from Stratford. From Henley he returned to Stratford by Midland Red, before the last Stratford Blue ride of the day on the 5.35 p.m. service 525 to Chipping Campden. Dr Lloyd noted that the bus, Titan No.5, did a 'double-run' into Lower Quinton and back, but in the darkness he could not tell exactly where the bus turned round.

After repainting in the blue and white livery with the Midland Red-style of fleet number, No.30 (2769NX) is seen on a quiet stretch of the A34 on its way to Oxford. (*P.M. Photography*)

His next Stratford Blue travels were on Friday 18 December, starting at Evesham Railway Station on the rail-replacement service 396. It came as no surprise that he alone boarded at the station, which he had reached on Midland Red's service 378 from Worcester. The 396 was operated by Tiger double-decker No.133, and served the defunct railway stations of Littleton & Badsey, Pebworth, Long Marston and Milcote (because this journey, the 9.03 a.m. from Evesham, was scheduled for double-deck operation it made a detour to avoid the low railway bridge at Broad Marston, adjacent to Pebworth Halt). After entering Stratford over Clopton Bridge Dr Lloyd carried on to the terminus at the railway station, the only passenger to do so. His short journey back to the town centre was on coach No.56 (AAC21B), a rare sight on local service work and a clear sign of a shortage of serviceable buses. Further evidence of this were glimpses of a Midland Red 'S14' single-decker, temporarily fitted with Stratford Blue blinds, and a 'D7' double-decker on service 90A which had to show 'A90' because of the configuration of Midland Red's blinds. After a trip to Alveston and back on

Another vehicle renumbered during 1969 was No.55 (5455WD), which became No.53, bringing the Tiger Cubs together in one block as Nos 40-53. This view shows it about to pass the Pump Room Gardens in Leamington while working service 90A from Stratford. It is now fitted for one-man-operation, with the destination blind moved to the offside and separate number blinds on the nearside. The sparkle which it had when new (see page 151) has certainly gone. (*T.W. Moore*)

Over the course of five days in December 1970 Dr Keith Lloyd travelled almost the whole Stratford Blue network, having learned of the company's imminent demise. On Thursday 24 December he rode on the normally Friday-only 12.45 p.m. journey to Exhall, worked by Tiger Cub No.49 (5449WD), which did not have Exhall on the blind and instead showed '5A Graftons', reasonably appropriate as it travelled via Temple Grafton and Ardens Grafton. This was the last Stratford Blue journey of all to Exhall, and the driver commented that it was the first time in eight years that he had actually carried anyone there! Dr Lloyd's photograph shows No.49 about to return to Stratford on the 1.21 p.m. journey from the terminus at Exhall, some way short of the village proper. (*Dr E.K. Lloyd*)

the L1, the only 'local' he had not yet travelled on, Dr Lloyd took the Friday-only service 12 to Bearley, which strayed only about half a mile off the A34 Birmingham Road to turn round by the church, returning the way it had come. Then came a trip on the 12.30 p.m. 339 to Alcester, which on Fridays ran via Wilmcote (the only day of the week that Wilmcote saw a bus) and Aston Cantlow, returning on the 1.20 p.m. journey from Alcester via the main road. Back in Stratford for only six minutes the insatiable traveller set off again on the 1.50 p.m. service 7 to Walton, another village which only had a service on Fridays. This returned to Stratford for 2.47 p.m., allowing a quick breather before the 3.05 p.m. service 9 to Claverdon and back, yet another Friday-only operation. This service included Dr Lloyd's favourite stretch of Stratford Blue route, down the steep hill from Claverdon to Langley and through a ford to Langley Green. Having now seen the majority of the Stratford-based services, Dr Lloyd turned to the Kineton routes, beginning with a journey to Kineton via Ettington on the 4.30 p.m. service 30. The 30 had no variants, all journeys following exactly the same route, but from Kineton Dr Lloyd was to travel on the 35, which had numerous variations although they all entered Banbury along the A41. The 5.22 p.m. journey followed the most direct route except for a diversion through Radway, and climbed Edgehill at the northern end of the escarpment.

Thursday 31 December 1970 was the very last day of Stratford Blue operation and on this occasion Dr Lloyd travelled on the 2.10 p.m. Banbury – Ratley journey on service 36, operated by Tiger Cub No.46 (3946UE). In the vicinity of Ratley he photographed the bus before it returned through the snow-covered landscape to Banbury. With little over an hour of daylight left, was this the last photograph ever taken of a true Stratford Blue bus? (*Dr E.K. Lloyd*)

Dr Lloyd's fourth day of exploration was on Christmas Eve, a Thursday. This time his first journey was on the 12.45 p.m. 5A to Exhall – normally another 'Friday-only' village, but when Christmas Day fell on a Friday the market-day services ran a day early. This journey was therefore of particular historical significance as the last ever Stratford Blue bus to the village, where Dr Lloyd noted that the terminus was some way short of the houses due to the lack of a suitable turning point. Inevitably he had to return on the same bus, but left it at Binton Turn to catch the afternoon service 6 back to Evesham. This was operated by the modified 'Alpine Continental' coach, No.55, and on the way Dr Lloyd managed to photograph it as the driver waited time at Pebworth – the last journey ever on Stratford Blue service 6. From Evesham his return journey to Stratford was also on No.55, on the 3.00 p.m. 5A. The final Stratford Blue journey of the day was on the 4.10 p.m. service 396 to Pebworth, his onward journey from there being by Midland Red.

The fifth and final day of this comprehensive study of Stratford Blue's services took place on the very last opportunity, New Year's Eve, when Dr Lloyd left Banbury with his 'Day Anywhere' ticket on the 12.00 p.m. service 34 to Kineton, taking him via Farnborough, Fenny Compton and Northend. The bus was Tiger Cub No.47, and similar No.46 took him back to Banbury, on the 1.05 p.m. service 35 via the length of Edgehill to Upton House and back, then diverting off the A41 to serve Hanwell, where the bus turned round in an icy field entrance. In Banbury Dr Lloyd stayed with No.46 for the 2.10 p.m. Thursday-only service

36 to Ratley via Horley, Hornton and Edgehill, which also carried a bundle of newspapers for delivery to Hornton. Before the return journey to Banbury Dr Lloyd photographed the bus in the snow at Ratley. Next he travelled on another service 35 journey, the 3.20 p.m. to Avon Dassett, which included the steep descent through Warmington village – on the return journey this section was avoided by turning round at the Plough and travelling back through the village to the A41. Arrival back in Banbury was scheduled for 4.23 p.m., in time for the 4.30 p.m. service 35 to Kineton, which, as it turned out, was worked by the same bus, Tiger Cub No.42, and took Dr Lloyd through Hanwell and Warmington again. At Kineton he began his very last Stratford Blue journey on the 5.20 p.m. service 32 via Gaydon and along the main road to Leamington. This journey was operated by yet another Tiger Cub (No.45) and was due in Leamington Bus Station at 6.00 p.m., exactly six hours before Stratford Blue's separate existence came to an end.

This completed the marathon five-day exploration which had covered the vast majority of the services and ensured that the essential flavour of Stratford Blue's operations, at least as they appeared in later years, was recorded for posterity.

As night approached on this final day the buses returned once more to their home garages, bringing to an end forty-four years and nine months of continuous 'Blue' operation. Despite the unfortunate decline of the last few years it is no exaggeration to say that without Stratford Blue, Stratford and the surrounding area would never be quite the same again.

# 11

# Midland Red and
# the Stratford Blue Revival
# 1971–1999

On New Year's Day 1971 the entire Stratford Blue fleet carried Midland Red legal ownership details, the necessary vinyls having been applied overnight, but the Stratford Blue fleetnames and numbers were untouched. No.6 may have been in full Midland Red colours but there was little else to indicate that Stratford's local bus company had passed into history!

All forty-four active vehicles transferred to Midland Red: twenty-three double-deckers, seventeen single-deck buses and four coaches (the single-deck buses and the three Atlantean double-deckers were fitted for one-man-operation). The Panthers were also transferred, but continued to languish in store in Birmingham. Midland Red already had over 200 Leopards (buses and coaches) and had previously operated Titans, but they had never before run Tigers, Tiger Cubs, Atlanteans or Panthers, so these did not fit in well.

The fleet was split between Stratford garage (thirty-two vehicles) and Kineton (twelve). On takeover Nos 9, 10, 20/29, 30, 41/43/45-49, 52/59 and 132-135 were still in the earlier blue and cream livery but the rest (except of course No.6) were blue and white. Titan No.2 and Tiger Cub No.41 received Midland Red colours in January and another two Titans soon followed, but the policy was now to add 2000 to the Stratford Blue numbers so these emerged as Nos 2003/2004, and Nos 2, 6 and 41 were similarly renumbered. By May twenty-six vehicles (all the Leopards and Panthers, two Tiger Cubs and the twelve newest Titans) had been painted red, but as it turned out no more were to be done.

The first former Stratford Blue bus withdrawn by Midland Red was Tiger No.134 (JUE350), which was already in the 'dump' behind Lichfield garage by 2 January, having probably suffered a major defect. It was sold to a Black Country scrap merchant by the end of the month. By that time Midland Red buses were already to be found at the Stratford Blue garages, with 'S14' No.4689 (689BHA) and 'LS18' No.5210 (5210HA) officially allocated to Stratford, and Banbury's 'S23' No.5941 (UHA941H) helping out at Kineton (sometimes on the author's afternoon school journey). The next withdrawals were in April/May when a cull of non-standard vehicles removed all Tiger Cubs (including the two which had been repainted red), the last three Tigers, the final rear-entrance Titan (No.20; TNX454) and the three-year-old Atlanteans. One of the latter (No.9) never ran for Midland Red, having collided head-on with a car transporter between Bidford and Welford in December 1970 and

The first 'Blue' bus repainted into Midland Red livery was Titan No.6, in December 1970. No.2 (669HNX) followed in January 1971, initially retaining its Stratford Blue number, but this was quickly changed to 2002. This bus was the only 'HNX' Titan to retain its original small destination display. Alongside it at the Red Lion is No.5209 (5209HA), a Midland Red 'LS18' class Leyland Leopard transferred from Sutton Coldfield garage in April 1971, on service 90A to Leamington. Neither is showing a service number, in time-honoured Stratford Blue fashion! (*Alan Broughall*)

The oldest buses repainted red were two 1959 Tiger Cubs, Nos 41 and 43. Both had very short careers with Midland Red and were withdrawn two days after this photograph was taken on 29 May 1971. No.2043 (2744AC) has just arrived at the Red Lion from Shipston on service 519 and shows the separate route number blinds which were a recent modification. After brief service with Potteries Motor Traction, No.43 ran for an operator in Lancashire and then became a contractor's site hut. (*Alan Broughall*)

The first of the Stratford Blue coaches to receive red livery was No.57 (AAC22B), in February 1971. As Midland Red No.2057 it is seen here at Gloucester Green, Oxford, en route for Coventry on an Associated Motorways express service. While with Midland Red both Plaxton Panorama coaches (Nos 2056/2057) worked from other garages, including Evesham, Ludlow and Worcester. In June 1974 they received white National Express livery, which they retained until withdrawn in January 1976. (*Author's collection*)

After repainting, No.2058 (DAC753C) looked virtually indistinguishable from Midland Red's 'LC7' class coaches, although drivers certainly noticed its manual gearbox. Initially it stayed at Stratford but in 1974 moved on to Evesham and then to Wellington before being withdrawn in January 1976. In the meantime it had gained white 'National' livery. By the end of 1976 it was in the hands of a Bloxwich scrap merchant, an early end for a 1965 coach. In this view at Stratford Bus Station a board is propped against the windscreen advertising the day's excursion, to Hidcote Manor Gardens and Chipping Campden. Behind the coach can be seen the very limited covered waiting area within the Red Lion Bus Station. Even this was of little use on a wet day with a westerly wind! (*R.F. Mack*)

then been taken to the Yorkshire Woollen District Transport Co.'s Dewsbury works for repair. The replacements at Kineton and Stratford included nine of the 100 Ford R192s then being delivered to Midland Red for use on rural services, four 'LS18' Leopards, three 'DD12' Daimler Fleetline double-deckers, and two elderly BMMO 'D7's. The Fords looked very distinctive with a cream waistband on their Plaxton 'Derwent' bodies, all other Midland Red service buses being plain red at this time. No doubt this varied intake caused some headaches for Stratford's fitters, who were used to working exclusively with Leylands.

Twelve of the displaced buses were transferred within the National Bus Company, the Atlanteans to City of Oxford Motor Services and the 'AC' and 'UE' Tiger Cubs to PMT. The rest went to independent operators – the older double-deckers to G&G Coaches in Leamington and the 'WD' Tiger Cubs (which were only nine years old) via a dealer to operators in Shropshire and Wales.

The infamous Panthers were officially struck off in July, possibly without so much as visiting Stratford and certainly without ever carrying a passenger for either Stratford Blue or Midland Red, despite having carried both liveries. Unlike most Leylands, Panthers were not well regarded and there were no takers within the National Bus Company so eventually they were sold to Preston Corporation Transport. The original registrations (XNX131-135H) were cancelled and they entered service in Lancashire in November 1971 with later Warwickshire registrations AUE309-313J and a cream and blue livery which would not have looked out of place in Stratford. In their new home they settled down to give over ten years' service.

Stratford Blue's last new vehicle, No.36 (XNX136H), retained its original livery for under twelve months, becoming No.2036 in Midland Red's all-over red livery in April 1971. As with the other coaches, silver transfers were carried, complementing the chromework on the body. No.2036 was immediately recognisable as the only Alexander coach in the very large Midland Red fleet and is seen here on excursion duty. (*M. Bennett*)

No.54 (CWD33C) was also repainted into Midland Red livery in April, complete with the silver fleetname and number transfers normally used on coaches and semi-coaches. This was probably an error in the paintshop and they were later replaced by the gold version used on service buses. This 1971 view shows it in use as a one-man bus on service L6 to West Green Drive via Masons Road. On 1 January 1972 the Stratford garage services were renumbered into the Midland Red series and the L6 became the 506. No.2054 completed over five years' service with Midland Red at Stratford garage, but despite its similarity to many more recent Midland Red vehicles it was withdrawn in May 1976 and sold for scrap. Its manual gearbox was probably its downfall. In the background to this Bridge Street view is the Anchor Inn, now known as the Encore. (*R.F. Mack*)

The final rear-entrance bus in the Stratford Blue fleet, Titan No.20 (TNX454), outlived its sister vehicles by almost three and a half years, Nos 21/22 having been sold to Green Bus of Rugeley in 1967. It was finally taken off the road by Midland Red at the end of April 1971, still in the earlier blue and cream livery. This view of No.20 (only the red buses carried the 2000-series numbers) was taken during its last few weeks in service, the clue being the decimal currency advertisement for Park Drive Tipped at 20½p for twenty. 'D-Day' was 15 February 1971, although Stratford Blue, like most other bus companies, only adopted the new currency six days later. Thirty years later a single cigarette would cost more than a packet of twenty did in 1971! (*Roy Marshall*)

Amongst the many Midland Red vehicles drafted in to Stratford in the early months of 1971 were a pair of 1957 'D7's. No.4759 (759BHA) came from Worcester garage in April and stayed at Stratford until September when it was withdrawn and replaced by a Daimler Fleetline. This view shows it turning into Bridgefoot on its way to Bridge Street to operate a journey to Blue Cap Road, which was served by an extension of the L3 (Justins Avenue) service from November 1968. Clopton Bridge is in the background, and to the right of the bus is the chimney of Cox's timber yard. (*Paul Gray*)

On withdrawal at the end of April 1971, the Marshall Tiger Cubs were parked up at the rear of Evesham garage to await sale. No.52 (5452WD) is seen here sandwiched between sister vehicle No.51 and a Midland Red 'S14', also withdrawn. Although these were the newest of the Tiger Cubs, dating only from 1962, there was no taker for them within the National Bus Company and they passed to Don Everall, the Wolverhampton-based dealer, for resale. No.52 later worked for an operator in the Wrexham area, while No.51 had a succession of operators in Shropshire. (*Alan Broughall*)

The twelve Titans delivered between 1963 and 1966 were the only double-deckers repainted red, the programme being completed during April 1971. Three of the 'EUE' batch are seen here together at the Bus Station, none of them showing service numbers! In line with established Midland Red practice Stratford and Kineton were given two-letter garage codes ('ST' and 'KN' respectively). These appeared on the destination blinds and this was the way to tell the allocation of a Midland Red bus. The 'ST' code is just visible to the left of the word 'Stratford' on No.2026 (538EUE). (*Alan Broughall*)

By June only the 1960 Titans (Nos 28-30; 2767-2769NX) remained in service in Stratford Blue colours – complete with fleetnames and numbers – but in August the axe fell on these too, and for the first time in forty-four years there were no blue buses in Stratford.

Isle of Man Road Services (IoMRS) had agreed to buy the PD3 Titans and took delivery of Nos 28-30 in November and December, after Midland Red had repainted them in IoMRS livery and fitted them for one-man-operation (despite their obvious unsuitability for such use). By January 1972 Nos 2001/2002 (668/669HNX) and 2024-2027 (536-539EUE) had joined them, and the final six (Nos 2003-2008) were taken off the road between May and July, reaching the Isle of Man in September. In their new home the former Stratford Blue Nos 1-8 and 24-30 were allocated Manx registrations MN44/45, MN63-66, MN2670/2671, MN57-60 and MN41-43 respectively. A mixed bag of Midland Red vehicles replaced them at the former Stratford Blue garages, including BMMO 'D9' double-deckers at Stratford garage and 'S17' single-deckers at Kineton. The presence of the D9s delayed the removal of rear-entrance buses from Stratford garage, originally planned for 1967, by several years.

Stratford Blue's final new bus order had specified three Marshall-bodied Leyland Leopards and these arrived in the spring of 1972 as part of Midland Red's 'S26' class (Nos 6461-6473; DHA461-473K). No S26s came to Kineton or Stratford, and it was impossible to identify which three constituted the Stratford Blue order.

By August 1972 the seven Leopards were the only former Stratford Blue vehicles left with Midland Red, and not all of these had stayed on home ground, No.2056 (AAC21B) having

The Northern Counties PD3s looked a little odd in Midland Red livery with their exposed radiators, a feature which had long since disappeared from native Midland Red vehicles. However, this revival was to be short lived as all four were withdrawn in November 1971 ready for despatch to the Isle of Man. No.2025 (537EUE) is seen here in Henley-in-Arden on its way from Birmingham on service 150. On the left is one of Johnson's lorries, operated by the family business that ran the Garner 'Patent BusVan' shown on page 19 and now runs several bus services from Stratford. (*Alan Broughall*)

The last Titans to leave the Midland Red fleet were Nos 2006 and 2008, which lasted until July 1972. No.2007 (GUE1D), which went a month earlier, is seen here at the Royal Well Bus Station in Cheltenham, ready to leave for Evesham on service 540 (service 64A became the 540 in Bristol Omnibus's new number series in June 1967). Leyland Titans returned briefly to the Midland Red fleet in 1974, when the business of Harper Brothers of Heath Hayes was acquired. (*M. Bennett*)

Midland Red sold all fifteen PD3 Titans to Isle of Man Road Services, the first of many second-hand double-deckers to operate on the island, and on its formation in October 1976 they passed to Isle of Man National Transport. One-time Stratford Blue No.36 (536EUE) is seen here at Douglas Bus Station as IoMRS No.57 (MN57), with a Willowbrook-bodied Tiger Cub of almost identical appearance to Stratford Blue's Nos.40-43 (2741-2744AC) in the background. No.57 was one of three converted to open-top for seasonal use on Douglas Promenade, and remained with IoMNT until 1982. (*Author's collection*)

The Ford R192s were introduced to Stratford garage very soon after the Stratford Blue takeover and were to form an important part of the fleet there and at Kineton for several years. No.6380 (YHA380J) had a very short spell of operation at Hereford before coming to Stratford in March 1971. The Fords were best suited to the rural services, but that did not stop them putting in appearances on the town services, as shown here in Bridge Street. The 505 was the old Stratford Blue L5 (West Green Drive) service. (*Author's collection*)

moved to Worcester. It seemed that the Stratford Blue fleet had been eliminated with almost indecent haste, and in about eighteen months operations at both garages had very much assumed a Midland Red appearance. This was emphasised by renumbering the services into Midland Red's series and by the appearance of new buses and a new culture which helped to ensure that the numbers were actually displayed.

The Kineton-area services were renumbered first, when they were 'revised' (in other words, cut) on 9 October 1971. The Stratford-area services followed on 1 January 1972. However, services 6 and 7 were no longer considered viable and were withdrawn before the new numbers were allocated. Also withdrawn were the Friday (market day) journeys on service 11, leaving only the school buses.

The final list of Stratford Blue services, with their new Midland Red numbers, is as follows:

| L1–L6 | Stratford local services | 501–506 |
|---|---|---|
| 5/5A | Stratford – Bidford – Broom/Evesham | 538/539/ |
| | | 541/542 |
| 6 | Stratford – Pebworth – Evesham | (Withdrawn) |
| 7 | Stratford – Loxley/Wellesbourne/Walton | (Withdrawn) |
| 8 | Stratford – Ilmington/Shipston | 521 |
| 9 | Stratford – Claverdon | 549 |
| 10 | Stratford – Alcester | 542 |
| 11 | Stratford – Hampton Lucy/Wellesbourne | 522 |
| 12 | Stratford – Bearley | 149 |
| 30 | Kineton – Ettington – Stratford | 530 |
| 31 | Kineton – Combrook – Stratford | 531 |
| 32/32A | Kineton/Northend – Gaydon – Leamington | 532/533 |
| 33/33A | Kineton – Moreton Morrell – Leamington | 534 |
| 34 | Kineton – Fenny Compton – Banbury | 510 |
| 35 | Kineton/Avon Dassett – Warmington – Banbury | Incorporated into 510 |
| 36 | Kineton – Ratley – Banbury | 511 |
| 44 | Stratford – Oxford | 544 |
| 90A | Stratford – Leamington | 591 |
| 90B | Henley-in-Arden – Leamington | 548 |
| 150 | Stratford – Birmingham | No change |
| 339 | Stratford – Alcester | 528/529 |
| 396 | Stratford – Honeybourne – Evesham | No change |
| 519 | Stratford – Shipston – Long Compton | No change |
| 525 | Stratford – Chipping Campden | No change |
| 540 | Evesham – Cheltenham | No change |

This list excludes Midland Red services on which Stratford Blue had scheduled workings, such as the occasional journeys on the 154 from Birmingham to Shirley and from Percy Estate to Warwick on the L45 Leamington local service.

In November 1972 the 'Alpine Continental' coach conversion, No.2055, was stood down and later transferred to City of Oxford, reducing Midland Red's stock of former Stratford Blue vehicles to six.

The National Bus Company had now been in existence for four years and in the fashion of the 1970s decided it needed a corporate identity. After a little experimentation it was decreed that coaches would be white and buses either 'poppy red' of 'leaf green'. 'Local coaches' (usually known as dual-purpose vehicles) would be red or green with a white roof. Naturally, Midland Red opted for red rather than green, although what would have happened if Stratford Blue had not already been wound up can only be guessed at. Of the surviving Stratford Blue vehicles, Nos 2036 and 2056-2058 were repainted in the white coach livery, No.2059 became red and white and No.2054 continued to the end in its previous Midland Red livery.

Service 544 between Stratford and Oxford was split at Chipping Norton in March 1971, after over twenty years of through operation, and City of Oxford's journeys between Chipping Norton and Oxford later reverted to using the number 44 (some instead became 35s). However in the spring of 1973 a through service was reinstated and linked with journeys on service 150 to create a through Birmingham – Oxford service (X50), running twice a day in each direction. Midland Red and City of Oxford each operated one round trip, although Midland Red soon began to supply both vehicles, one of which stayed overnight at City of Oxford's Chipping Norton garage.

The next change to affect the surviving Stratford Blue vehicles was not until January 1976, when coaches 2056-2058 (AAC21/22B and DAC753C) were withdrawn, followed in May by No.2054 (CWD33C). Only No.2054 had remained at Stratford, the coaches having served at various other Midland Red garages. After five years, only two former Stratford Blue vehicles now remained with Midland Red – Nos 2036 (XNX136H) and 2059 (HAC628D).

Another type to appear in Stratford in some numbers was the 'D9', the last of a long line of Midland Red-built double-deckers. One of the first to arrive was No.5380 (AHA380B), transferred from Bromsgrove in November 1971, and seen here working service 538 from Evesham to Stratford. (*R.F. Mack*)

Not surprisingly the seven Leyland Leopards outlasted the other former Stratford Blue vehicles with Midland Red, but in November 1972 No.2055 (436GAC) was the first of these to go and in early 1973 it was transferred to City of Oxford Motor Services. In January 1972 services 5/5A were renumbered and 539 denoted a journey via the Graftons or Cranhill. No.2055 is shown in Evesham High Street in June 1972, about to leave for Stratford. (*Author's collection*)

With the introduction of NBC's corporate liveries from 1972, four former Stratford Blue coaches received National Express white livery. No.2036 (XNX136H) was one of them and is seen here in Hales Street, Coventry, on a National Express service to Llandudno. (*P.M. Photography*)

After a spell in NBC's 'dual-purpose' livery No.2059 (HAC628D) received the poppy red bus livery, relieved by a white band below the windows. This view shows it in Banbury Bus Station on one of Kineton's occasional stints on the town services, still with its Stratford Blue blind. It stayed at Kineton, its home base from new, until January 1977 and then ran briefly from other Midland Red garages, including Bromsgrove, before it was withdrawn from passenger service in May 1978. Later it was used for several years as a driver training vehicle and was then restored as closely as possible to its original condition by an owner in Upton-on-Severn. (*R.F. Mack*)

During the late 1970s former Stratford Blue No.36 (XNX136H) was busy working from Midland Red's Digbeth (Birmingham) garage on the longer-distance stage carriage services. For this purpose it had been fitted for one-man-operation with number blinds, and painted into the red and white version of NBC livery. This view shows it in Navigation Street, Birmingham, nearing the end of a journey from Derby on service X12. (*Author's collection*)

The Mark 1 Leyland National was the epitome of National Bus Company standardisation, especially in the all-over poppy red colour scheme which was rigidly adhered to in the mid-1970s. Examples were used at both the former Stratford Blue garages, but for a time No.624 (PUK624R), supplied new in April 1977, was the only one at Kineton. This view shows it at the Red Lion, ready to return to its home base on what had been Stratford Blue's service 30 via Ettington, becoming Midland Red's 530 in 1972 and then the 210 with the 'Avonbus' revisions of May 1977. Almost twenty-four years after it entered service No.624 was at work on city services in Hull! (*P.M. Photography*)

In the meantime many changes had affected Midland Red; in 1973 the Birmingham and Black Country operations (and 413 buses) were sold to the West Midlands Passenger Transport Executive, and in March 1974 the historic title Birmingham & Midland Motor Omnibus Co. Ltd was changed to the simpler Midland Red Omnibus Co. Ltd, at last reflecting the popular name. In the following month large parts of Warwickshire disappeared into the newly created West Midlands metropolitan county.

During 1976 Midland Red conducted extensive market research on its Stratford-based services, and after consultation with Warwickshire County Council a completely new network was introduced on 28 May 1977 – the biggest shake-up Stratford's bus services had ever seen outside wartime. The new services were marketed under the title 'Avonbus', inspired by the success of the 'Reddibus' name used for services in Redditch.

One of the main changes was the replacement of the long-established 150 Birmingham service by a new limited-stop X20. This cut the journey time from seventy-two minutes to fifty-eight, reducing operating costs significantly. For through-passengers the faster journey time was a welcome improvement, but to achieve it many little-used stops on rural stretches of the A34 (as it was then) were removed, a decision which angered many people who had caught the 150 for more than two generations but could now only stand and watch as the X20 went flying past their stop. The X50 Oxford service was incorporated into the basic hourly frequency.

Other changes included the loss of the Alveston and Banbury Road local services (501 and 504). The Alveston service had operated continuously for just over fifty years since the start of Stratford-on-Avon Motor Services in April 1927; it was replaced by rerouting the 518 (Stratford – Wellesbourne – Leamington – Coventry) through the village. The other local services were replaced by a complex pattern of routes (205-207) covering Justins Avenue, West Green Drive and Shottery. The country services were also much altered and, except for the Leamington services, were renumbered into the 200-series, for example 209 for the Friday-only service to Kineton via Combrook (latterly 531 and before that the Stratford Blue 31) and 218 for the Evesham service. Many services were timed to connect at the Red Lion Bus Station with the X20 to and from Birmingham.

The fleet at Kineton and Stratford had been progressively updated and for the Avonbus launch a number of Leyland Nationals (NBC's standard single-decker) were introduced, complementing some dual-purpose Leopards delivered earlier. By the end of the year most buses displayed the 'Avonbus' title, usually towards the rear of a broad white band above the lower-deck windows. This represented one of the earliest breaks anywhere from the rigid uniformity of NBC's corporate liveries.

The 'Avonbus' scheme was part of Midland Red's Viable Network Project, aimed at separating the profitable core from the loss-making services which would only survive with local authority support. The project successfully achieved these aims and the methods were later applied across the whole company, and elsewhere within the National Bus Company, by this time known as MAP (Market Analysis Project).

No.627 (PUK627R) was one of Stratford's Leyland Nationals, and is shown here in the garage yard with its blind set for the journey from Birmingham on the limited-stop X20 service. The white band above the windows, to carry the 'Avonbus' logo, considerably enhances its appearance. No.627 later spent several years at Nuneaton garage while Stratford did without Leyland Nationals, but towards the end of its career, in the late 1990s, it was back again. (*Author's collection*)

No.2036 was the only Stratford Blue vehicle to continue in passenger service with Midland Red until the company was split up in September 1981. It then passed to Midland Red (North) (as did the author!) where it mostly ran from Ludlow garage. After sale it provided transport for a Scout group in the Telford area for some years before being bought for restoration by a private owner. In its final years with Midland Red it carried NBC's poppy red bus livery together with the 'Hotspur' local identity name used for services in the Shrewsbury and Ludlow areas. This view shows it at the Shire Hall in Hereford, picking up passengers for Leominster on service 292. (*Malcolm Keeley*)

The Leamington-area services, including those run from the old Stratford Blue Kineton garage (not covered by the Avonbus scheme), were surveyed during November 1977. It took until May 1980 to launch a new network, under the unimaginative 'Leamington & Warwick' banner (a sharp contrast to some of the bizarre local identity names which were dreamed up, such as 'Wendaway' for the Evesham operations). The Leamington & Warwick scheme spelled the end for Kineton garage, which was closed after operation on Saturday 30 May. Latterly Kineton had only had six buses and closure had seemed inevitable. According to Midland Red's press release, 'as social changes have reduced the need for many buses, so the importance of Kineton garage has got less ... there just aren't enough passengers in the area to keep the garage open any longer'. Tribute was paid to the staff of eight drivers and an inspector, supported by cleaners and mechanics. Some transferred to other garages but others left, and a tradition which stretched back to Charles Hunt's Kineton Green Bus Service was lost. Amongst those transferring to Leamington was Vic Kinnin, who was awarded the British Empire Medal in 1985 in recognition of forty years' accident-free driving, thirty-five of them at Kineton.

The late 1970s were dominated by the MAP schemes which tried desperately to reverse the decline in patronage (and gave the author his first experience of work in the bus industry), but in 1981 it was announced that Midland Red was to be wound up and replaced by five smaller companies, one of which would only run coaches. The other four were Midland Red (East), (North), (South) and (West) Ltd, and took over from Sunday 6 September 1981.

Midland Red (South) Ltd was the smallest, with 163 vehicles operating from garages at Banbury, Leamington, Nuneaton, Rugby (the head office) and Stratford.

Neither of the surviving Stratford Blue buses passed to the new owners of Stratford garage. No.2036 (XNX136H), which had been converted for one-man-operation in 1977, initially in dual-purpose livery, went to Midland Red (North). It lasted until December 1982, latterly at Ludlow garage in bus livery. No.2059 (HAC628D) had ended its passenger-carrying days in May 1978 but was converted into a driver training bus and in this capacity it went to Midland Red (West), lasting another ten years. Fortunately both these vehicles have been rescued and restored as reminders of the last years of Stratford Blue.

Midland Red (South) (MR(S)) also acquired the Leamington & Warwick Transport Co., which although it had operated its last bus forty-four years earlier was still credited with the receipts from the operation of its monopoly routes, and this remained the case until 1986.

Little change was evident at first, although the legal address shown on Midland Red (South) buses was that of the Northampton-based United Counties Omnibus Co., which provided some administrative support. By 1986 MR(S) had gained more autonomy and the legal address was altered to Railway Terrace, Rugby.

From early 1982 the word 'South' was added to the Midland Red fleetname on the buses, but standard NBC poppy red was retained. The following year it was announced that the local

From September 1981 operations from Stratford garage were carried out by Midland Red (South) Ltd, which started out with just eighteen double-deckers, all Daimler Fleetlines. At first there was little visible difference and NBC poppy red livery was retained, as seen here on 'D13' No.6197 (UHA197H), but the various local identity names, including 'Avonbus', were dropped. It is seen here at the Red Lion, one-man-operated, on service 218 to Evesham. Several Fleetlines ran from Kineton and Stratford in Midland Red days, including examples of the earlier single-door 'D11' and 'D12' classes. No.6197 put in an impressive twenty years' service between September 1969, when it was new to Leamington garage, and June 1989 when it was withdrawn from use at Stratford. (*Author's collection*)

identity names, including Avonbus, would be phased out as buses were repainted or withdrawn. A new livery was developed for dual-purpose vehicles from 1984, mostly white but with a broad poppy red band and interlocking horizontal stripes in a darker red. This complicated style was completed by black skirt panels and was carried by Leopard single-deckers and Olympian double-deckers at Stratford garage.

By late 1985 Stratford Blue had been gone for almost fifteen years, so many people were taken aback when a second-hand Leopard with Willowbrook 'Spacecar' body appeared in a two-tone blue version of the new dual-purpose livery, with bold Stratford Blue fleetnames. Naturally No.64 (SAD127R) was placed in service at Stratford, where it caused a flurry of nostalgia, even if the livery was nothing like the original. In truth the only similarity was the use of a certain amount of blue paint, and even that was not the right shade! Although used as a coach by previous owners National Travel and later the revived Black & White Motorways of Cheltenham, No.64 was used as a one-man bus at Stratford. Its usual duties were the X20 and some of the former Stratford Blue rural services, particularly to Evesham and Shipston.

An interesting development for the summer of 1986 was the 'Castles Tour', an open-top tourist service linking Stratford with Kenilworth and Warwick and operated in conjunction with Guide Friday Ltd. The MR(S) vehicle was a Daimler Fleetline – one of two converted

Midland Red (South) No.961 (B961ODU) was one of two coach-seated Leyland Olympians delivered in October 1984, the first double-deckers to carry the new dual-purpose livery of white with poppy red, maroon and black. It is shown here at Gloucester Green, Oxford, at the end of a three-hour journey from Birmingham via Stratford on service X50. The through service between Birmingham and Oxford had begun in 1973, often using standard service buses, although the dual-purpose Olympians and earlier Leyland Leopard single-deckers were much more suitable. In the background are a City of Oxford Bristol VR, in standard NBC poppy red, and a pair of Heyfordian Travel coaches. (*Author's collection*)

in 1985 – and was based at Stratford garage. Guide Friday was a Stratford-based company which had been set up by Roger Thompson in 1975. He began with a 20-seat Bedford coach, but in 1978 he acquired a Leyland Titan from Leicester City Transport and had it converted to open-top for the Stratford town tour. This was a great success and Guide Friday went on to introduce similar services in many other tourist centres. For several years they also operated the 'Shakespeare Connection' between Stratford and Coventry Station, part of an integrated coach/rail service between Stratford and London Euston. However, while Guide Friday went from strength to strength with their open-top tours, earning Mr Thompson an OBE for services to tourism, Midland Red (South) lost interest and after a few short seasons the open-toppers were sold. Guide Friday later used one of them in the Lake District.

By now Margaret Thatcher's Conservative government had passed the 1985 Transport Act, which deregulated the bus service market. From 26 October 1986 any licensed bus or coach operator would be able to run whatever bus services it wished, provided that six weeks' notice was given. If a local authority felt a need to supplement these 'commercial' services the Act required this to be done by competitive tendering, offering operators a second way to enter the market.

Like many established operators Midland Red (South) was initially fearful of competitive attacks. To ward these off various strategies were adopted and in January 1986 a new company

Midland Red (South) No.52 (XTF819L) carried a unique yellow and black 'Cotswold Link' livery for the services between Stratford and Cheltenham/Gloucester which ran between 1983 and 1986. It was a 1973 Leopard with Duple Dominant body, acquired ten years later from National Travel (West), and had here found its way to Oxford on the X50. The X50 operated between Stratford and Oxford continuously from 1973 until 2001, but in many different forms, the original joint operation with City of Oxford Motor Services lasting only until 1986. In 1990 Midland Red (South) also pulled out and the service was then reduced to Stratford – Oxford only and maintained under contract to the local authorities successively by Burman Travel of Tamworth, City of Oxford and then Midland Red (South) again. In April 1998 it was extended back to Birmingham and increased to hourly as a Stagecoach Express service, but for the final two years it reverted to running Stratford – Oxford only, as a Stagecoach Oxford operation. (*Author's collection*)

Less than a year after Stratford Blue was taken over in January 1971, the blue buses and the familiar name were gone. Fourteen years then elapsed before nostalgia demanded a return of the old name, initially only on Midland Red (South)'s No.64 (SAD127R), an eight-year-old former National Travel Leyland Leopard with Willowbrook 'Spacecar' body. At Stratford it was used as a service bus, painted in a unique two-tone blue version of the contemporary dual-purpose livery. This view shows it at the Red Lion after a run from Birmingham on the X20. (*Author's collection*)

was registered with the title Stratford-upon-Avon Blue Motors Ltd (the original company had been dissolved in 1977), in order to prevent anyone else from capitalising on the name.

As MR(S) formulated its strategy for deregulation, the Red Lion Bus Station, which had been in continuous use for well over fifty years, was vacated. This happened from late April/early May 1986, and all bus services were moved to the stops on either side of Bridge Street and one on Guild Street, close to the garage but hardly convenient for the majority of passengers. The Guild Street stop was short-lived and by 1987 Wood Street had become the major terminal point for services leaving Stratford via Clopton Bridge or Warwick Road.

In the event the new Stratford Blue company was never used, but MR(S) had some imaginative plans for deregulation including a 'Stratford Blue' minibus network. This began on 'D-Day', 26 October, replacing the previous town services, which had changed little from the 'Avonbus' network of 1977. The services used five brand-new Freight Rover Sherpa 16-seaters (Nos 468-472; D468-472CKV) painted in a vibrant 'electric blue' livery with darker blue 'Stratford Blue' fleetnames on a white stripe above the windows. After six months they were joined by the identical No.474 (D474CKV) which had initially run in plain white. Minibuses were appearing in vast numbers up and down the country at this time, following the success of NBC's first large-scale experiment in Exeter, and they were generally greeted by a mixture of bemusement and derision from passengers. There was no disguising the fact that they were basically vans fitted with windows, seats and a bus-type folding door, so they were often referred to as 'bread vans'. Despite their faults they were nippy and manoeuvrable, and allowed services to operate along suburban roads which had never previously seen buses.

Under the privatisation programme of the late 1980s Midland Red (South) was acquired by Western Travel in December 1987, and in 1988 a new livery was introduced. This used the same poppy red as before, but with grey lower panels and larger areas of white. This is illustrated by Leyland Olympian No.907 (A547HAC), at Pool Meadow, Coventry, at the start of a service X18 journey to Stratford via Kenilworth, Leamington, Warwick and Wellesbourne. The photograph was taken on 22 August 1993. (*Author*)

They were also cheap to run and – perhaps the greatest attraction – offered scope to negotiate a lower rate of pay for drivers, who were now selected for their ability to deal with passengers rather than their proficiency at driving large vehicles. All of this encouraged a 'cheap and cheerful' atmosphere. The new buses must have brought a wry smile to the face of many older residents who could recall the first 'Stratford Blues' in the late 1920s, and comparisons with Grail and Joiner's 14-seater Chevrolets running round in an unregulated environment were inevitable. Could this really be sixty years of progress?

The new services only ran on Mondays to Saturdays and were numbered S1 (West Green Drive) and S2 (Justins Avenue), each advertised as running about every nine minutes during the day and every twenty minutes in the evening. The sixth minibus was needed from 27 April 1987 when new half-hourly services S3 (Bridgetown) and S4 (Old Town) started. Further expansion came on 5 December with the S5 to Cherry Orchard, S6 to Joseph Way and S7 to Clopton Road. These were less frequent; the S6 ran hourly and the S5 and S7 each three times a day. At the same time the S3 was extended to Tiddington and increased to every twenty minutes, but the S4 dropped to hourly. This represented the high point of the minibus network, although in July 1989 the S1 was extended to include Shottery.

The 1985 Act also required the break-up and privatisation of the National Bus Company and in December 1987 Midland Red (South) was sold to Western Travel Ltd, who had already bought the Cheltenham & Gloucester Omnibus Co. from the NBC. The new owners introduced a revised livery for MR(S) during the second half of 1988, keeping a poppy red base but now with white and grey relief. A new fleetname and logo was also introduced, giving almost equal prominence to 'Midland' and 'Red', with 'south' appearing below in smaller lower-case lettering.

In October 1989 MR(S) made several cuts to the Stratford Blue minibus network and the rural services. In some cases the County Council stepped in to secure replacements and Anthony's Coaches of Stratford and Smiths (Shenington) Ltd (who traded as Smiths of Tysoe but were actually based at Alcester!) both had some success. MR(S) had mixed fortunes with competitive tendering, and early successes allowed a small outstation to be opened at Kineton in October 1987. This closed again in 1990 when David Grasby of Oxhill won several contracts, and for the next few years most services around Kineton were run by his distinctive bright yellow coaches. Mr Grasby had run coaches since 1958 but his first move into bus operation came when Reg Rouse retired in December 1972.

In October 1988 No.64, which had started the Stratford Blue renaissance, was taken out of service, leaving just the minibuses to carry the name. However, in the spring of 1990 Western Travel introduced a Stratford Blue version of the contemporary MR(S) livery, using a mid-blue instead of poppy red and with 'Stratford Blue' shown in the same style as 'Midland Red'. Leyland Olympian double-decker No.964 (C964XVC) appeared first, carrying a large swan logo on each side and the name *Roxanne* (apparently after one of the swans nesting on the Avon at the time). A Leopard coach (No.4; 230 HUE, originally BVP786V) and a Leyland National (584; NOE584R) soon followed, with the names *Rachel* and *Rosemary*. The swan was originally intended to form part of the livery, but was dropped after the Olympian.

The revival of Stratford Blue was part of a strategy to win back passengers and in June 1990 there was a press launch to help get the message across. Timetables appeared in the local free papers with a variety of special fare offers. The new Stratford Blue network was much different from the original, consisting of three local services (to West Green Drive/Shottery, Justins Avenue and Bridgetown/Tiddington), interurban routes to Birmingham, Coventry and Leamington, and rural routes to Shipston (service 50), Alcester (212), Broad Marston (215), Bearley (217), Evesham (218) and Studley and Redditch (228). Many traditional Stratford Blue destinations were not on the new network, including the whole of the Kineton area and Banbury, although by way of compensation Coventry and Redditch did feature.

The intention now was to extend the new image to all Stratford garage buses, but the next bus to be treated, in December, was quite a surprise. No.955 (OJD136R) was a 1976 Leyland Fleetline double-decker bought from the Staffordshire independent operator Stevensons of Uttoxeter. It had started life as a member of London Transport's ill-fated 'DMS' class, passing to Stevensons after only six years in London. This type of second-hand purchase seemed like a throwback to pre-war Stratford Blue buying policies and emphasised that bus operation in the deregulated era would not attract the level of investment it had seen in the post-war boom years.

During 1991 the new Stratford Blue fleet was enlarged with another three repainted Olympians (Nos 961-963; B961ODU and C962/963XVC) and six brand new Mercedes-Benz 811Ds (Nos 407-412; J407-412PRW). These had 33-seat bodies built in Northern Ireland by Wrights of Ballymena and were somewhat optimistically described by the company as 'luxury midicoaches'. They replaced full-size buses on a variety of duties, including turns on the X20 Birmingham service.

Other buses to gain the new livery included Leyland National No.504 (JOX504P), now fitted with a wheelchair lift to operate Warwickshire County Council 'Flexibus' services, Olympian No.905 (A545HAC) and a second former London Transport and Stevensons Fleetline (No.953; OJD241R).

The new generation of Stratford Blue buses had become a familiar sight but were never to be seen in two of the most familiar locations for the original fleet. The Red Lion Bus Station, which closed in 1986, had by now been transformed into the pub's beer garden and children's playground, and in July 1990 it was the turn of the Warwick Road garage, which was closed and replaced by premises at Avenue Farm Industrial Estate, off Birmingham Road. The old garage was sold, parts of it later finding use with a tyre company and a tool hire business.

From May 1992 the Stratford local services were 'rebranded' as the 'Avon Shuttle', and in September services 1 and 2 (previously S1 and S2) were combined into a single un-numbered service. This ran every twelve minutes and covered West Green Drive, Shottery, Justins Avenue and the recently opened Maybird Centre (Bridgetown and Tiddington had been dropped from the town service network in November 1991). Five minibuses were given a white and blue livery and the swan logo was resurrected and applied over the side windows. Stratford Blue fleetnames were carried, along with a route diagram and frequency details in English, French, German and Japanese! There was also a multilingual pocket timetable, targeted mainly at visitors to Anne Hathaway's Cottage. The minibuses concerned were Nos 376/378-380/382 (C706/709-711/719FKE), Ford Transit 16-seaters acquired from the East Kent company in Canterbury to replace the less reliable Sherpas.

The 1990 relaunch of Stratford Blue resulted in several different types of bus receiving the new livery, a direct equivalent of the poppy red version used at Midland Red (South)'s other garages. The first double-decker treated was Olympian No.964 (C964XVC), and the second was this well-travelled second-hand acquisition, No.955 (OJD136R), which had previously carried the red livery of London Transport and the yellow of Stevensons of Uttoxeter. In an attempt to give the buses a touch of individuality some were given names, No.955 becoming *Josephine*. It is seen here on 29 June 1994 making the right turn out of Rother Street into Wood Street, on a mid-day journey from Evesham on service 218. This view makes a fascinating comparison with the 1950s photograph of Stratford Blue Titan No.39 at the same location on page 122. (*Author*)

The summer of 1991 saw the delivery of six Mercedes midibuses, the only brand new vehicles to carry the new livery. They were 33-seaters (only one seat less than the PS1 Tigers of 1948/1949, which were very much full-size buses at the time) and found use on a wide variety of services although the Stratford 'locals' were left to the 16-seat Sherpas and Transits. An unexpected use was on Coventry city service 7 to Sewall Highway, on which Midland Red (South) operated certain journeys under contract to West Midlands PTE. Prior to deregulation the city services had been the sole preserve of the PTE, and before that the city's own transport department. No.411 (J411PRW) is seen here at Pool Meadow, before setting out for Sewall Highway on 6 October 1991. (*Author*)

By 1991 the revival of Stratford Blue was in full swing and another three Olympians with coach seats were repainted blue. These included *Jean* (No.963; C963 XVC), here seen passing the entrance to the Jephson Gardens in Leamington while working the X16 Coventry – Stratford service on 8 February 1992. Nostalgia was big business in the 1980s and 1990s and, just as Midland Red (South) 'reinvented' Stratford Blue, so too Whitbread revived the Flowers name for a number of their beers and promoted it widely for the first time since the early 1960s. Unfortunately perhaps, the combination of 1990s Stratford Blue livery and advertising for Flowers' Original or IPA was not to be seen. (*Author*)

223

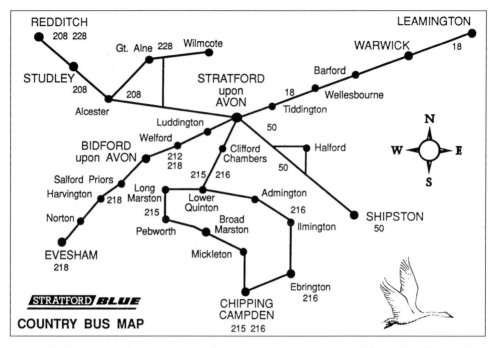

REDDITCH
208 228

Gt. Alne 228  Wilmcote

STUDLEY
208        208

Alcester

Luddington
Welford

BIDFORD
upon AVON      212
                218

Salford Priors
Harvington    218  Long
                    Marston
Norton              215

Pebworth

EVESHAM
218

STRATFORD *BLUE*
COUNTRY BUS MAP

STRATFORD
upon
AVON

Tiddington

50

Clifford
Chambers
                50
215  216

Lower
Quinton

Broad
Marston

Mickleton

Admington

216

Ilmington

Ebrington
216

CHIPPING
CAMPDEN
215 216

LEAMINGTON

WARWICK       18

Barford

18  Wellesbourne

Halford

SHIPSTON
50

N
W — E
S

The Stratford Blue country bus map, 1990s style, reproduced from a 1992 timetable booklet. The swan logo had been intended to form part of the livery, but only appeared on the first Olympian. This was a much smaller network than the original company had operated, without Cheltenham or any of the Kineton-area services. However, as well as the services shown, the X16 to Coventry and X20 to Birmingham were also run by Stratford Blue vehicles. The only 'gains' were Redditch and Studley, and Ebrington, none of which was served by the original Stratford Blue.

Another vehicle repainted was No.91 (CDG213Y), a Leyland Tiger with a Plaxton coach body transferred from the Cheltenham & Gloucester Omnibus Co. in 1991, which received an all-over blue livery with bold 'Stratford Blue Coaches' fleetnames in September 1992 and was used on local bus duties when not needed as a coach.

In 1993 Midland Red (the 'South' had been dropped again from the trading name in 1992) acquired several unfamiliar Bristol VR double-deckers and put them into service in the colours of their previous owners. These included No.940 (PEU511R) in yellow and green Badgerline livery and No.944 (HUD475S) in the red, white and black of City of Oxford, both of which looked rather odd with Stratford Blue fleetnames! They also looked somewhat shabby and were not worthy recipients of the name, but before they could be repainted blue – if that was the intention – the company changed hands again.

The new owners were Stagecoach Holdings plc, at the time Britain's largest private sector bus group, who bought Western Travel in December 1993. Stagecoach had operating subsidiaries throughout the UK and beyond, but its origins went back little further than 1980 when it was a small Perth-based coach operator. Expansion was rapid, especially after the National Bus subsidiaries came onto the market in the late 1980s, and the Stagecoach livery of orange, red and blue stripes on a white background was already familiar in many parts of the country.

This was swiftly adopted for the former Western Travel fleets, removing the prospect of further buses in Stratford Blue colours. Developments under the new régime were slow at first, but more Bristol VRs were drafted into Stratford, this time from other group companies and already wearing Stagecoach stripes, and other buses started to lose Stratford Blue colours in favour of the corporate scheme. Initially no fleetname was carried pending a review of corporate styles, but during 1994 'Stagecoach Midland Red' and 'Stagecoach Stratford Blue' started to appear on the buses, sometimes only as window vinyls. Stagecoach Stratford Blue proved to be very short-lived as it was quickly decided that all buses should carry the Midland Red title, and this seemed to spell the end for the Stratford Blue revival. By 1996 the blue, grey and white livery was extinct again apart from 'Flexibus' Leyland National No.504, but even this now carried the Midland Red name rather than Stratford Blue.

As a small compensation the Avon Shuttle town service was retitled the 'Stratford Blue Shuttle' in July 1995, and five brand-new Mercedes 25-seaters soon replaced the Ford Transits (the former East Kent buses had been replaced in the meantime by similar vehicles from the Cheltenham & Gloucester, which were not in Avon Shuttle livery). The Mercedes (Nos 360–364; N360-364AVV) carried standard Stagecoach livery but with 'Stratford Blue Shuttle' on the sides and across the top of the windscreens, keeping the name alive in a small way.

Western Travel's ownership of Midland Red (South) ended in 1993. One of their last acts was to draft in several ageing Bristol VRs, and more appeared after Stagecoach acquired the company. The latter included former East Midland bus No.949 (DWF189V), which arrived already in Stagecoach livery and gained a 'Stagecoach Stratford Blue' vinyl in its windscreen. This June 1994 view shows it passing the American Fountain in Stratford, at the end of the 1.10 p.m. journey from Evesham on service 218. (*Author*)

Under Stagecoach ownership the Stratford Blue revival was abruptly halted, and No.91 (CDG213Y) was amongst the first vehicles to lose its blue livery in favour of the Stagecoach livery of white with orange, red and blue stripes. By now it was carrying the 'retro' Warwickshire registration 420GAC, reminiscent of Stratford Blue's Alpine Continental coach, 436GAC. Initially Stagecoach seemed undecided on fleetnames and here No.91 shows only the small 'Stagecoach Stratford Blue' name in its windscreen. This view in Wood Street on 7 June 1995 shows it after operating from Redditch on service 228. (*Author*)

The new ownership is revealed by a discreet 'Stagecoach Stratford Blue' sticker in the windscreen of No.963 (C963XVC), one of five Leyland Olympians to carry Stratford Blue livery. It is nearing the top of Bridge Street after a journey from Coventry on service X16 on 6 June 1995. (*Author*)

No.504 (JOX504P) was the second Leyland National to receive Stratford Blue colours and was used on Warwickshire County Council's network of 'Flexibus' services, with a wheelchair lift for less mobile passengers. It was the last survivor in the Western Travel version of Stratford Blue livery, but finished its days with Midland Red fleetnames. This view shows it parked in the approach to the old Leamington Bus Station on 7 March 1997, after operating a Flexibus service. (*Author*)

After the 1995 takeover of Grasby's services, Stagecoach Midland Red resumed a greater presence on the former Stratford Blue services in the Kineton area. A typical vehicle was this Leyland National 2 (No.818; BVP818V) delivered to Midland Red in 1980 and seen at Kineton Church on 31 January 1998. Service 274 ran to Leamington via Gaydon, Moreton Morrell and Bishops Tachbrook, combining elements of the old Stratford Blue 32 and 33 services. (*Author*)

Some Midland Red (South) Leyland Nationals had very long lives, helped by having their original engines replaced by DAF units. No.628 (PUK628R) was new in April 1977, the month before the X20 replaced the long-standing 150 service from Stratford to Birmingham. Almost twenty-one years later, on 31 January 1998, it is seen at Bridge Street at the start of yet another trip along the Birmingham Road – by now demoted to the less important-sounding A3400. This length of service was never expected in Stratford Blue days! (*Author*)

Stagecoach consolidated their presence in the area in September 1995 by acquiring David Grasby's services, most of which were centred on Kineton and were successors to the old Kineton garage routes. For a very short time the title 'Stagecoach David R. Grasby' was used, but 'Stagecoach Midland Red' soon appeared instead.

The very limited use of the Stratford Blue title continued until April 1998 when Stagecoach revised its Stratford-based services again, reversing the trend of many years by a cautious expansion, especially towards the Cotswolds. The town services now gained numbers again (1 and 2 for Shottery and 3 for Justins Avenue), but the 'Stratford Blue Shuttle' title was dropped and all services were now operated under the Stagecoach Midland Red banner. Most of the other Stratford garage services were renumbered into the 21–28 range in place of the 200-series numbers which had survived from the 'Avonbus' era.

This officially marked the end of a thirteen-year revival for Stratford Blue, during which time many more blue buses had travelled the roads familiar to their predecessors, but in practice the name lingered on as the 'Shuttle' lettering remained *in situ* on at least some of the minibuses used on the town services.

Also in April 1998 a new X50 Stagecoach Express service was introduced between Birmingham, Stratford and Oxford, operating hourly seven days a week. This ambitious new service replaced the X20 between Stratford and Birmingham, the 50 to Shipston and the previous three-times-a-day X50 between Stratford and Oxford. Stratford garage needed six coaches for the service.

The decision to buck the trend and improve the services around Stratford was laudable but it created a need for more drivers at an extremely difficult time for recruitment. Very soon the company was in the embarrassing position of being unable to cover all scheduled journeys and by July the situation was so desperate that drivers were borrowed from Stagecoach depots as far away as Morecambe to work the X50! The problem was not only with drivers, as the demanding timetable proved too much for some of the coaches (not-so-new Leyland Tigers), which often had to be replaced by elderly and totally unsuitable double-deckers.

Perhaps the expansion was a final attempt to reverse the declining fortunes of Stratford garage, but unfortunately it only seemed to accelerate them and in a dramatic about-turn a major reduction of services was announced in November 1998, which would leave just a few core services and would culminate in the complete closure of the garage by April 1999. Coming so soon after the expansion in the spring the announcement met with shock from the staff and local bus users alike, but Stagecoach stuck to its decision.

The plan was swiftly put into effect and the first phase took effect from 31 December, when services 21 (Bourton-on-the-Water via Moreton-in-Marsh), 24 (Bearley/Snitterfield) and 27 (Broad Marston/Pebworth) ran for the last time. On the same date the X50 Stagecoach Express was withdrawn and the previous pattern with the X20 running to Birmingham and the 50 to Shipston reinstated (the Stratford – Oxford leg of the X50 passed to Stagecoach Oxford). The next phase was on 30 January 1999, when the town services in

An expansion of Stagecoach Midland Red services around Stratford took place in April 1998, when many services were also renumbered into a new series, such as the 25 to Alcester via Wilmcote. By this time Stagecoach had brought in many of their standard Volvo single-deckers with Alexander bodywork, including No.230 (P558ESA), which had first operated for one of the group's Scottish fleets. This view shows it picking up in Wood Street on 8 May 1999 while a traction engine and trailers pass the other way – a sight more common during the early years of Stratford Blue. (*Author*)

After 1995 the Stratford Blue title was extinct except for the 'Shuttle' branding used for the town services. This was carried by five Mercedes minibuses delivered in Stagecoach livery in 1995, although the name was officially dropped with the service changes of April 1998. Despite that, No.361 (N361AVV) carried it right to the end of town service operation by Stagecoach, and is seen here picking up for Shottery on the penultimate day, 29 January 1999. Beside it in Bridge Street is a Volvo on service X20 to Birmingham, showing the style of Stagecoach fleetname used in Scotland, from where the bus had recently been transferred. (*Author*)

Stratford finished, and on 13 February the Kineton-area services, many of which had been regained with the acquisition of Grasby's business, ceased. The final phase was on Good Friday, 2 April, when services 22 to Broadway and 23 to Brailes were axed.

The Avenue Farm garage was then closed, seventy-two years and a day after Stratford-on-Avon Motor Services had started its first service, and a direct link with Grail and Joiner's pioneering initiative was lost. Stagecoach Midland Red continued to run several main-road services centred on Stratford, principally those to Birmingham (X20), Coventry (X16/X18), Shipston (50), Evesham (28) and Studley and Redditch (25/26), but these were now operated from Leamington garage.

Stagecoach could no longer be seen as the town's local bus operator, and the way was clear for others to step in.

# 12

# The Name Lives On
# 1999-2003

Many of the services which disappeared as Stagecoach Midland Red wound down its Stratford operations were far too important to disappear altogether, and Warwickshire County Council secured replacements from other operators – potentially a difficult task given Stagecoach's previous near monopoly in the area. However two local operators, Guide Friday and Newmark Coaches, seized the opportunity to move into bus service work for the first time.

Newmark Coaches (Expertpoint Ltd) was owned by Alan Newland, Midland Red (South)'s local manager at Stratford during the Western Travel era and the man behind the reinvention of Stratford Blue in 1990. Now he decided to do it again, but with his own company. His bids for services 21 (now only to Moreton-in-Marsh), 24 (Bearley and Snitterfield) and 27 (Pebworth and Broad Marston) were successful, and Newmark took them over from 2 January 1999, followed by the majority of the Kineton area services in February and service 22 to Moreton-in-Marsh at the beginning of April. They also began two town services from the end of January.

Newmark had little time to prepare for their move into bus operation and started off with a motley selection of minibuses and ageing coaches, mostly in previous owners' liveries and without fleetnames. Only two vehicles were needed from the beginning of January but by April the requirement had risen to at least ten, on top of the vehicles used for coach work and other commitments. Newmark were serious about becoming Stratford's new local operator, and clearly needed some far more suitable vehicles so leases were was arranged for three Mercedes Vario minibuses (S716/717KNV and T455HNV) and four low-floor Dennis Dart single-deckers (S719-722KNV), all with Marshall bodies. These were in the leasing company's plain white but before long they all gained a blue 'Stratford Blue – A Newmark Company' fleetname. Use of the Stratford Blue name apparently attracted no objection from Stagecoach, perhaps a little surprising given that they were the direct successors to the original company and had used the title so recently themselves.

The town services were a better financial proposition than the rural services, and Newmark felt able to run these without recourse to subsidy. However they had not reckoned on Guide Friday deciding to do the same! This resulted in head-on competition between the two operators, finally bringing a 'bus war' to Stratford more than twelve years after deregulation had introduced the possibility. Both companies operated to Justins Avenue and West Green Drive, although they each had their own route pattern; Guide Friday ran a half-hourly service which combined the two destinations, whereas Newmark had separate services, both running at twenty-minute intervals (the 1 to Justins Avenue and the 2 to Shottery and West Green Drive). Neither operator ran in the evening or on Sundays, but nor had Stagecoach before them. Guide Friday needed two buses, and their service began on Saturday 30 January, running alongside Midland Red on their last day, while Newmark's three-bus operation followed on the Monday.

Guide Friday had been operating from Stratford for twenty-four years and whilst their open-top tour business had now expanded as far as Berlin, Paris and Seville, they had never before catered for the daily needs of people in their home town. For the town services four second-hand MCW Metrorider minibuses were bought from the Wilts & Dorset bus company and painted in the familiar dark green and cream livery with a diagrammatic map of the route on the side and clear 'Town Bus' labelling. Guide Friday's first success with a County Council contract was with service 23 to Ilmington and Brailes, which started in April and was later branded 'The Stour Valley Bus', using another specially-liveried Metrorider.

Competition on the town services lasted seven months. Alan Newland had predicted that there was not enough business to support two operators and experience proved him right. Guide Friday, whose vehicles had always looked the more professional, won the battle and Newmark withdrew gracefully after Friday 3 September, to concentrate on the rural contracts and a new hourly service to Alveston. This mirrored one of the very first Stratford-on-Avon Motor Services destinations of 1927, but this time the service was short-lived.

Stagecoach's withdrawal from Stratford gave Newmark Coaches the opportunity to launch another reincarnation of Stratford Blue, and in February 1999 they took over the Kineton-area services. A new pattern of operation included service 77, which ran from Stratford to Leamington via Kineton, and Newmark's Marshall-bodied Dennis Dart S721KNV is seen on the service in Bridge Street on 14 August 1999, complete with Stratford Blue fleetnames. (*Author*)

The only new vehicles in Newmark's Stratford Blue fleet were leased, and operated in plain white; three Mercedes minibuses (S716/717KNV and T455HNV) and four Dennis Darts (S719-722KNV). At least the fleetname ('Stratford Blue – A Newmark Company') was in blue! Both types had bodies by Marshall of Cambridge, who had supplied bodywork to the original Stratford Blue during the 1960s. S716KNV is shown here in Wood Street, about to operate service 22 to Moreton-in-Marsh, on 14 August 1999. The 22 was only introduced by Stagecoach in April 1998, but lasted to the very end of Stratford garage, passing to Newmark after the final closure on 2 April 1999. (*Author*)

Like Newmark Coaches, Guide Friday saw Stagecoach's withdrawal from their base in Stratford as the ideal opportunity to move into bus service work. Their second-hand MCW Metroriders bought from Wilts & Dorset included E54HFE, which had originally run for Grimsby Cleethorpes Transport. They were neatly repainted and this view shows the detailed route plan carried on the sides as part of the livery. The bus is about to leave Bridge Street for Justins Avenue on 19 February 2000. (*Author*)

Fears of competition on deregulation in 1986 had come to nothing, and the 1999 'bus war' between Guide Friday and Newmark was the first aggressive bus competition which Stratford had seen in seventy years. It lasted seven months, from February to September. On 14 August the competition is illustrated in Bridge Street by Guide Friday Metrorider F351URU and Newmark's Mercedes T455HNV, both heading for West Green Drive although the Newmark bus is just showing 'Town Service' on its blind. (*Author*)

Only Newmark had served Shottery, but from 4 September Guide Friday amended their town service to provide peak-hour journeys to and from the village. As an off-peak service could not be provided without affecting the frequency or needing an extra bus, an unusual solution was tried; Shottery residents were offered a special season ticket which was valid to and from the town centre on the Stratford Tour buses, but they were requested to travel downstairs and not to interrupt the guide's commentary! The journey into town via its rather roundabout route took half an hour, but the return journey was a more acceptable twelve minutes. Only eight-week passes were available which did nothing to help infrequent passengers, or visitors, and later the facility was withdrawn, as were most of the peak-hour buses.

In addition to the leased vehicles Newmark's Stratford Blue fleet was expanded with four elderly Leyland National 2s which were painted in a bold blue and white livery with the fleetname in large white capital letters, creating a recognisable company image which was later applied to at least one of the Dennis Darts. Other vehicles, including more National 2s, coaches and minibuses, were also acquired but did not receive Stratford Blue livery. There were even some Nationals in Stagecoach colours, causing much confusion among the Stagecoach Midland Red vehicles in Stratford.

The Stagecoach withdrawal also gave opportunities to other operators, perhaps most significantly to Travel West Midlands, the National Express subsidiary whose ancestry stretched back through the days of West Midlands PTE to Birmingham City Transport. Although Stagecoach kept the X20 to Birmingham on weekdays they withdrew the Sunday service.

Newmark initially replaced this under a short-term contract but TWM took over from May 1999, using modern double-deckers. Other operators on the X20 were Caves of Solihull and Pete's Travel of West Bromwich, who later replaced TWM on the Sunday service. Despite the emergence of these other operators Stagecoach Midland Red retained a sufficient number of services to remain the majority operator from Stratford.

Barely eighteen months after the launch of Newmark's Stratford Blue it became clear that there were financial problems, and in June 2000 the recently formed Status Group announced that it had acquired the company, with Alan Newland staying on as manager. Status had bus operations dotted around the country, including in County Durham, Lancashire, London and Milton Keynes, and within days buses from each of these areas were to be seen on the Stratford services. Some were in the Status Group's yellow livery with 'Stratford Blue' labels in the windscreens, while others were in a miscellany of liveries, mainly those of previous owners. Amongst them was a minibus from a London subsidiary, Tellings Golden Miller, in a livery of white with blue and yellow stripes which was later adopted for the Stratford Blue fleet. Newmark's leased Dennis Darts and Mercedes swiftly disappeared, although at least some of the Nationals remained, still in the Newmark Stratford Blue livery.

The Status group began the services using the licence of another Status company in the West Midlands, Midland Choice Travel, but a new company was soon formed with the title

Guide Friday's dark green and cream open-top tour buses were a familiar sight in Stratford from 1978 to 2002, and from the late 1980s they became increasingly familiar in many other tourist spots in the UK and in Europe. The buses came from a wide variety of sources and some were quite old; USJ254 had begun life as a normal closed-top double-decker with Plymouth City Transport in 1962, then registered WJY759. It is shown on a wet day in August 2000, outside the Pen & Parchment (previously the Unicorn) at Bridgefoot. (*Author*)

Stratford Blue Travel Ltd. Unfortunately it got off to a bad start, without any of the hoped-for investment and with poor standards of reliability. Six months later things were no better so in December 2000 Warwickshire County Council terminated the contract for most of the Kineton-area services, including the 77 (Stratford – Kineton – Leamington) which needed three buses. One of the problems was said to be the number of breakdowns. Operation of service 77 passed to Stagecoach Midland Red, but on a reduced frequency. In the meantime the new Status version of Stratford Blue livery of white with blue and yellow stripes and a blue and yellow fleetname was applied to at least six vehicles, including three elderly coaches (GSU554, LIB6352 and WCA942W), two Leyland Nationals (TOF695S and MDS868V) and a former Brighton Borough Transport Leyland Lynx (G995VWV).

Earlier in the year Warwickshire County Council took the unusual step of ordering four 'state-of-the-art' Mercedes Citaro citybuses for use on new contracts which were due to start in September 2000, including for services around Stratford such as the 23 to Brailes and Whichford, and the 212 to Bidford and the Graftons, both of which were then operated by minibuses. Stratford Blue bid for the contracts, but without success, and the work went to Guide Friday and Johnson's of Henley, who each received a pair of Citaros in the county council's new green and yellow County Links livery.

The writing was on the wall for Stratford Blue Travel after the loss of the 77, and it soon emerged that on re-tendering, First Midland Red, as Midland Red (West) had become, had

An unexpected consequence of Stagecoach's withdrawal from Stratford was the appearance of Travel West Midlands on Sunday X20 journeys between Stratford and Birmingham. Their modern double-deckers included No.4020 (T420UON), a low-floor DAF with Optare bodywork built in the same Leeds factory as the body on Stratford Blue's first double-deck Leyland Tiger conversion (No.16; JUE353) in 1961. It is seen here at Bridge Street, picking up for the return journey to Birmingham, on 13 August 2000. (*Author*)

The Status Group acquired Stratford Blue in June 2000, bringing the prospect of increased investment to improve the image of the fleet. Early signs were not hopeful however, and Newmark's nearly-new vehicles disappeared, to be replaced by a hotchpotch of second-hand vehicles in a variety of liveries, including this scruffy 1981 Dennis Falcon supplied new to Leicester City Transport. Although it showed 'Stratford Blue' in the windscreen, the blue livery was pure coincidence; this was the livery of a recent owner, Islwyn Borough Transport! It is shown in Bridge Street on the infrequent and short-lived town service 4 to Flower Road, on 8 August 2000. (*Author*)

won the contract for services 21/22 (Stratford – Moreton-in-Marsh). This started in February 2001 and deprived the company of its other main routes at a time when they were also having difficulty finding alternative premises; they were operating from a yard off Birmingham Road which had only a short lease. The inevitable consequence was a complete shutdown; the bus services ran for the last time on Saturday 17 February and Stratford Blue Travel ceased trading a week later – an ignominious end to another brave attempt to recreate Stratford's own bus company, which had lasted barely eight months. Most of the remaining local routes were transferred to other companies, including Johnson's and Welcombe Garages, but a few were not replaced. Warwickshire County Council later reported that patronage had increased as a result of the more reliable service given by the replacement operators.

This seemed like the final curtain for Stratford Blue, but yet again the name was to re-emerge. Soon after the closure of the Stratford operation the Status Group sold what was left of Stratford Blue Travel to Peter Newman of Ensignbus, who also ran open-top tours under the City Sightseeing title. City Sightseeing already competed with Guide Friday at other locations and Newman had decided there was room to compete with Guide Friday's Stratford Tour. Ensignbus also had considerable experience of running bus services in London and the South East, although latterly most of these had been sold. On 25 May 2001 City Sightseeing Stratford-on-Avon was launched, with a fleet of bright red open-top double-deckers, contrasting with the sedate green and cream Guide Friday livery. Although the trading name was City Sightseeing and the vehicles were red, the legal ownership was shown as Stratford Blue Travel Ltd, of Purfleet, Essex!

Guide Friday responded to the competition by introducing a 'Boat and Bus' tour, but this achieved only limited success. After an aggressive battle for the tour bus traffic, not only in Stratford, City Sightseeing gained the upper hand and in June 2002 Ensignbus bought Guide Friday Ltd, acquiring the majority of its worldwide operation. This led to a swift rationalisation of the open-top tours in Stratford, much to the relief of local residents who had campaigned vigorously for a reduction in the number of buses. As part of the deal City Sightseeing took over Guide Friday's local bus services around Stratford – both the County Council contracts and the commercial town services. Clearly City Sightseeing was not a suitable name for this type of operation so a new name would have to be found; after much debate Stratford Blue was chosen yet again, despite the poor standards associated with the previous two revivals.

In July a bright and attractive new Stratford Blue livery was unveiled on a former Guide Friday Optare Metrorider which had originated with Reading Buses (No.613; H613NJB). Within weeks this was followed by several more vehicles, all finished to a high standard in a mid-blue and silver livery with prominent Stratford Blue fleetnames. These included similar ex-Reading Optare Metrorider No.611 (J611SJB) and a further Metrorider from Arriva

The 'County Links' Mercedes Citaros obtained by Warwickshire County Council for use on some of their contracted services are impressive-looking buses. Guide Friday's pair are seen here in Wood Street on 25 January 2002, the leading bus (X438KON) on service 212 to Bidford via Welford and X439KON on the 23 to Whichford via Ilmington. Both services cover villages served by the original Stratford Blue but which had latterly been operated with ageing minibuses; the improvement was dramatic. (*Author*)

After acquisition by Ensignbus a new mid-blue and silver livery was introduced for Stratford Blue, and former London MCW Metrobus No.129 (BYX129V) illustrates the double-deck version. It is shown outside the Guide Friday office on Rother Street on 6 September 2002, before taking up duty on the Town Centre Shuttle between the Bridgefoot coach park and Bridge Street, an operation introduced by Guide Friday. This was a market day and the stalls are visible in the background. (*Author*)

(No.653; K853RBB), and by September the trio of Metroriders had transformed the image of the town services. There were also four elderly MCW Metrobus double–deckers, used mostly on schools services but also on the former Guide Friday Town Centre Shuttle, which during the summer months carries visiting tourists between the Bridgefoot coach terminus and Bridge Street and must be one of the shortest bus services in Britain. By the end of January 2003 three other vehicles carried the blue and silver livery: a Dennis Dart (No.688; H588NOC) and a pair of Leyland Tigers, No.739 (WPH139Y), which had been rebodied in 1989 with an East Lancs bus body and No.767 (B167XBU), with a Plaxton coach body. The Tigers were also primarily for schools services, but saw occasional stints on the county council contracts in lieu of the Mercedes Citaros, while the Dart was bought to operate the town services alongside the Metroriders.

The blue buses carried the legal address of Stratford Blue Travel Ltd in Essex, but this was later amended to Avenue Farm, Stratford, after the company had negotiated a move from the former Newmark premises on Birmingham Road to the old Stagecoach garage, which had stood empty for a lengthy period. However Guide Friday Ltd continued to hold the Operator licence so the buses carried notices stating that they were operating on hire to Guide Friday. Later the legal lettering reverted to Guide Friday Ltd, trading as Stratford Blue, again using the Purfleet address!

Other than school contracts the small network of services operated by Stratford Blue in January 2003 was as follows, all except the commercial town service running under contract to the County Council and generally being maintained by the Mercedes Citaros in County Links livery:

| | |
|---|---|
| 23 | Stratford – Shipston – Brailes – Whichford |
| 25/26 | Stratford – Alcester |
| 28/29 | Stratford – Bidford – Evesham |
| 212 | Stratford – Welford – Bidford – Temple Grafton – Stratford |
| (no number) | Stratford town service (Justins Avenue and West Green Drive) |

None of these operates on Sundays, and on weekday evenings only one bus is in operation. This operates services 25/26/28/29, which Stagecoach operate commercially during the daytime.

Perhaps the final irony is that by January 2003 Stratford Blue had outlived Midland Red, the latter name now surviving only in company titles thanks to the marketing strategies of the major groups. On the brink of the Midland Red centenary in 2004, Midland Red

Thanks to the efforts of individuals who have rescued them for preservation, at least two Stratford Blue vehicles have been restored to something close to their original condition, including the last vehicle to enter service with the original Stratford Blue, No.36 (XNX136H). This picture shows it at the Aston Manor Transport Museum in Birmingham on 25 November 2001, operating a special service for museum visitors. An Atlantean, a PS1 Tiger and a PS2 Tiger double-deck rebuild are also held by museums with a view to ultimate restoration to their former glory. These survivors will ensure that an important piece of Stratford's transport heritage remains for future generations. (*Author*)

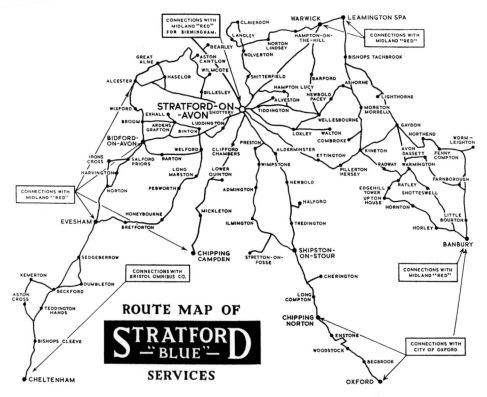

A Stratford Blue route map, as featured in an early 1960s edition of the timetable. Service 150 to Birmingham is not shown, perhaps because the Road Service Licence was still held by Midland Red.

(South) Ltd remains in Stagecoach ownership, running services from Stratford, but a corporate rethink during 2000 led to the local operations being rebranded as 'Stagecoach in Warwickshire' rather than Stagecoach Midland Red. At about the same time First decided to drop all local names completely, despite Midland Red (West) Ltd having been retitled to First Midland Red Buses Ltd in 1999, and the buses operating services 21/22 from Stratford to Moreton-in-Marsh now only use the 'First' title.

With its heavy dependence on county council contracts the present Stratford Blue company may have a less secure future than its celebrated predecessor, but given the experience of its present owners the current revival may prove to be the most promising yet.

Even so, it is obvious that time has moved on and that the heyday of Mr Agg's Stratford Blue of the late 1940s and early 1950s cannot possibly be recreated in an era when the vast majority of local residents never even contemplate travelling by bus.

# Appendix

# The Stratford Blue Fleet

This appendix gives details of the 180 or so vehicles which made up the Stratford Blue fleet over the years from 1927 to 1970. It also includes those which have carried various 'revival' liveries during the period from the 1980s to 2003.

The listing is split into forty-eight chronological groupings, which range from individual vehicles up to the thirty Leyland Tigers and Titans bought in 1948-1950.

Stratford Blue's vehicle-buying policy went through several distinct phases, partly reflecting the different periods in the company's history.

Grail and Joiner bought eleven new buses in 1927/1928 but followed these with vehicles bought on the second-hand market. Under Balfour Beatty ownership vehicles were either transferred from other group companies, or were acquired with the businesses of Frank Martin of Cheltenham in 1930 and Reliance of Bidford in 1932. After Midland Red bought the company in 1935 second-hand Tillings were initially the norm, with two large batches in the late 1930s: eighteen from North Western in 1936/1937 and sixteen from West Yorkshire in 1938. Surprisingly perhaps, none of the Kineton Green vehicles were acquired. There were also five second-hand Maudslays during this period.

A handful of vehicles arrived during the war (two second-hand acquisitions and three long-term loans), and to tide the company over in the immediate post-war period eight more second-hand Tillings were bought.

The late 1940s saw an end to the policy of buying second-hand and the previous fleet was replaced by thirty brand new Leylands between 1948 and 1950. Thereafter all fleet additions were new except for a Bedford coach acquired with the Warwickshire County Garage tours business, and all were Leylands apart from this and a Thames Trader coach. After replacement of the initial post-war fleet was completed in 1963 vehicles were added either in smaller batches or individually.

Over the years new and second-hand vehicles were roughly equal in number – about ninety of each – with all but one of the second-hand purchases being made between 1929 and 1946. All vehicles bought new carried Warwickshire registration letters; there were sixteen 'AC's, thirteen 'NX's and fifty-four 'UE's, but only seven 'WD's. A few second-hand vehicles from local operators also carried these marks, as did three of Midland Red (South)'s 'revival' fleet of the 1990s (420GAC, 230HUE and A545HAC). Because so many second-hand buses were bought, all but one of the Warwickshire marks were outnumbered in the fleet by the twenty-six Stockport-registered 'DB's operated between 1936 and 1950.

Since the disappearance of the original Stratford Blue company in 1971 there have been six distinct revivals of the name, as detailed under headings 43-48. Three of these were by Midland Red (South), each during a different period of ownership, while the other three

STRATFORD-UPON-AVON BLUE MOTORS LIMITED.

FLEET LIST - MAY 1966.

| FLEET NO. | REGISTRATION NO. | CHASSIS NO. | CHASSIS TYPE (LEYLAND) | BODY MAKE | BODY TYPE | SEATING CAPACITY | YEAR OF INTRODUCTION |
|---|---|---|---|---|---|---|---|
| 1 | 668 HNX | L.02477 | PD3A/1 | Willowbrook | D/D | 73 | 1963 |
| 2 | 669 HNX | L.02478 | " | " | " | 73 | 1963 |
| 3 | 670 HNX | L.02479 | " | " | " | 73 | 1964 |
| 4 | 671 HNX | L.02480 | " | " | " | 73 | 1964 |
| 5 | 672 HNX | L.02481 | " | " | " | 73 | 1964 |
| 6 | 673 HNX | L.02482 | " | " | " | 73 | 1964 |
| 7 | GUE 1 D | L.43176 | " | " | " | 73 | 1966 |
| 8 | GUE 2 D | L.43177 | " | " | " | 73 | 1966 |
| 20 | TNX 454 | 556413 | PD2/12 | " | " | 63 | 1956 |
| 21 | TNX 455 | 556415 | " | " | " | 63 | 1956 |
| 22 | TNX 456 | 556416 | " | " | " | 63 | 1956 |
| 24 | MAC 571 | 521521 | " | Leyland | " | 58 | 1952 |
| 25 | MAC 572 | 521522 | " | " | " | 58 | 1952 |
| 28 | 2767 NX | 592208 | PD3/4 | Willowbrook | " | 73 | 1960 |
| 29 | 2768 NX | 592229 | " | " | " | 73 | 1960 |
| 30 | 2769 NX | 592230 | " | " | " | 73 | 1960 |
| 31 | JUE 353 | 495825Y | PD2/1 | Roe | " | 63 | 1961 |
| 32 | JUE 348 | 495826Y | " | Northern Counties | " | 63 | 1963 |
| 33 | JUE 349 | 495827Y | " | " | " | 63 | 1963 |
| 34 | JUE 350 | 495828Y | " | " | " | 63 | 1963 |
| 35 | JUE 351 | 495829Y | " | " | " | 63 | 1963 |
| 36 | 536 EUE | 623278 | PD3/4 | " | " | 73 | 1963 |
| 37 | 537 EUE | 623279 | " | " | " | 73 | 1963 |
| 38 | 538 EUE | 623593 | " | " | " | 73 | 1963 |
| 39 | 539 EUE | 623594 | " | " | " | 73 | 1963 |
| 40 | 2741 AC | 587177 | PSUC1/1 | Willowbrook | Dual Purpose | 41 | 1959 |
| 41 | 2742 AC | 587178 | " | " | " | 41 | 1959 |
| 42 | 2743 AC | 587190 | " | " | " | 41 | 1959 |
| 43 | 2744 AC | 587191 | " | " | " | 41 | 1959 |
| 44 | 2745 AC | 587193 | " | " | Saloon | 45 | 1959 |
| 45 | 3945 UE | 606329 | " | Park Royal | " | 45 | 1960 |
| 46 | 3946 UE | 606330 | " | " | " | 45 | 1960 |
| 47 | 3947 UE | 606365 | " | " | " | 45 | 1960 |
| 48 | 3948 UE | 606366 | " | " | " | 45 | 1960 |
| 49 | 5449 WD | 617455 | " | Marshall | " | 45 | 1962 |
| 50 | 5450 WD | 617540 | " | " | Dual Purpose | 41 | 1962 |
| 51 | 5451 WD | 617468 | " | " | " | 41 | 1962 |
| 52 | 5452 WD | 617469 | " | " | " | 41 | 1962 |
| 55 | 5455 WD | 617541 | " | " | " | 41 | 1962 |
| 56 | AAC 21 B | L.04272 | L2 | Plaxton | Coach | 41 | 1964 |
| 57 | AAC 22 B | L.04273 | " | " | " | 41 | 1964 |
| 59 | 436 GAC | L.00178 | PSU3/3R | Duple | " | 49 | 1963 |
| 60 | CWD 33 C | L.21695 | " | Weymann | " | 49 | 1965 |
| 61 | DAC 753 C | L.40355 | " | Duple | " | 49 | 1965 |
| 62 | HAC 628 D | L.60880 | L2 | Marshall | " | 41 | 1966 |

Nos.20 to 25 have rear enclosed platforms

Nos.31 to 35 are 7'6" wide, being conversions to double-deck of 1950 single-deck bus.

Nos.56 to 62 are 8'2½" wide.

Except where otherwise stated all vehicles are 8'0" wide and have front entrances.

Midland Red used to produce pocket-sized fleet list books which were both for internal use and also available for sale from the Bearwood offices. These made no reference to the Stratford Blue subsidiary fleet and an occasional duplicated sheet was all that was available for those with an interest in Stratford Blue. This example shows the fleet at its maximum size of forty-five, after the delivery of No.62 in May 1966.

have been by separate companies since the closure of Midland Red (South)'s Stratford base in 1999. These revivals have been characterised by very varied fleets of second-hand vehicles, and the only new vehicles to be supplied throughout this time in any version of Stratford Blue livery were the six Mercedes bought during Western Travel's ownership of Midland Red (South). Please note that in all cases with the 'revival' fleets other vehicles have been operated; the only ones listed are those which have appeared in some form of Stratford Blue livery.

In the listing which follows vehicle details are given as below:

COLUMN 1        Operator's fleet number(s) (any changes are detailed in the notes)

COLUMN 2        Registration number(s)

COLUMN 3        Chassis manufacturer and model

COLUMN 4        Body manufacturer

COLUMN 5        Body layout, using the following abbreviations:

B        Bus
C        Coach
DP       Dual-purpose bus/coach
H        Highbridge double-decker

Followed by seating capacity (upper deck first for double-deckers)

C        Centre entrance
D        Dual entrance
F        Forward or front entrance
R        Rear entrance
RD       Rear entrance with platform doors fitted
L        Wheelchair lift
T        Vehicle fitted with a toilet

COLUMN 6        Date new (usually date of first registration)

Anyone wanting further details of the vehicles listed is recommended to contact the PSV Circle, whose very comprehensive records have been consulted extensively during the preparation of this book.

# Listing of Stratford Blue Buses 1927 – 2003

## 1. Grail and Joiner's initial fleet, 1927/1928

| | | | | | |
|---|---|---|---|---|---|
| 1-7 | UE3403/<br>3897/4189/<br>4664/4665/<br>4933/4934 | Chevrolet LM | Allen | B14F | 1927 |
| 8/9 | UE5283/5749 | Thornycroft A2-Long | Hall Lewis | B20F | 1927/1928 |
| 10/11 | UE6494/6734 | Thornycroft A2-Long | Hall Lewis | B20D | 1928 |

Nos 1–11 were bought new by Stratford-on-Avon Motor Services.

## 2. Second-hand Thornycrofts, 1929/1930

| | | | | | |
|---|---|---|---|---|---|
| 12 | TX1498 | Thornycroft A1-Long | Northern Counties | B20F | 1926 |
| 13 | UT411 | Thornycroft A1-Long | Vickers | B20F | 1927 |
| 14 | NR9527 | Thornycroft A1-Long | Challands Ross | B20F | 1926 |
| 15/16 | TX598/647 | Thornycroft A1-Long | Hall Lewis | B20F | 1926 |

Nos 12/15/16 had previously operated for Barry Associated Motorways, Barry, Glamorganshire. Nos 13/14 had previously operated for V.J. Wheeler, Kirby Muxloe, Leicestershire.

## 3. Buses acquired from Frank Martin, Cheltenham, November 1930

| | | | | | |
|---|---|---|---|---|---|
| 17 | DF4771 | Thornycroft A2-Long | Hall Lewis | B20F | 1928 |
| 18 | TR1866 | Thornycroft A1-Long | Wadham | B20F | 1926 |
| 19 | RU1931 | Morris | Kiddle | B14F | 1925 |
| 20 | DG127 | Ford AA | ? | B14F | 1930 |
| — | HO6332 | Thornycroft BT | Bartle | B26F | 1924 |
| — | UE4933 | Chevrolet LM | Allen | B14F | 1927 |
| — | DF2319 | Graham-Dodge A | ? | B20F | 1927 |

These buses were acquired with Martin's business. HO6332, UE4933 and DF2319 may not have been used by SoAMS, although they were acquired. Nos 18/19 and HO6332 were acquired by Martin from Hants & Dorset, Bournemouth, who had bought No.19 new; No.18 was new to Godfrey, Southampton, and HO6332 to Croucher's Yellow Bus Service, Lyndhurst. Nos 17, 20 and DF2319 were new to Martin and UE4933 had been acquired from SoAMS. One other vehicle is thought to have been acquired and may have been either PY241 (a Vulcan) or DF9216, which has been recorded both as a Guy and as a Reo; it is unlikely to have been used by SoAMS.

#### 4. Tilling-Stevens transferred from Midland General, 1931

| | | | | | |
|---|---|---|---|---|---|
| 19-22/ 24 | RA3869/ 3538/3870/ 3959/3958 | Tilling-Stevens Express B9B | Strachan & Brown | B30F | 1927 |

These buses have also been recorded as B10B models, and some as having Brush bodies, but Strachan & Brown is thought to be correct. No.20 returned to Midland General in 1933 in exchange for FG5227.

#### 5. The Albion demonstrator, 1932

| | | | | | |
|---|---|---|---|---|---|
| 23 | WD3338 | Albion Valiant PV70 | Cowieson | DP32F | 1932 |

This vehicle was on hire from Albion for six months, although registered in Warwickshire in the name of Stratford Blue. It may not have carried its allocated fleet number.

#### 6. Buses acquired from Crompton & Longford (Reliance), Bidford-on-Avon, June 1932

| | | | | | |
|---|---|---|---|---|---|
| 7 | UE6467 | Star Flyer VB | Willowbrook | B20F | 1928 |
| 18 | UE7973 | Star Flyer VB4 | Willowbrook | B26F | 1929 |
| — | UE5447 | Chevrolet LM | Willowbrook | B14F | 1928 |
| — | UE9319/9816 | Guy OND | Guy | B20F | 1929/1930 |
| — | UY6470 | Bean | ? | B20F | 1929 |
| — | WD1171 | Ford | ? | B14F | 1930 |
| — | YF8295 | Guy FBB | Vickers | B32R | 1927 |

These buses were acquired with the Reliance Garage's bus services; it is thought that only the two Star Flyers and possibly YF8295 ran for Stratford Blue. UY6470 was new to Hays, Redditch; YF8295 was new to the Great Western Railway and was then acquired by Western Welsh Omnibus Co., Cardiff; the others were new to Reliance.

#### 7. The Commer transferred from Midland General, 1933

| | | | | | |
|---|---|---|---|---|---|
| 20 | FG5227 | Commer F4 | Hall Lewis | C32F | 1929 |

No.20 was new to the General Motor Carrying Co., Kirkcaldy, Fife (another Balfour Beatty company); it was transferred to Stratford Blue in exchange for the previous No.20 (RA3538). The body was described as a 'sun saloon' but it may be more correctly recorded as B32F.

## 8. The AEC demonstrator, 1933

| | | | | | |
|---|---|---|---|---|---|
| 23 | AMD739 | AEC Regal | Harrington | C32R | 1933 |

This vehicle was on hire from AEC for six months.

## 9. Daimlers transferred from Leamington & Warwick, 1933/1934

| | | | | | |
|---|---|---|---|---|---|
| 20 | UE9916 | Daimler CF6 | Strachan & Brown | B32F | 1930 |
| 23 | UE9323 | Daimler CF6 | Strachan & Brown | DP30F | 1929 |

Although painted in Stratford Blue colours, Nos 20/23 were only on long-term hire from the Leamington & Warwick Electrical Co.; they later returned to that fleet.

## 10. Guys transferred from Cheltenham District, 1934

| | | | | | |
|---|---|---|---|---|---|
| 14-16/ | DG1312/1317/ | Guy Conquest | Guy | B28F | 1930 |
| 20 | 1316/1310 | | | | |

## 11. Former Red House Maudslays, 1936

| | | | | | |
|---|---|---|---|---|---|
| 17 | WK9631 | Maudslay ML4B | Willowbrook | B32F | 1929 |
| 18 | VC7801 | Maudslay ML3BC | Willowbrook | B32F | 1931 |
| 23 | WK9708 | Maudslay ML3B | Willowbrook | B32F | 1929 |

These buses came from Midland Red, who had acquired them with the bus services of the Red House Garage, Coventry; they were not used by Midland Red. The bodies on Nos 17 and 23 dated from 1932 when No.17 was converted to forward-control ML3 specification; the original bodywork was by Midland Light Bodies and Vickers respectively. WK9631 may have been numbered 7 rather than 17 although always recorded as the latter.

## 12. Tilling-Stevens acquired from Trent, 1936

| | | | | | |
|---|---|---|---|---|---|
| 11 | VT34 | Tilling-Stevens Express B10A | Willowbrook | B32F | 1927 |
| 12 | VT580 | Tilling-Stevens Express B10A2 | Willowbrook | B32F | 1927 |

Trent had acquired these buses in 1935 with the business of Kingfisher Services, Derby; the Willowbrook bodies dated from 1933. No.11 was new to Tilstone, Tunstall, Staffordshire, with a Lawton B32F body; No.12 was new to Pritchard, Stoke-on-Trent, also with a B32F body.

### 13. Tilling-Stevens acquired from North Western 1936/1937

| | | | | | |
|---|---|---|---|---|---|
| 1–10/ | DB5141/ | Tilling-Stevens | see below | B31R | 1928 |
| 14–21 | 5152–5154/ | Express B10A2 | | | |
| | 5184/5162/ | | | | |
| | 5157–5159/ | | | | |
| | 5140/5147/ | | | | |
| | 5130/5156/ | | | | |
| | 5177/5155/ | | | | |
| | 5163/5190/ | | | | |
| | 5166 | | | | |

These buses had a mixture of Brush and Tilling bodies, most, if not all, of which dated from 1930/1931 and had been transferred from other buses; the original bodies had also been supplied by Brush (Nos 1/6/9, 10/15/19, 21) and Tilling. Nos 20/21 have also been recorded as 35-seaters with Stratford Blue. No.5 was renumbered 22 in 1939.

### 14. Tilling-Stevens acquired from West Yorkshire, 1938

| | | | | | |
|---|---|---|---|---|---|
| 1 | WX2121 | Tilling-Stevens Express B10A2 | Tilling | B32F | 1930 |
| 2–4 | WX2131/ 2126/2134 | Tilling-Stevens Express B10A2 | United | B32F | 1930 |
| 5–7 | WX2120/ 2152/2151 | Tilling-Stevens Express B10A2 | Tilling | B32F | 1930 |
| 8 | WX2148 | Tilling-Stevens Express B10A2 | United | B32F | 1930 |
| 9 | WX2125 | Tilling-Stevens Express B10A2 | Tilling | B32F | 1930 |
| 10/14/ 15 | WX2130/ 2118/2133 | Tilling-Stevens Express B10A2 | United | B32F | 1930 |
| 16 | WX2144 | Tilling-Stevens Express B10A2 | Tilling | B32F | 1930 |
| 17–19 | WX2141/ 2153/2150 | Tilling-Stevens Express B10A2 | Roe | B32F | 1930 |

### 15. Former Owen of Abberley Maudslays, 1938

| | | | | | |
|---|---|---|---|---|---|
| 20 | WP8277 | Maudslay ML3K | Beadle | C32R | 1935 |
| 21 | WP3425 | Maudslay ML3F | W.D. Smith | C32R | 1933 |

Nos 21/22 were acquired from Owens when they sold their bus operations to Midland Red.

### 16. AEC double-decker acquired from City of Oxford, 1940

| | | | | | |
|---|---|---|---|---|---|
| 22 | JO2354 | AEC Regent | Park Royal | H24/24R | 1931 |

No.22 was the first double-decker in the fleet.

### 17. Wartime transfers from Midland Red and Majestic Express, 1944/1945

| | | | | | |
|---|---|---|---|---|---|
| 23 | HA4942 | SOS M | Ransomes | B34F | 1929 |
| 24/25 | JA6972/6973 | Leyland Tiger TS7 | Harrington | C32F | 1936 |
| 26 | AHA619 | SOS OLR | Short | B34F | 1935 |

No.23 was acquired from Midland Red in 1944. Nos 24/25 were on long-term hire from Majestic Express, Stockport, although they were repainted in Stratford Blue livery; they may have been 30-seaters. No.26 was on long-term hire from Midland Red and remained in red livery.

### 18. More Tilling-Stevens from North Western, 1946

| | | | | | |
|---|---|---|---|---|---|
| 20/21/ | DB9375/ | Tilling-Stevens | Eastern Counties | B31R | 1930 |
| 26-31 | 9377/9395/ | Express B10A2 | | | |
| | 9368/9362/ | | | | |
| | 9380/9389/ | | | | |
| | 9397 | | | | |

The bodies on these buses dated from 1935; originally they had Tilling bodywork except for No.28 which had a Brush body.

### 19. The new Leyland fleet, 1948-1950

| | | | | | |
|---|---|---|---|---|---|
| 32-39 | GUE238-245 | Leyland Titan PD2/1 | Leyland | H30/26R | 1948 |
| 40-49 | GUE246-255 | Leyland Tiger PS1 | NCB | B34F | 1948/1949 |
| 50-53 | JUE348-351 | Leyland Tiger PS2/3 | Willowbrook | DP35F | 1950 |
| 54/55 | JUE352/353 | Leyland Tiger PS2/1 | Willowbrook | B34F | 1950 |
| 26-31 | JUE354-359 | Leyland Titan PD2/1 | Leyland | H30/26R | 1950 |

Nos 26-55 were all bought new, as were all subsequent fleet additions with one exception. They replaced all previous vehicles in the fleet. Nos 50-53/55 were later rebodied as double-deckers (see below).

## 20. The 'MAC' Leyland Titans, 1952

| 23-25 | MAC570-572 | Leyland Titan PD2/12 | Leyland | | H32/26R | 1952 |

Nos 23-25 were fitted with platform doors in 1955 (becoming H32/26RD).

## 21. The 'Seagull' coaches, 1954

| 56/57 | OUE11/12 | Leyland Royal Tiger PSU1/16 | Burlingham | C37C | 1954 |

## 22. The 'TNX' Titans, 1956

| 20-22 | TNX454-456 | Leyland Titan PD2/12 | Willowbrook | H35/28RD | 1956 |

## 23. The first Leyland Tiger Cubs, 1959

| 40-43 | 2741-2744AC | Leyland Tiger Cub PSUC1/1 | Willowbrook | DP41F | 1959 |
| 44 | 2745AC | Leyland Tiger Cub PSUC1/1 | Willowbrook | B45F | 1959 |

## 24. The first 30ft Titans, 1960

| 17-19 | 2767-2769NX | Leyland Titan PD3/4 | Willowbrook | H41/32F | 1960 |

Nos 17-19 were renumbered 28-30 in 1965.

## 25. The Park Royal Tiger Cubs, 1960

| 45-48 | 3945-3948UE | Leyland Tiger Cub PSUC1/1 | Park Royal | B45F | 1960 |

## 26. The Thames Trader coach, 1961

| 58 | 3958UE | Ford Thames Trader 570E | Duple | C41F | 1961 |

## 27. The first double-deck rebuild, 1961

| 16 | JUE353 | Leyland Tiger PS2/1 rebuild | Roe | H35/28F | 1961 |

No.16 was built on the chassis of 1950 Leyland Tiger No.55 (see above); it was renumbered 31 in 1965.

## 28. The Marshall Tiger Cubs, 1962

| 49 | 5449WD | Leyland Tiger Cub PSUC1/1 | Marshall | B45F | 1962 |
| 50-52/ 55 | 5450-5452/ 5455WD | Leyland Tiger Cub PSUC1/1 | Marshall | DP41F | 1962 |

No.49 was modified to B43F in 1969 and No.55 was renumbered 53 in the same year.

## 29. The former Warwickshire County Garage Bedford, 1962

| 59 | 8222NX | Bedford SB3 | Duple | C41F | 1960 |

No.59 was acquired with the coach tours business of the Warwickshire County Garage.

## 30. More double-deck rebuilds, 1963

| 32-35 | JUE348-351 | Leyland Tiger PS2/3 rebuild | Northern Counties | H35/28F | 1963 |

Nos 32-35 were built on the chassis of 1950 Leyland Tigers Nos 50-53 (see above); they were renumbered 132-135 in 1970.

## 31. The Northern Counties Titans, 1963

| 36-39 | 536-539EUE | Leyland Titan PD3/4 | Northern Counties | H41/32F | 1963 |

Nos 36-39 were renumbered 24-27 in 1969.

## 32. The 'Alpine Continental' coach, 1963

| 59 | 436GAC | Leyland Leopard PSU3/3R | Duple (Northern) | C49F | 1963 |

No.59 was renumbered 55 in 1969, and modified for use as a service bus in 1970.

### 33. The 'HNX' Titans, 1963/1964

| | | | | | |
|---|---|---|---|---|---|
| 1-6 | 668-673HNX | Leyland Titan PD3A/1 | Willowbrook | H41/32F | 1963/ 1964 |

### 34. The Plaxton 'Panorama' coaches, 1964

| | | | | | |
|---|---|---|---|---|---|
| 56/57 | AAC21/22B | Leyland Leopard L2 | Plaxton | C41F | 1964 |

### 35. The first dual-purpose Leopard, 1965

| | | | | | |
|---|---|---|---|---|---|
| 60 | CWD33C | Leyland Leopard PSU3/3R | Weymann | DP49F | 1965 |

No.60 was modified to B53F and renumbered 54 in 1969.

### 36. The Duple 'Commander' coach, 1965

| | | | | | |
|---|---|---|---|---|---|
| 61 | DAC753C | Leyland Leopard PSU3/3R | Duple (Northern) | C49F | 1965 |

No.61 was renumbered 58 in 1969.

### 37. The final Leyland Titans, 1966

| | | | | | |
|---|---|---|---|---|---|
| 7/8 | GUE1/2D | Leyland Titan PD3A/1 | Willowbrook | H41/32F | 1966 |

### 38. The second dual-purpose Leopard, 1966

| | | | | | |
|---|---|---|---|---|---|
| 62 | HAC628D | Leyland Leopard L2 | Marshall | DP41F | 1966 |

No.62 was renumbered 59 in 1970.

### 39. The Leyland Atlanteans, 1967

| | | | | | |
|---|---|---|---|---|---|
| 9-11 | NAC415 -417F | Leyland Atlantean PDR1/1 | Northern Counties | H44/31F | 1967 |

### 40. The Alexander 'Y-type' coach, 1970

| | | | | | |
|---|---|---|---|---|---|
| 36 | XNX136H | Leyland Leopard PSU3A/4R | Alexander | C49F | 1970 |

## 41. The Leyland Panthers, 1970

| 31-35 | XNX131 -135H | Leyland Panther PSUR1A/1R | Marshall | B41D | 1970 |
|---|---|---|---|---|---|

These buses were ordered but never used by Stratford Blue; because of the delays in entering service the registrations shown above were voided and they became AUE 309-313J instead. Their first user was Preston Corporation Transport, who bought them from Midland Red.

## 42. More Leyland Leopards

Three Leyland Leopards with Marshall bodies were ordered before the company was absorbed by Midland Red, and these were delivered as part of Midland Red's thirteen-strong 'S26' class (Nos 6461-6473; DHA461-473K). It was not possible to identify which had been ordered by Stratford Blue.

## 43. Midland Red (South) buses painted in versions of Stratford Blue livery during NBC ownership, 1985-1987

| 64 | SAD127R | Leyland Leopard PSU3D/4R | Willowbrook | C47F | 1977 |
|---|---|---|---|---|---|
| 468-472/ 474 | D468-472/ 474CKV | Freight Rover Sherpa 365D | Rootes | B16F | 1986 |

No.64 was acquired from Black & White, Cheltenham, in 1985; Nos 468-472/474 were new to Midland Red (South).

## 44. Midland Red (South) buses painted in versions of Stratford Blue livery during Western Travel ownership, 1989-1993

| 4 | 230HUE | Leyland Leopard PSU3E/4R | Plaxton | C49F | 1980 |
|---|---|---|---|---|---|
| 91 | CDG213Y | Leyland Tiger TRCTL11/3R | Plaxton | C46FT | 1983 |
| 376/ 378-380/ 382 | C706/ 709-711/ 719FKE | Ford Transit 190D | Dormobile | B16F | 1986 |
| 407-412 | J407- 412PRW | Mercedes-Benz 811D | Wright | DP33F | 1991 |
| 427 | H912XGA | Mercedes-Benz 814D | Reeve Burgess | DP31F | 1990 |
| 504 | JOX504P | Leyland National 11351A/1R | Leyland National | B49DL | 1976 |
| 584 | NOE584R | Leyland National 11351A/1R | Leyland National | B49F | 1977 |

| 905 | A545HAC | Leyland Olympian ONLXB/1R | ECW | H45/32F | 1983 |
| 953 | OJD241R | Leyland Fleetline FE30AGR | MCW | H44/29F | 1977 |
| 955 | OJD136R | Leyland Fleetline FE30AGR | Park Royal | H44/29F | 1976 |
| 961 | B961ODU | Leyland Olympian ONLXB/1R | ECW | DPH42/30F | 1984 |
| 962-964 | C962-964XVC | Leyland Olympian ONLXB/1RH | ECW | DPH42/29F | 1986 |

This list only includes vehicles which carried a version of blue and white livery and 'Stratford Blue' fleetnames; buses which carried Stratford Blue fleetnames on previous owners' or advertising liveries are excluded. No.4 (as No.786, with original registration BVP786V) was acquired from Midland Red (North) in 1981; No.91 was acquired from Cheltenham & Gloucester in 1991; Nos 376/378-380/382 were acquired from East Kent in 1992; No.427 was acquired from Lofty's, Bridge Trafford, in 1993, and Nos 953/955 were acquired from Stevensons of Uttoxeter in 1989/1990. The remaining vehicles (Nos 407-412, 905/961-964) were new to Midland Red (South). Although able to carry forty-nine passengers No.504 generally operated with some seats removed in its capacity as a wheelchair-accessible 'Flexibus'.

Several of these vehicles carried names as detailed below:

| 4: | *Rachel* |
| 407-412: | *Penny, Crown, Farthing, Sovereign, Shilling, Florin* |
| 584: | *Rosemary* |
| 905/955/961-964: | *Mary, Josephine, Dorothy, Ron Ingram, Jean, Roxanne* |

## 45. Midland Red (South) buses delivered in Stagecoach livery with 'Stratford Blue Shuttle' fleetnames, 1996

| 360-364 | N360-364AVV | Mercedes-Benz 709D | Alexander | B25F | 1996 |

## 46. Newmark buses which carried versions of Stratford Blue livery, 1999/2000

| — | NAT198V | Leyland National 2 NL116L11/1R | Leyland National | B49F | 1980 |
| — | JCK849W | Leyland National 2 NL106AL11/1R | Leyland National | B44F | 1981 |
| — | SVV589W | Leyland National 2 NL116L11/1R | Leyland National | B49F | 1980 |
| — | RDC739X | Leyland National 2 NL116AL11/1R | Leyland National | B49F | 1981 |

| | | | | | |
|---|---|---|---|---|---|
| — | S716/<br>717KNV | Mercedes-Benz<br>Vario 0.814 | Marshall | B31F | 1999 |
| — | S719-<br>722KNV | Dennis Dart SLF | Marshall | B43F | 1999 |
| — | T455HNV | Mercedes-Benz<br>Vario 0.814 | Marshall | B31F | 1999 |

This list only includes vehicles which carried Newmark's white and blue Stratford Blue livery, or carried Stratford Blue fleetnames on plain 'dealer' white. The Leyland Nationals were acquired second-hand and had been new to National Bus Company subsidiaries East Yorkshire (NAT198V), Ribble (JCK849W), United (RDC739X) and United Counties (SVV589W). The Dennis Darts and Mercedes were leased from a dealer and operated in plain white, although one Dennis Dart later carried the Newmark Stratford Blue livery.

## 47. Status Group vehicles painted in their Stratford Blue livery, 2000-2001

| | | | | | |
|---|---|---|---|---|---|
| — | GSU554 | Leyland Tiger<br>TRCTL11/3R | Plaxton | C51F | 1983 |
| — | LIB6352 | Leyland Leopard<br>PSU5C/4R | Duple | C53F | 1978 |
| — | TOF695S | Leyland National<br>11351A/1R | Leyland National | B49F | 1978 |
| — | MDS868V | Leyland National<br>NL116L11/1R | Leyland National | B52F | 1980 |
| — | WCA942W | Leyland Leopard<br>PSU5D/5R | Plaxton | C57F | 1980 |
| — | G995VWV | Leyland Lynx<br>LX112L10ZR1R | Leyland | B47F | 1990 |

This list only includes vehicles which carried the Status Group white, blue and yellow livery with Stratford Blue fleetnames (TOF695S is confirmed as carrying the livery but may not have had fleetnames). All vehicles were acquired second-hand and were new to Bostocks of Congleton (WCA942W), Brighton Borough Transport (G995VWV), Central SMT (MDS868V), Cheltenham & Gloucester (GSU554; originally registered A213SAE), Midland Red (TOF695S) and National Travel (South West) (LIB6352; originally registered AAD185S). The seating capacity of GSU554 and LIB6352 is not confirmed.

## 48. Ensign Group buses painted in their Stratford Blue livery, from 2002 (to the end of January 2003)

| | | | | | |
|---|---|---|---|---|---|
| 112 | GOG223W | MCW Metrobus<br>DR102/18 | MCW | H43/30F | 1981 |
| 129 | BYX129V | MCW Metrobus<br>DR101/9 | MCW | H43/28D | 1979 |

| 164/174 | WYW64/74T | MCW Metrobus DR101/9 | MCW | H43/28D | 1979 |
|---|---|---|---|---|---|
| 611 | J611SJB | Optare Metrorider MR07 | Optare | B25F | 1991 |
| 613 | H613NJB | Optare Metrorider MR07 | Optare | B25F | 1991 |
| 653 | K853RBB | Optare Metrorider MR07 | Optare | DP28F | 1992 |
| 688 | H588MOC | Dennis Dart 8.5SDL3003 | Carlyle | B28F | 1990 |
| 739 | WPH139Y | Leyland Tiger TRCTL11/2R | East Lancs | B51F | 1982 |
| 767 | B167XBU | Leyland Tiger TRCTL11/3RH | Plaxton | C50F | 1985 |

This list only includes vehicles which received the Ensign blue and silver/grey livery with Stratford Blue fleetnames. All vehicles were acquired second-hand and were new to London Country (WPH139Y, but rebodied in 1989 while with Midland Red (North)), London Transport (WYW64/74T, BYX129V), Metroline Travel (H588MOC), Northumbria Motor Services (K853RBB), Reading Transport (H613NJB, J611SJB), Southern National (B167XBU; originally registered B896YYD) and West Midlands PTE (GOG223W). WPH139Y was originally No.439.